Thumbsticks, Boots and a Carrier Bag

by

Graham Pollard

Best wishes from Graham

Published by LR Publishing

This edition published in 2010
by LR Publishing

ISBN 978-0-9555919-5-2

©Graham Pollard

Also by this author
Left or Right, Ron?
Are We There Yet, Ron?

A CIP catalogue for this title
is available from the British Library

Paperback ISBN 978-0-9555919-5-2

Typeset by author Times New Roman 11
Printed and Bound by PrintonDemand-worldwide.co.uk
Published by LR Publishing, 4 Rockall Drive, Hailsham BN27 3BG

PREFACE

It was sometime ago that I had my heart attack. That's the first one. Oh, yes, I've experienced more than one! After the first, in 1990, I had to change my lifestyle. I stopped smoking, but could so easily start again. I had to stop eating fried food but still, to this day, dribble over the smell of a cooked breakfast in the morning. I also had to eat healthier, but a cheese burger is still a tempting substitute for a low calorie bar. Do I miss all those tempting things? Of course I do but sometimes I gave in to temptation. I do try to keep to a healthy diet, but invariably fail. I did kick the habit of smoking and with a price of cigarettes the way it is, at the moment, I really think that I might not be able to afford to smoke now. I started to take regular exercise. I went walking with Ron over various parts of Sussex. I wrote a book about our walks titled 'Left or Right, Ron?'[1] which became so popular that another was expected. We continued our round of walks and produced another book titled, 'Are We There Yet, Ron?'[2] finding little known villages and I thought I was doing really well. No smoking, healthy diet (?) and plenty of exercise. So why did heart attack number two happen?

"You didn't always take your medication!" my wife reminds me. "You used to have late night feasts," she continues. "You are always rushing around to get things done, and you don't relax. You work long hours, you drink too much, and you don't listen to a thing I say!" Familiar to anyone? But she was right. I thought I was doing everything I should but all the things my wife and family chastised me for are true. So, when I get the 'all clear' after heart attack number two I promise to look after myself. Honest!

This brings me to book number three. As I write this I haven't got a title for the book but one will 'crop up' as Ron and I progress. The idea for these pages came about whilst I was convalescing and, finding time on my hands, decided to join the local Library. I love books. Not any book but I look for certain authors like Candace Robb with her great stories about an archer and Magda Digby. Jonothan Kellerman with Alex Delaware to name just two but what I found myself looking at was not this type of book at all but I was drawn to the many books on Sussex. Within the shelves of local books I noticed that there are books on hill walks, pub walks, town walks and river walks but not one that packs them all into one cover. So, I suggested to Ron that our next venture should be walks with a theme. We have used a number of publications to compile these stories and have also gone a bit up market and purchased maps and a compass. Ron has suggested that we will have to go back to school to discover how to use these marvels of modern science. Both Ron and I hope that you will all enjoy another episode into walking mayhem, where left could mean right, and where being geographically challenged may be a thing of the past. Although in the next pages, I'm sure, I'll be proven wrong again.

Should anyone follow our progress and attempt to complete the same walk as us, you are hereby warned that things can change overnight. Paths disappear, stiles are dislodged and hedges can be destroyed. Thankfully, neither Ron nor I have any control over this phenomena which can make a short walk longer than expected and, therefore, cannot be blamed, sued or chastised, if it does, as on some occasions, with Ron and me, it all goes wrong.

---

[1] Published by LR Publishers
[2] Ibid

Acknowledgements

You are all aware of my 'event' by now. With the help of some masochistic young ladies in the Physiotherapy Department at our local hospital I may not have been able to participate in the following pages. So my 'thanks' (?) go to Hilda, Shirley and the volunteers who put me through 6 weeks of torture, two hours per session with two sessions a week so that Ron and I could continue with our hobby.

My family are my world and without them I would not be able to complete all that I have in my life. Growing older isn't easy. My body has started to tell me that I can't do things that I want to do. Without the love, understanding, encouragement and advice from my wife, Mele, these pages would not be sitting here, with you, now. My two children Michelle and Anthony are my inspiration and I can't thank them enough for all the encouragement they have given me. Chloe, Megan, my fantastic granddaughters, along with little Harry, my grandson, are the apple of my eye. It is obvious they get their good looks and charm from their mum, Nicole.

Of course there is Ron. What can you say about Ron that already hasn't been said? He is what he is. What you see is what you get. He doesn't put on any airs or graces. He is one of the best friends I have had and completing this book with him, has been a joy.

Lastly the book couldn't be put together without help. Print on Demand who have managed to get into print my ramblings, I believe, have completed a great job in producing the actual book. I must also thank Lyn, my very own proof-reader for again ensuring that I don't get into trouble with my p's and q's and steering me clear of any law suites.

I must also acknowledge the assistance given in Chapter 5 of this book. The Enrichment Walk wouldn't and in fact, couldn't have happened without the backing and consent of Langney Primary School, its Headmaster and the parents of the children involved. I think the walk was a great success, and the pictures, every one taken by the children, were exceptional. How they managed to reduce the number of photographs from the 570 they took to the 14 that I actually used I will never know. But, from the feedback I have received from my daughter Michelle, the children really enjoyed the experience.

Finally, all those people who have been brave enough to come for a walk with us or have met us on our walks deserve not only a mention but also an award. Thank you all for making two old men very happy.

I hope we manage to bring just one smile to your face as you read our stories because that is all we ask.

Please enjoy the book and should you see two old codgers, out along a country lane, both with Thumbsticks, wearing Boots and one holding a Carrier Bag stop us and have a chat, we'd love to meet you and say hello.

Graham

CONTENTS

Romantic Walk

Some may not see Ron as a 'romantic' but deep down I think we are all romantics to some extent, even Ron. I've seen the way he swoons whenever Pip looks at him at our local hostelry! But, unfortunately, being with Ron on a 'Romantic Walk' in some beautiful Sussex countryside doesn't seem right to me, so I have invited someone else to walk with me. No I am not admitting to some secret passionate affair, but am, of course, inviting my long-suffering wife, Emelia.

Due to my recent event (that's what the hospital calls it!) my confidence has been a little knocked. So we, that's the wife and I, thought I should try a little something to instil some confidence not only in myself but also in my wife. After all we seem to forget that our loved ones are also affected by such 'events'. I have suggested an evening of passion and frivolous activity but, apparently, my confidence isn't the only thing that needs some tender loving care. What the wife has suggested is a familiar walk, just the two of us, not too far, just the two of us, perhaps a meal afterwards, just the two of us, and we could see where it leads………. Again, just the two of us.

I believe that romance comes in different forms. A cherished moment could be seen as being romantic. A place once visited can hold fond memories. That is why, when

The Yew Tree Inn, Arlington

Emelia suggested a familiar walk, I immediately thought of Arlington Reservoir. It was the first walk completed by Ron and me when we started our walking, oh so many months ago. It was the start of all our writings and stories, the funny and the not so funny. But that walk does hold fond memories for me and I wanted to see if the scenery would be any different, in the middle of summer compared with when Ron and I completed the walk, at the start of a very cold January. I was also a little more experienced in the taking of photographs so I was hoping to catch some better (?) images or something I missed altogether. The walk is only a few miles from home, so not a long way to travel and the walk was relatively short, being only 3 miles, and mostly on the level. Halfway round was a country pub, ideal for a romantic meal, and a rest should the whole experience be too much for me. But I am currently undergoing cardiac physiotherapy, twice a week, at the hospital so I'm certain that 3 miles isn't going to tax me too much.

We are told that the pub halfway round the walk, The Yew Tree, does good traditional food, but we would be advised to book a table in advance. But I know better. It's a Wednesday; it's the middle of the week so we won't have a problem getting a table.

For those unfamiliar with Arlington Reservoir I will give a little background information. Anyone that is familiar with the surroundings, please bear with me: cutting off a meander in the Cuckmere River formed the whole 120 acres of what is now designated as a Site of Special Scientific Interest. It is the favourite haunt of many birds and up to 10,000 wildfowl spend their winter here. The reservoir is also home to a successful trout fishery and bream, roach, perch and eels make up the underwater population.

The area was originally planted with more than 30,000 native trees, including oak, birch, wild cherry, hazel and hawthorn. The grassland area along the shoreline has been left uncut to enable and encourage many kinds of moth and butterfly to thrive in their natural habitat.[3] The reservoir is also said to be the home of fallow deer but, although I have not visited the site all that often, I have not seen them. There are numerous places along the walk to stop, to look and admire the fabulous scenery, wooden tables and chairs are supplied should you decide to take a picnic. But be warned that if you take your dog for a walk around the reservoir he/she must be kept on a lead.

The entrance to the car park

So, that describes where we are going. Mele (Emelia) and I shall be using the original book of instructions[4] for today's walk, just as Ron and I did with the first Arlington Reservoir walk[5] but I'm hoping that my memory isn't as affected as other parts of me are, and that I will be able to find my way about with little trouble (?)

So at just past 3 o'clock we head towards Arlington. I decided that we would head towards the pub first. If we started our walk at the pub, and finished at the pub, we could enjoy a pleasant drink as well as an intimate meal towards the early evening. I had calculated that the walk should take no longer than 1½hours. But should we feel the 'urge' to stop somewhere, for any reason (?), it would take a little longer, so I allowed 2hours. This meant we should be back at the pub at about 5.30. Nice time for a quick pint before dinner. I pulled up outside The Yew Tree and for some reason completely

Mele. on animal

changed my mind on starting the walk here. "I've a better idea," I explain to Mele, "let's start at the car park in the reservoir and stop at the pub halfway round. We can have a quick drink to refresh ourselves, book a table for this evening, and finish the walk back to the car and then drive back to the pub for dinner." So that was the plan.

We arrived at the car park to find nothing has changed. It still costs money to park here so I decided to park on the road. It's not that I'm tight it's just a pet hate of mine to have to pay to park my car in an area owned by South East Water. They must be one of the only companies that charge you, in advance, for a supply of water, and then when they can't supply you with the water you've already paid for make excuses about not having enough supplies

One of the miniatures

---

[3] 50 Walks in Sussex, an AA guide, first published in 2001, ISBN 0 7495 2876 1, PAGES 47/8
[4] Ibid
[5] Left or Right Ron? Published by LR Publishers 2007, ISBN 978 0 9555919 0 7 Chapter 1

because I've wasted my own, paid for supply. Yet leakages from their very own pipelines account for millions of gallons of water lost every week. But enough, let's go for a walk.

The sun is very hot today and I expect it to get hotter. Mele is dressed in casual gear and I've just discovered that I've left my trusted thumb stick at home. "You won't need a stick today, will you?" enquires Mele. "Not for walking but just in case we come up against some animals that aren't so friendly," I casually reply. You could see the colour drain from her face. "Animals," she says, "you never said anything about animals. What sort of animals? Don't tell me there might be cows. You know I don't like cows. If you've got cows you've got bulls and I like bulls even less than I like cows. No, you never mentioned animals." I manage to calm her down with comforting words and, with a little hesitation; we make our way towards the signed entrance to Arlington Reservoir.

Mele convinced – it's sheep

The start of this 3-mile walk, around the reservoir, actually takes you away from the water and leads you down a tarmac lane towards Polhill's Farm. To our right are open fields and, in the distance, you can clearly see the magnificent South Downs. The area certainly has some stunning scenery. Mele has started waiving her arms about. "Are you ok?" I ask my true love. "Something's buzzing round my head," she replies. "It's probably only a fly. Probably from the miniature horses in the field over there," I offer in the way of explanation. But the only thing that stops her from waiving her arms about is for me to hold her hand. (Now I'm a true romantic!)

There is a diversion of the path that takes us away from the farmhouse and is well signposted "The last time I walked along here was with Ron," I explain, "Because it was in January it was very muddy and slippery and the fields were full of pigs." We pass around Polhill's Farm and come out by the waters edge. Here we turn right and head towards a kissing gate. "Don't we pass through the gate?" asks Mele.

True love

"No," I reply, "the instructions tell us to pass the kissing gate and find a stile about 100 yards further up the lane, on the left." "Shame," says Mele "could've used that kissing gate." But her meaning escaped me, or it did at the time.

Once at the stile Mele's first question was, "There aren't any animals in here, are there?" A quick look over her shoulder and I can honestly reply, "Yes, there are some sheep shading under the tree but they won't hurt you." I'm beginning to sound like Ron.

Arlington Church, in the distance

I expect I'll soon start saying 'don't run' or 'don't show 'em yer scared' which are Ron's normal tips on animal psychology. Once over the stile we head slightly to our right, towards a pond where we find another stile. Again Mele asks about animals and this time I can assure her that all is clear. "Mind you, when we were here last this field was full of cattle. The mud was up over our shoes and Ron promised himself some decent footwear." It doesn't seem that long ago that both Ron and I walked this route and the memories still come back to me. Once over yet another stile we are out onto the road that would take us to The Yew Tree Inn. But, of course, that would be too easy. What we actually need to do is walk up the road for a few yards, round the bend and cross the bridge over the River Cuckmere. Once over the bridge we turn left, onto the Wealdway. The traffic along this road tends to come at you as if it was a game where each car has to see how close it can get to you. As there is no footpath you should get onto the verge and stay there until you reach the bridge. Once on the bridge you look down onto what used to be a navigable river, The Cuckmere. Now, in places it is just a trickle of a stream but it did give Mele and me the opportunity to take a break and, with the sun behind us, the thought of a romantic meal and evening together, soft music playing..........

But we need to get on. Turning left onto the Wealdway we now head, slightly uphill towards some houses. Mele starts to pick grasses and what looks like dead or dying plants. "What are the grasses for?" I ask. "I need them for a display," Mele replies, "I'll show you later," and she gives me that look! You know what I mean lads, that look. That very special look. The look that says nothing but means everything. Or you hope it does, or, perhaps it wasn't 'that' look at all and now your confused. Am I getting a message or did I miss-read 'the' look? Either way, Mele is still picking dead flowers?????

Once by the houses we need to cross another stile to our left. Once across the stile, and a little further into the field you get a glimpse of Arlington church spire, right in front of you. I can hear Ron say to me that '....all them 'undreds o'years ago people would walk ter church along this very path....' and I'd ask why they would walk to Arlington when they had really nice church at Berwick. Our instructions tell us to head to the right of the church where we find another stile that leads us out to the road and the welcome sight of The Yew Tree Inn. And it's closed. "I don't believe it,"

The Church of St Pancras, Arlington

Over the bridge and the Cuckmere

I say in true Victor Meldrew style. The temperature is soaring, the sweat has poured out of me and the one place that could offer us some refreshment is closed. Because of this we have another change of plan. I'll have to find somewhere else to eat this evening. But where? "Let's not worry about it now," I say to Mele, "we'll think of somewhere," and we head back up the road to the Church.

Some churches that Ron and I have had the pleasure to visit are usually old, obviously (?), but the church at Arlington is old with a capital 'O'. The Saxons originally built the Church of St Pancras. The first written record of the church is in the wardens accounts dated 1455. These records are now preserved in the British Museum. At that time the church possessed 30 cows, which were let out to the local farmers and paid for in beeswax (2lbs per cow per year)[6]. If you ever get the chance to have a look around any church you will always find interesting stories about the church itself or of its parishioners. Arlington is no different. Thankfully the church was open so Mele and I could have a good look round. When Ron and I came here last the church was locked so we didn't get the opportunity to marvel at this beautiful old church. So today was a bit of a bonus for me.

One of the things that I really enjoy about writing about these walks is the stories and fables that can be found about the villages. All it takes is a little bit of research. I have a book which tells of little known facts about some of the villages not just in Sussex, but in England as a whole and is a fascinating read. For example, who has heard of a place called Burlow Castle? Apparently this castle was situated in the Cuckmere Valley just south of Arlington. By the mid 19th century only earthy mounds remained. The locals, at the time, thought the area was the home of Pharisees (fairies) and nobody would go near the place after dark. One day Charles Packham, along with his mate Harry, were ploughing a field alongside this area when they heard '.a queer sort of noise right down under the ground'. It turned out to be a fairy, calling for help, because she was baking bread and had broken her peel (wooden shovel) and didn't know what to do. 'Put it up and I'll try to mend it' said Charles, and up through a crack in the dry ground came a little peel no bigger than a cheese knife. Charles, trying not to laugh mended the peel with his pocket-knife and a couple of tintacks and laid it back in the crack in the ground. Harry, unaware of what had

The Long Man in the distance

---

[6] Gathered from information given in the hand-held guide material at the church

happened, laughed at Charles when he related the story to him. The next day Charles heard the voice again and saw, standing close to the crack, '..a liddle bowl full of summut dat smelt a hem-an-all better dan small beer.' Charles drank the liquid and meant to keep the bowl to show Harry, who was unaware of these events, but the bowl slipped out of Charles hand and smashed to pieces. When Charles related these events to Harry, he again just laughed and ridiculed Charles. But Harry eventually paid the price for being so disbelieving: he fell ill, could no longer work, became just skin and bone and died, a year later, at the very same day and hour when the little voices were first heard[7]……………………… But to continue with our walk.

We leave the church at the far end of the churchyard, through a kissing gate and head back, the way we came until reaching the stile we turn sharp right and head towards a metal bridge. Mele is still collecting dead flowers (?) but I noticed that 'the look' is no longer there. Perhaps she feels that she isn't going to get fed now? Or the walk is a bit of a disappointment, or it's not going too well or, of course, I could be looking too deep into the situation and she could be thinking of the flowers she's picking? Who knows? When we arrive at the bridge she cheerfully says that she thinks she has enough flowers now and, did I see that look again (?), we head across the bridge, back over the Cuckmere.

As I said, memories come back as we walk, now slightly uphill. When I was with Ron on this walk I'm sure there were more stiles on this stretch. Our instructions say there are but we are now walking in open pasture, with not a stile in sight. Mele has started to slap her own face!! "What are you doing that for?" I ask. Frantically, as she proceeds to push her index finger up her nose she says, "Somfing's just shot up me nose." "Well jamming your finger up there won't get it out," but after a few seconds of pushing, sniffing and the blowing of nose in her tissue she manages, after wiping the tears from her eyes, to get back her self control. "I'm ok now," she assures me as we head, uphill, towards another kissing gate, which was used by other means, other than walking through in typical Mele fashion.

We are now back within spitting distance of the reservoir and pass the bird hide that was opened in 1996. Mele has decided that a rest is needed, so sits on one of the many wooden seats that are scattered throughout the park. The sun is really beating down now and we both wish we had brought some water with us. "But I thought we could stop in the pub for a drink," I explain, "How was I supposed to know they'd be shut?" "If you'd have phoned like it was suggested you would have found out the opening times, wouldn't you?" says Mele and, of course she's right (again!) But there's nothing we can do about that now. We decide to carry on, along the well-marked path and head back to the car. This part of the walk is a real picture. Looking over the mass of water towards the South Downs has to be seen to be believed. I have taken a few pictures but I really don't think it does justice to the peace and tranquillity of the surroundings. By looking in a straight line, over the man-made bird island in the middle of the reservoir, you could clearly see the Long Man of Wilmington which, of course is a legendary story in itself.

Back at the car we have to decide what to do for a meal. We could drive round to The Yew Tree and hope they are open but, then again, we've been there twice and found it shut. We could go to a place that I know Mele enjoys, Frankie and Bennies, on Sovereign Harbour but Mele thought that it would be too hot and stuffy. I also suggested one of the restaurants on the harbour and we could eat outside and admire all the boats

---

[7] 'The Lore of the Land' by Westwood & Simpson Published by Penguin ISBN 0141021039 Page 722

Mele, with her dead flowers

that I could never dream of owning, but instead, we decided to go to 'The Treacle Mine'. We had both heard good and bad reports about this place but our son raved about it on his last visit. My son is the type of person who will not eat in a restaurant if the knives and forks he is to use have got to the table before he has. He will demand a clean set before he orders a meal. So if he says The Treacle Mine is a nice place to eat, it must be a nice place to eat. And I have to say we were not disappointed. The food was good, tasty, hot and well presented. The service was good and the restaurant was cool, clean and welcoming. And should Ron be interested they serve liver and bacon and have cask beer. What more does he need?

Well, that is the end of this walk. I think I've proved to myself that I am able to complete a walk. Mele is pleased that I have come through it unscathed and both our confidences are lifted. Mele has made me promise that I will never go out for a walk on my own and I must teach Ron how to use a mobile phone before she is happy to let us continue with our walks. I think that is a small price to pay. Although teaching Ron how to use a mobile phone is going to be a totally different challenge!

Pub Walk (1)

As the title implies there is likely to be more than one walk which involves a visit to a hostelry. Everyone knows that both Ron and I are partial to a drop of liquid refreshment so the fact that a few pub walks are completed within these pages should come as no surprise. I will, however, try to limit the actual number of pub visits as the book progresses.

So, what has been happening? Since the first chapter I have undergone a regime of cardio-vascular exercises. Every Tuesday and Thursday Hilda and her team at the Eastbourne District General Hospital have put me through my paces. The exercises involve work in a gymnasium and although I wouldn't admit it to Hilda I have to say that all the sweat and tears has been worth it. After twelve, two hour, sessions I have been released to the world and have had to promise to exercise regularly to ensure that a healthy Graham cannot drain the purse of our wonderful National Health Service again. I have also been back to The Conquest Hospital, in Hastings, and been given the 'all clear' from my Cardiologist, Dr. Dickinson, although I am warned that I still have a small blockage at the lower, front of my heart which she will operate on if and when it's necessary. Some other good news is that the DVLA have advised me that I can continue to drive the mini-bus for the school. So, all in all, if I can come through all of this, teaching Ron how to use a mobile phone is going to be 'a piece of cake', isn't it? The

Sussex Ox, with driver

fact was it was a very simple and easy process. Ron comes over as a bit of a stick in the mud where modern technology is concerned but even at the age of 102 he still has all his faculties and he mastered the use of my mobile with little to no effort. I have also instructed him about the use of my GTN spray, and the recovery position but, of course, he will not need to use it but everyone seems a lot happier now that he is instructed in all things cardiac. Finally everything is in place and settled. My wife is happy, my family can't wait to get me out the door and heading for God knows where in Sussex, and Ron is keen and eager to start our walks again.

For our first walk together I have chosen a walk starting and finishing at The Sussex Ox. A number of reasons helped me make this decision. The first is obvious, it's a pub, and although I have heard a lot about The Sussex Ox at Milton Street, I've never visited it, which is

strange because I like to take my wife out for the occasional meal and I'm told that The Sussex Ox 'do a good spread'. I think one of the reasons for us not to eat there may be that with pub meals you can end up with a huge plate full, and I can remember my father-in-law saying that you eat with your eyes. One look at a large dinner and both me and the wife would be finished. So it will be interesting to see what the food is like at the end of the walk. The other reasons for choosing this walk is that it is reasonably close to Hailsham so we will not need to travel too far and the walk is reasonably short (3 miles) and includes a stroll along the River Cuckmere. We have also returned to the habit of walking on a Wednesday, because as Ron says, 'it don't rain in Sussex on a wensdi afternoon'.

The pub, now known as the Sussex Ox, used to be called The Royal Oak up to the 1940's. Before then it was thought to be a slaughterhouse and butchers shop. It is situated in the back of beyond and to say that the pub has little passing trade would be an understatement, although when Ron and I got there to start the walk there had been a very nasty accident (again!!) by Drusillas roundabout and all the traffic was being diverted past The Sussex Ox so traffic was, in fact, non-stop. Various friends of ours have visited the 'Ox' and recommend it for good food as well as good beer. Ron has called in before (surprise, surprise!) and tells me that sitting out in the garden offers some of the very best views of Sussex. So I can't wait.

The Sussex Ox

I will admit that the walk is not one of my own design but taken from one of our regular books 'Pub Walks in East Sussex'[8] and is described as '…*mostly good underfoot and not over strenuous which makes it an ideal walk for all the family*'. This worries me slightly because prior to starting the walk I've looked at the instructions and hills are mentioned, as is 'The South Downs Way'. And if you mention hills and The South Downs Way in the same sentence that usually means steep. But let's get to our first walk in a couple of months. I'm beginning to get withdrawal symptoms

I collect Ron from The Kings Head and head for Milton Street. Ron was playing for The Kings Head in a darts competition last night and his mood was a little subdued when he climbed into the car. "Dart match not go too well last night?" I ask, "Got beat," he replies, "but we expected that," he continues. "T'was second leg an' we 'ad ter beat 'em 9 – 2. Didn't stand much ova chance against this team 'cause they're good. But we put up a fight an' only lost 6 – 5. But at the end, someone fell out with the captain. Said

The Sussex Ox, Milton Street

'eed never throw a dart for 'im again. Sad way ter end a match, that is. But let's not worry about that now. We've got a walk ter do." And with that, he brightened up and the rest of our short journey was taken up with idle chitchat.

Once at the 'Ox' we decide to park the car in the pub car park. After all, we expect to have a meal later, and we're sure the landlord wouldn't mind. I park the car and Ron has his door open before I have chance to put the brake on. "Bugger me!" he exclaims, "if you'd a parked the car 5 inches further over I'd a missed this," and he bends out the door and comes back up, clutching a one pound coin. "People are so posh out 'ere they drop money they don't bother ter look for it," he chuckles. "I'll just wander about the car park, while you change yer shoes. Never know, might find enough ter pay fer the meal." And off he goes, rummaging about the car park looking for coins. Whilst I'm changing shoes I can hear him kicking stones but he didn't manage to find any more coins and with instructions in hand we set off for our walk. As we come round the corner of the car park the landlord (?) was watering the plants so we let him know

[8] 'Pub Walks in East Sussex' by Mike Power - ISBN 1-898073-04-X - Walk No. 25 on page 60

that we would be back for a meal later and hoped that parking the car in the car park was ok. We were greeted with a pleasant smile and he told us that we were welcome to leave the car, hoped we had a pleasant walk and looked forward to seeing us later. "Seems like a nice man," comments Ron.

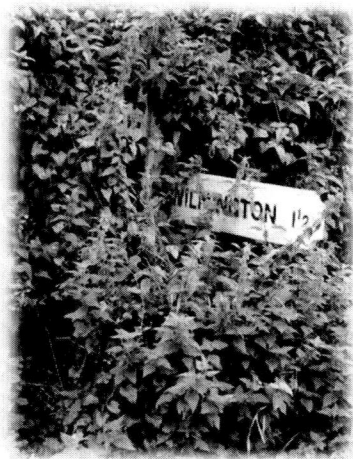

Overgrown sign

We leave the front of the pub and turn right. It is now that we realise that 'something' must be amiss. Traffic is everywhere. The road is very narrow so care is needed as we head down the road looking for our first stile, on the left. "I 'ope the instructions, in that book, are a bit clearer than that road sign," says Ron pointing out the overgrown sign, on the corner, in the hedge. "I'm not promising anything," I reply, "your guess will be as good as mine. Mind you," I continue, "just in case, I've brought a compass with me. I'm going to see if I can work out how to use one. Now the first thing I've got to do is take a bearing" "Yer need a decent map to do that," says Ron. "I know," I reply, "I've brought an Ordinance Survey map with me, as well." So I get the map out, put the compass on it, line up the lines with the compass...... and then I have absolutely no idea what I'm doing. "Put the b*£&&8y thing away," says Ron, "we can get lost just as easily without one o'them compass thingies as we can with one. Never bothered with one before, why bother with one now."

Our first stile

Of course he's right but one day, in my dreams, we'll need to know how to use a compass. And I'll be the expert (?).

The stile we need to find is on the left-hand side of the road as our instructions state. So that's a good sign from the start. Hopefully the remainder will be just as good, who knows. From this stile we cross, diagonally across a field. The path is clear and, because the weather has been reasonable it is easily followed. The view to our right and front is stunning. Lush green trees and fields greet us as we pass what I think is the area known to be Burlow Castle (see Romantic Walk). The only thing currently visible is a vague earth worked mound, which according to books is the remains of a 12th century mote and bailey castle, or perhaps a ring work fortress. Fragments of 12th and 13th century pottery, along with Prehistoric flints from all periods have been found on its large platform[9]. All the books and pamphlets I have read tell me that the site is visible from this path we are now on but, to be perfectly honest, I couldn't see it. Perhaps I was looking in the wrong direction? Do you think that a compass might help?? I decide not to mention the compass again.

---

[9] www.castleuk.net/castle_lists_south/199/miltoncastle.htm - visited 27/08/08

Nice building - nice price

Once across the field we come to a lane. Here we turn left and pass a place, on our right, which gives the name to Milton Street. Milton Court is a rather resplendent property with an arched driveway and next to it is the even larger gravel drive leading to Milton Farm. Just passed this dwelling is a kissing gate, on our right, that will lead us towards Alfriston and the River Cuckmere.

Anyone familiar with our walks will remember Alfriston. I'll just mention the pie shop and hope that this will jog your memories. Because no trip to Alfriston would be complete without Ron's trip to the local shop for a supply of pies for his week's dinners. Today was going to be no exception as we stride up the bank of what used to be a navigable river and now is nothing more than a trickling stream. "Surely we can't blame 'global warming' for the lack of water in The Cuckmere?" I ask. "I can remember coming here a couple of years ago and the river was much higher than it is now." We are amazed at how low the water level has dropped, and it didn't look as if it got any higher than the current trickle. But why it should be like that we have no idea. Just before we arrive at The Tye we detour to the 'pie shop' and are greeted like long-lost relatives. "Of course we remember you," says the owner, "come here Ron, and give us a hug," and he's practically leaping over the counter. The shop is now bigger; they've knocked an internal wall down, and the whole shop looks lighter and airier than it did when we last visited. A vast improvement plan is in place where they are opening the top of the shop as a museum. At the moment there is just a massive hole in the ceiling and the owner explains that the staircase is due to arrive within the next few weeks. Ron brought enough pies to last him the month but I was a good boy and had to refrain. I must admit I was very tempted.

In the year 1555 a victim of religious intolerance was a certain Richard Hooke of Alfriston who was condemned at Chichester in the reign of Queen Mary[10].

Previously known as Plonk Barn

...of devilish iniquity, on account of his manifest wicked errors, detestable heresies, and damnable opinions opposed, and contrary and repugnant to the Catholic Faith...Since Holy Mother Church can do nothing further against such a putrid member, we have handed over to your Royal Highnesses...the said Richard Hooke as a heretic to be punished and broken....

---

[10] Hailsham and its Environs, by Charles A Robertson – Page 60

All that Shredded Wheat

Elderberries by the bucket

Unfortunately his fate is not recorded, but I'm sure he didn't get community service! But you can imagine what might have been the outcome of poor Richard.

Alfriston is a lovely village that seems to be able to keep its olde worlde charm. From the market cross to the village pubs it is steeped in history yet seems to move with the times. Steamer Trading is one of the more modern establishments within the old buildings yet doesn't seem out of place. However when Ron checked out the price of a Sunday Roast at The George he found the prices a little high, "Don't think we'll be stoppin' 'ere fer a Sunday Lunch," said Ron, "Bit out ov our price range."

We continue along the main street until a sign directs us to the left and towards The Tye. Another beautiful area of Alfriston where the church is situated. If you haven't visited Alfriston before, spend a few minutes to look around this beautiful Sussex village. Every time Ron and I visit we find something new to discuss or marvel at. The people are friendly and the scenery is stunning. Just by the church is the old Clergy House, now owned by the National Trust. Just to visit this house is worth the trip in itself. A true gem of a place.

We find our way to the left of the church and continue our walk back over The Cuckmere, via the white bridge, and follow the path until we reach what is described in our walk instructions as 'Plonk Barn'. Unfortunately this barn, built around the 1600's, had been renovated in 1985. It appears that it was also re-named 'Great Meadow Barn' but they forgot to inform the writers of walking books. This not only confused us but also confused a couple who were walking behind us. They actually asked Ron for advice on the route they were taking and Ron, being Ron, started a debate on Sussex and it's history along with the weather, the time of year, the books we had written and when the couple told us that they were from Gloucestershire he didn't bat an eyelid, just simply said, "that's one 'ell 'ov a walk to 'ere," and bid them farewell. The look on the woman's face was a picture.

We part company with the Gloucestershire couple as they head towards Lullington Church. We bear left into one of the largest corn fields I have ever seen. It's enormous. What is strange is that the corn has not been collected. I think the correct term is that it hasn't been harvested. Yet we are at the end of August. Surely the harvest must be late, or was it too wet when harvest time came? We have no idea but not only has this very large field not been harvested but neither had the next. Our path was clearly marked through use but I hate to think how much it must have cost the poor hard-up farmer to sow this much wheat, just to see it wither and die in the field, or is there some reason for it? Ron was trying to work out how many boxes of shredded wheat a field this size could produce but eventually had to admit defeat. Again, the views from up here were stunning but the memory of '*not over strenuous*' was not strictly true.

Alfriston Village

Our next instruction was, once we had exited the fields, to turn right and head along the lane until we reached the road. We believe this to be the road that would, if you turned right, lead you towards Lullington Church. But we have to cross the road and head up Wilmington Hill, part of the Folkington Manor estate. Again I will refer to our early description of this walk. Anyone who knows the area will agree when I say that this is uphill. Admittedly it is not unnecessarily steep but it is very uneven, underfoot (the path is flint and chalk) and I would have difficulty in pushing a buggy up this slope. In fact I had problems pushing myself up this slope. Some radio control pilots, greeting us on their way down, confirmed that it was steep, windy at the top, but ideal flying conditions. But the struggle was worth it because at the very top, looking down, Ron and I could see The Sussex Ox. One of the most welcome sights for anyone.

Through the gate, we turn left, and head down the steep slope towards a gate at the bottom. Our instructions should have told us to turn left after the second gate. We turned left too soon. The downward slope we were on was steeper, so much steeper, than the slope we had come up and I can guarantee that no child would have been able to descend this part of the walk in safety. But once at the bottom it was just a short walk, across the road, and onto a bridleway opposite. If anyone makes home-made wine, this bridleway is the place to come for elderberries. I have never seen so many; the bridleway is full of them. "Trouble is," says Ron, "Yer need ten buckets full o' fruit before yer get a pound in weight!" At the end of the bridleway we turn left and head back to The Sussex Ox.

Now you must remember that I have never been to the Sussex Ox. I've never driven past it, called in for a pint nor eaten there, yet I expected something different when I walked through the door. People who have described The Sussex Ox to me have gone orgasmic about the place. Nothing I have heard was bad, far from it, so I expected plush, I expected wall-to-wall Axminster and I expected people to match. You know the type of people and place I mean. But I didn't get any of that. I got more! The welcome we received was as if we were the only customer living. The young lady behind the bar was both pleasant and courteous. No, there wasn't carpet on the floor, this was a real pub. It smelt like a real pub and it served real beer. The menu changes regularly and the board was constantly changed while Ron and I tried to decide what to eat. All around the bar area are old photographs, taken from the area which adds to the feeling of 'old'. We both ordered the chicken and were directed to the dining area. Ron had already explained to me about the view from the patio but when he last visited the trees weren't in leaf so you could see a little bit more. But the fenced garden is very well maintained and is a credit to them. If you arrive with children you can be sure of their safety which is always a consideration in today's way of life.

Whilst waiting for our food another diner struck up conversation. Ron, again being Ron, is not afraid to speak and, after idle chat eventually, offers to show the books that we are involved with. When his meal arrived we left him to enjoy his steak and ale pie and Ron returned to our table. "Tell me," says our fellow diner, "are you on holiday or just down for the day?" "We ain't neither," says Ron, "We're both 'ailshambornanbred." "I'm sorry, I didn't catch that," "'ailshambornanbred, we are" repeats Ron, "No," says our new friend, "I still didn't catch that, did you say you were from Eltham?" "No I didn't, I said we both 'ailshambornanbred," repeats Ron again. He looks at me for help so I turn to the man and say, "what Ron is trying to tell you is that we both come from Hailsham." "Oh, Hailsham," says our friend, "you're both Hailsham, born and bred. Now I understand." "Didn't I just bloody say that?" Ron asks me under his breath. "Yes you did, Ron. Just leave it."

Our food was excellent, the service was both fast and efficient and I would not hesitate in taking my wife and family to the Sussex Ox. It is true what my late father-in-law says, you eat with your eyes, and everything we saw today looked

A safe garden for the children

Wheelchair Walk

For some reason wheelchair walks aren't too popular in Sussex. I only managed to find three in East Sussex but had more success in the West of our County. Ron and I have decided on a 3 mile stroll near Graffham which is recommended for wheelchair users. The walk will include, we are told, some spectacular views, some spectacular horses (at stud), a pretty church and, hopefully, a welcoming pub.

We are joined today by Mally (pronounced Rally with an 'm'). Mally uses a wheelchair. Not all the time, but he has a little breathing problem which means he can't walk very far without getting very breathless. As if that wasn't bad enough he is also an ardent football supporter who can talk about the 'sport' non-stop, if you let him. Stockport in Cheshire is where Mally was born so it is obvious that he has supported Stockport County since birth. Edgeley Park is the home ground, which, I believe, isn't far from that other well- known club, Manchester United. Mally used to take his sons to watch Stockport County play their home games but before he was allowed to go home he had to take his sons the extra 6 miles so they could just touch the gates at Old Trafford.

Ron and I have known Mally, and his wife Sheila, for some time and they have both been following our walks and our stories with interest. Both are regulars of our favourite pub, The Kings Head, and we have whiled away a few hours in their company discussing all manner of things. One of the stories told by Mally was of a football match he was at, many years ago, against a team from Wivelsfield Green. "I used ter carry the bucket an' sponge fer Geebro in them days," says Mally, "but this team were good, played us off the park they did," Mally relates, "beat us nineteen, one. T'was unbelievable. But at the end of match I walked in 'ter the Wivelsfield dressing room and asked if we could 'ave man-o' the match. An' they agreed to give man o' the match to our goalie because 'at least 'e tried' cheeky buggers!" The name of the goalie was Kevin Loveland, our very own and well-respected florist. Mally has also told me of some underhand stories on how to cheat at flower shows (another book in the pipeline??). And, would you believe that there is a connection between Stockport, in Cheshire, and our very own Hailsham. No, I didn't know there was a link either.

Road leading to Graffham Church

But, many years ago, Mally can't remember how many, there were two gentleman by the name of Mr Hawkins and Mr Tipson who visited a mill in Cheshire, where Mally's grandfather and father worked. The pair purchased some machines and then had them transported to Hailsham. Unfortunately, the people of Hailsham hadn't a clue how to work the machines so…….. 'Me granddad 'ad ter come down 'ere an' teach you Southerners 'ow ter use machines.' This was the start of what I remember as 'H & T Marlow', once one of the biggest employers in Hailsham.

As I said our walk today is a wheelchair walk at Graffham. For those unsure of the location of Graffham it is near Petworth, on the A285 to Chichester. The walk was taken from the Internet[11] and is part of a collection of walks carried out by Jenifer (sic) Fox, who is a Multiple Sclerosis sufferer. Should anyone wish to see all of the other walks from Jenifer (sic), please go to the web site listed below or give me a call and I can forward a copy? It's well worth it if you have anyone confined to, or in need of, a wheelchair and if you want to go somewhere different. Unfortunately, for us in East Sussex, a car is needed to get to the walks in Jenifer's list unless, of course, you can use public transport.

First we need to put it together

So, on a gloriously warm October Saturday morning I collect Ron from you-know-where and then head off to pick Mally up from his house. We are informed that Mally's family have hired a wheelchair from the local Red Cross. All I hope is that we can fit it into my car! When we arrive at his house he's waiting outside, with a dismantled wheelchair, a wrap-around blanket, a coat and an overcoat. Mally's wife also informs me that he will be wearing thermals???? It is

View across the Stud Farm

obvious to both Ron and I that Mally must feel the cold because today is one of the hottest October days in years. "I thought I'd stand out 'ere and wait fer yer," explains Mally, "'cause the wife's at work an' the dog gets a bit excited with strangers." With that, a big Alsatian leaps towards the window and starts barking at us and you all know my love(?) of animals. But, thankfully, we are able to get everything into the car and we are soon heading off. "I've been lookin' forward ter this," says Mally as he relaxes in the front seat, "but before we get too far out of town do you mind if we pull up somewhere so that I can buy some ciggies? Don't worry," he quickly says, "I won't smoke in yer motor. But if yer could get near the shop door so that I don't have ter walk too far, that u'd be grand."

The trip to Graffham will take us just over 1½ hours so we while away the time chatting about this and that. 'Stockport County have bought another striker…' 'Brighton and Hove are playing a team from the bottom of the table…' 'Our local's getting' more like a disco….' Just talking about things in general, to while away the time. If anyone can remember the last time I headed towards the far west of our county you will remember that I got hopelessly confused around the one-way system in Petworth. Thankfully, with both Mally and Ron navigating, we managed to find our way round without problems. And Graffham is only a few miles away from here so we managed to find our way to the Church within minutes of leaving Petworth. But once parked the fun started. We now have to put Mally's chair together. It might have been easier if we had

---

[11] www.westsussex.gov.uk/leisureandtourism/prow/pdfs/Wheelchair_Walks_in_WS.pdf visited 01/10/2008

Mistletoe growing high in the branches

seen how it was taken apart. Then it would have been a case of reversal, but Ron described it as 'puttin' a deckchair together, but 'avin' ter attach the wheels'. But he persevered with the task and won in the end. We decided to call in to the church on the way back to the car, so we set off, past the church entrance and head towards the gates of Lavington Stud Farm. Here we turn left and walk along the tarmac driveway. The views to our left are outstanding. You can see for miles. Luckily the weather is very bright and sunny. Our instructions tell us that because this driveway is not used very often we may actually see some deer. At the moment all we have seen, apart from the fabulous views, are pheasant running for cover. I try to avoid the subject of pheasant shoots by pointing out to Mally the view of Petworth in the far distance but it's no good. Ron has started on about '..Fattenin' up the poor buggers all year, then a load ov ooray enries turn up ter scare the $*it out ov em and blast em out the sky. Call that sport??' Then he changes the subject immediately by pointing his thumb stick towards the top of a tree, narrowly missing Mally's ear, and exclaiming, "Look at 'ow much Mistletoe is on the top of that tree. I've never seen so much Mistletoe on one tree." As we all look up I, personally, couldn't see it. It was obvious that both Mally and Ron could. They were

getting excited and I couldn't understand why. I know I'm a townie but I assumed, obviously wrongly, that Mistletoe grew on a Mistletoe Tree. "'ave you ever seen a Mistletoe Tree?" asks Mally. "No," I admit, "that's because they only grow in time for Christmas." And to be honest the fact that Mistletoe is about at that time of year, frankly, has never bothered me so I'd never really thought about it. "It's a parasite," explains Mally, "birds eat the berries that grow on the Mistletoe, but the seeds pass through the bird natural like, and sticks ter branch in tree. Next year another bunch of Mistletoe appears. If yer not careful it can kill the tree ain't that

Foals showing and interest

right Ron?" "Certainly is, Mally. Mistletoe can take all the water an' nutrients from the host tree and in time the tree'll die. But there must be 'undreds o'pounds worth up there. And if yer look, lots o' the other trees are covered as well." When I got back home I looked up the plant on the Internet and found that there are over 900 species of the plant and the sticky substance, from the berries, is used in some countries for medicinal purposes and is shrouded in mystery and myth. One such myth is that Mistletoe should be cut with a golden sickle and it loses its power if it touched the ground. The loving custom of actually kissing under the Mistletoe is of Scandinavian origin.[12]

---

[12] http://en.wikipedia.org/wiki/Mistletoe visited 19/10/2008

Unfriendly sign?

We continue our walk along the drive until we come to the large stud buildings on our left. Our instructions tell us that we could continue along the drive, to the school buildings and then come back to the church. This would make for a relatively short walk of just over a mile so we opt for the longer, circular walk and turn left, through the gate and head towards and to the right of the stud buildings.

All around are signs advising us that dogs must be kept on leads and warnings not to touch the horses. To our right is a large paddock with a number of foals, doing what foals do. "Bet they're worth a pretty penny," says Ron. "'Tis a lovely life, though Ron," says Mally, "Bet they're kept well-fed an' watered. Just look at the place. It's bloody spotless. Not a bit o' litter, grass is mown, leaves are swept up off the driveway the place is immaculate. An' all you've got ter look forward too, in yer old age, is yer next mare ter come strollin' past and wallop, fill yer boots, son." All the buildings, to our left are painted white and Mally is right; the place is spotlessly clean and tidy. Of course Ron, as always, has an explanation for this, "t'is obvious, they don't get any yobs this far in the countryside to mess it up!" Of course he may be right.

Just pass the foals Mally notices something placed on top of one of the fence posts. "Perhaps they don't like too many people walking across their land," he chuckles as we see the object of his comments; a glove positioned in a 'v' sign.

We continue past the glove and the path turns left. It is now that I realise that it is Ron who is doing all the pushing of the wheelchair as I stroll along taking photographs. I offer to take my turn but Ron insists that he's ok. We are now going down hill so the push is a little easier. "I've brought Mally a little something," says Ron, "this'll 'elp us as we push 'im in the chair," says Ron as he fumbles about in his always present carrier bag. "What's that, then Ron?" asks Mally. "It's a roll o' sticky tape. Saw it in the shop this mornin' an' thought o' you!" Ron produces, from his carrier bag, a large roll of brown

Makes Mally more aerodynamic

sticky tape. "What the 'ells that for?" asks Mally. "Make yer a bit more aerodynamical," says Ron. "If we stick them ears o' yours down we'll 'ave a bit less wind resistance. Make yer easier ter push!" I promised Mally that I wouldn't mention his ears. But both Mally and I couldn't stop laughing at Ron. Anyone who knows Mally will be aware of his ears. Mally, himself, is not slow in taking the Mickey out of the size them. But just to make sure he was ok with the joke Ron asked, "Yer not offended are yer, Mally?" "Don't be daft," says Mally, "t'was bloody good laugh, that." And we continue, downhill towards a right-hand turn in the drive.

St. Giles Church, Graffham

"Aren't the clouds low?" says Mally, "being such a nice day, and all, I'm surprised that the clouds are that low." "It ain't the clouds being low, Mally," answers Ron, "t'is us bein so high up. If you look over there," Ron points to our left with his thumb stick, again just missing Mally's ear, "you can see we're almost level with the top o' the South Downs." I had noticed, on our instructions that as we started our walk it is possible to turn right and head up towards the South Downs Way and then head back towards the village. Obviously not a good idea with a wheelchair. But now I notice that our driveway has started to go uphill and Ron has handed over the chair to me.

We continue, along the driveway, passing more horses in the paddocks and fields until we reach what looks like another stable block. The view, to our left is now of the church in the distance. Behind the church is a wall of green trees and time is taken to just stand and marvel at the beauty of the scene before us. "There ain't enough colours in a paint pot ter be able ter paint a picture like that," says Ron, and we all just stand and admire.

We finally pass through an electric gate and exit Lavington Park and Stud and now head back, uphill, towards the church. I think the main impact to me, personally, about the area is how clean and tidy the area is. We have seen no rubbish at all, no graffiti, no dog pooh hanging in plastic bags from branches. The place is spotless and a credit to the people of Graffham. As is St. Giles Church although, again this is a personal thing; I felt it lacked that certain something for me. The church is beautiful, "'ow long must it 'ave taken to point all them stones in that wall?" asks Mally, pointing to the stonework on the outside, "it must 'ave taken 'em years." In fact, although some of the interior is believed to date back to Norman times the church was practically rebuilt in the early 1800's.[13] Which must be about the time that a notorious footpad known as Allen was relieving the local farmers of their purses as they returned from market? His daring made him the terror of West Sussex. Eventually the Militia was called to try and capture him. They managed to corner him near a pond in Graffham where he was spotted by his pursuers. The captain of the Militia, a Captain Sargent, called for Allen to give himself up. But his reply was a single shot which killed the Captain instantly. The other soldiers then opened fire and killed Allen[14]. So far we haven't come across a pond on our walk.

Mally, sits awhile

We leave the church after a little wander and sit down. Both Ron and Mally signed the visitors book. "The last person ter sign book came from Australia," says Mally, "people come from all over the world to see that church." Unfortunately we couldn't find any literature about the church so the odd

---

[13] http://www.geograph.org.uk/photo/52698 visited 17/10/2008
[14] People of Hidden Sussex by Swinfen & Arscott a BBC Radio Sussex Guide

snippet of information has had to come from the Internet. Again, the place is spotlessly clean and perhaps that was what was wrong for me. It was a bit clinical and white.

There are not many gravestones within the church grounds but most of the stones and graves can be found through the gate on the opposite side of the road. What is unusual, and a very welcome addition to the graveyard, should you be researching your family history in Graffham is the map of the graveyard including the names of the interred and where the grave can be located. All done on an alpha and numerical map, very civilised.

Our next stop on this walk is, of course, the pub. We dismantle the chair, in record time, stow it in the back of the car and head for The White Horse. But when we arrive we find that the pub is called The Forrester's Arms? That's odd; perhaps the name has been changed. We receive a very cheery greeting from the young lady behind the

The distant Church

bar. The pub is a Free House and Ron is pleased to see that there is a Harvey's on offer. Unfortunately it's not his favourite tipple but "…it's a pale ale type o' brew, but I'll give it a try." Mally says he'll try a pint of the same and I push the boat out with an orange juice and lemonade, with ice! The pub looks reasonably old and the main focal point has to be the very large open fireplace with logs the size of small trees. But in true 'Left or Right'[15] fashion although we're not lost we are in the wrong pub. I discovered this when I asked the young lady if the name had been changed from The White Horse. "Good heavens no," I'm told, "The White Horse is up the road, in the middle of the village. Just turn left, before the Church." Now that explains everything, doesn't it? It was about now that a menu was placed on our table, just in case? I have to admit that I thought the prices a bit steep and hoped that Ron would agree. The fact that Ron's pint was flat also helped persuade us to head back towards the church and turn left.

Again, in true Left or Right[16] fashion, when we headed back to the church we couldn't find a left turn. "Ask that young lady by the letter box," suggests Mally. I pull over and it's obvious that the young lady is a lad, who directs us back down the road and in the right direction. "Blimey," says Mally, "he was a good lookin' feller weren't he?" Now I'm beginning to get worried about Mally.

As we turned into the car park of The White Horse we are greeted with a helicopter 'parked' in the car park. "Look at that," says Ron, "your wife's actually sent out a search party

Mally feels the cold

---

[15] 'Left or Right, Ron?' by Graham Pollard
[16] Ibid

for us, Graham,' which is the usual comment from Ron whenever we get geographically challenged. But there it was. A small helicopter which was just begging to be used in this chapter. Mally headed for the door of the helicopter and I took his picture. "We'll tell 'em all at the Kings Head that we swapped 'is wheelchair for the chopper," chuckles Ron. "Don't you dare," says Mally, "we 'ad ter put a £20 deposit on that chair!"

After a good giggle we set off for the bar. Again a cheery welcome was received and this time Ron and Mally couldn't decide on which ale to try. The young lady behind the bar, who used to work in a Harvey's pub, recommended an ale called Betty Stogs. She poured a small amount of the ale into a couple of glasses and let them both try before they brought. Both agreed that '…it was a nice bit o' tipple' and ordered a pint each. I, again, decided to save myself and ordered the usual orange juice and lemonade. A quick look at the menu and the prices were more like our style and the food on the menu sounded very appetising. Poor Mally couldn't eat too much so went for just a 'soup of the day', Ron decided on liver and bacon and I settled on roast chicken. All came fabulously presented on hot plates and was very tasty. If you ever find yourself in the area give this pub a visit. It's in the middle of nowhere but is everything a true British pub should be. The staff was friendly, polite and knowledgeable and did not patronise us but showed a genuine interest in their customers. One strange thing happened whilst we were at The White Horse. Mally asked what was in Ron's carrier bag. That, in its self isn't odd, but what Ron then did was strange. He actually took out items from the bag to show Mally. First was a Newspaper, next a small sweet, "in case we meet a dog", then a bottle of water, next came a miniature bottle of whisky, "fer medicinal purposes", some raw plugs "ter repair signposts", a length of string, a packet of plasters and a bandage then a hammer. Next was a packet of tissues. By the time Ron brought out the toilet roll Mally was laughing so much, tears were running down his face. "You must be honoured, Mally" I tell him, "a number of people have asked what's inside that bag and as far as I can remember he hasn't told a soul, let alone shown them." "Changes every week," says Ron, "it'll be different on the next walk."

By the way, the helicopter that landed in the car park a little before we got to the pub is owned by a member of a big pheasant shoot which is due to happen later in the day. For legal reasons I can't print what Ron had to say about that!! But I think we had a great day. Mally, certainly seemed to enjoy himself. It is now just turned three o'clock and we must head home. Mally looks tired, perhaps you can have too much of a good thing.

Look what Mally got for his wheelchair

Friends Walk

This walk has been suggested by Lee, another of our drinking companions from The Kings Head. Like Mally in our previous walk, I have tried to get a little background information on Lee but had little success. He makes cables at a local factory for a living. The cables are used in machines that use cables. He has made cables for a long time. He has two sisters, one does not live locally but he lives in Hailsham. He plays darts, enjoys going to speedway at Arlington, is fascinated with spooky phenomena and drinks Harvey's Best. He is, normally, a very quiet individual but has been known to get a little upset at times. You now know just as much about Lee as Ron and I do. Another companion who wishes to join us today is totally the opposite of Lee. Sally is very outgoing, a lady who also likes her 'pint of Harvey's', and isn't afraid to say what she thinks and sometimes gets into trouble for saying it. One of the funniest live shows I've ever seen was Sally's stand-up, one woman comedy show at our very own Pavilion in Hailsham. The place was packed and her jokes and observations about everyday life and some of her friends and colleagues were hilarious. She also has a very serious side. At the Cremation of one of our very dear friends, Sean Snee, she read out a poem, written by Ron. A great number of mourners were deeply moved by the poem and the way in which Sally read Ron's words. Sally now resides in Canada with her husband, Rob, but has taken the time to visit her home town and join us, just for today.

Approaching St Mary's Church, Rye

As I said the walk was chosen by Lee. He liked the look of the walk[17] because it has some history at Rye, some religious connection at Winchelsea and we pass a castle at Camber. When the walk was arranged, some time ago, I didn't realise that the clocks would go back one hour and it would be dark by five o'clock. Not a massive problem but I don't finish work until one, it will take us over an hour to get to Rye, and the walk is 6½ miles long. It'll be dark before we finish. Both Ron and I have problems finding our way about in broad daylight. Can you imagine how dangerous we could be in the dark? So, with time against us, I have decided, at great expense to myself, to take the day off from work so that we can leave home at ten o'clock. This will give us ample daylight hours to complete the walk. The last time Ron and I walked around Winchelsea we got soaked.

Sally in her pink loafers

---

[17] 'Classic Walks in Sussex' by Ben Perkins – SB Publications – Page 23 Walk 4

The Old Grammar School

Let's hope history doesn't repeat itself.

At the allotted time on a very cold October Wednesday morning I collect Ron, Sally and Lee and we head towards Rye. The drive will take about an hour, Lee and Sally had never met so introductions were carried out. The journey is completed with some idle chit-chat. Discussions include Sally's home, in Canada and her life with her husband Rob. How she misses England but especially the 'Harvey's'. Apparently beer in Canada isn't too good. Sally lives near Lake Eerie which is said to be the 12th largest lake in the world. It is bordered by Canada in the North and by four states in America in the South, Michigan, New York, Pennsylvania and Ohio. The lake is 57 miles wide and two hundred and forty-one miles long[18] which makes any of our lakes sound a bit like puddles. Sally also described her house and even that sounds enormous. But with all the chat it didn't seem too long before we had passed through Hastings and were parking at Rye Railway Station, as suggested by our instruction book[19]. Although it is a pay-and-display car park I was amazed that it was only £1.50 for the whole day. When I looked at our ticket I noticed it expired at 4 o'clock Thursday morning. Was that a sign that we would be getting hopelessly lost??

It was obvious from our attire that the men in this group had walked before. I changed into walking boots and carried an extra jacket; Ron had an anorak, stout walking boots and a knitted hat, Lee was adorned in a very nice and warm looking coat and wore walking boots. But Sally decided on a

Just one of the stained glass windows

coat and hat which would have graced any cat walk (?) with bright pink cloth trainers (I believe they could be called loafers (?)) and we were heading out across marshland for the next 6½ miles. Let's hope it doesn't rain.

The first part of our walk is around the beautifully cobbled streets of Rye. Heading away from the Station we come to a junction and make our way up Market Street to join the High Street. Here we turn left. We need to look out for the Old Grammar School which dates from 1636. The school was founded by Sir Thomas Peacocke as a free school '*for the better of Education and Breeding of Youth in good*

---

[18] http://www.articlesbase.com/sports-and-fitness-articles/a-lake-eerie-perch-fishing-guide-559418.html visited on 30/10/08
[19] 'Classic Walks in Sussex' by Ben Perkins Page 24 of Walk 4

Literature'. The building functioned as a school until 1907.[20] The ground floor i s now occupied by a record shop aptly named Grammar School Records. Here we turn right and head up Lion Hill, towards St. Mary's Church. This has to be one of the most tightly compact churches we have seen yet, in its way, it is truly beautiful. First you have to walk towards the very large and imposing doorway. As we approach the door everyone around us is doing the tourist bit, Sally and me included, where you just have to have photographs. To the right of the impressive church entrance is a very quaint tea shop, which belittles its previous existence, somewhat. Above the large, old window is a very large, hanging sign with a picture of the said John Fletcher which reads:

FLETCHERS HOUSE
in this ancient vicarage
John Fletcher
was born in 1579
Jacobean dramatist and
collaborator with
Beaumont, Shakespeare
and Massinger

The vicarage, as it was then, was owned by his father, Richard Fletcher, who later became Bishop of London and Chaplain to the Queen. It was in 1606, at the age of 27, that it is recorded that John Fletcher was one from a group of literary men who used to meet with William Shakespeare at The Mermaid Tavern.[21] It is very obvious that the place is steeped in so much history that it would take pages to go through it all, and here and now is not the time, but we all just had to stop and stand outside this church and take it all in. If anything, inside the church is a little disappointing. Sally and Lee seemed to love the place but both Ron and I said at the same time, "It's not a sit down church." But it does have its own beauty. The stain glass windows are marvellous and, I'm sure, the view from the tower is spectacular, but I don't believe in having to pay for a view, so we declined to climb the steps.

West Street

I noticed some of the brickwork around the church is a strange pink colour. From brochures purchased at the church we are told that in 1377 the town was invaded by France. The church was set on fire and the bells taken back to France. The fire was so severe that the roof collapsed. The pink colour is where the fire affected the brickwork all those years ago.

---

[20] http://www.urban75.org/photos/rye/rye056.html visited 31/10/2008
[21] http://www.luminarium.org/sevenlit/fletcher/fletchbio.htm visited 31/10/2008

We manage to drag Sally away from the church by telling her that this is the start and we have a lot of walking to do before we get home. Reluctantly she stows her camera and we set off down the cobbled West Street towards Lamb House, once owned by the writer Henry James (?). Here we come to the junction with Mermaid Lane, with its famous Inn. Our instructions tell us to pass the Inn and I knew, long before we got here, that I might have trouble getting past the pub. But as luck (?) would have it, the place looked as if it was closed, so I took a few photographs and kept walking.

The Mermaid Inn, restored in 1420

With disappointment written all over them we pass the Inn and continue down the hill. When we reach the bottom we come to the very busy A259, near the Town Information Centre. We now need to follow the A259 over the River Tillingham and turn left at the mini-roundabout. Our instructions now say '...*For some of the way there is now an unofficial alternative path beside the river...*' so we head along this path, beside the river.

Many followers of our walks will be aware of my reaction to abandoned machinery on farmland and listening to the bleating of some 'hard-up farme rs'. I've found another 'pet hate'. Boats just left to rot and spoil. This boats name was 'Maserati' and according to the stern was out of Teignmouth. It must have cost the best part of a lot o'dosh. But it looked as if it hadn't seen open water for years. It was filthy, the red boat attached to it was falling apart and what you could see of the interior was battered and torn. Ron insisted that the boat had been seized by Customs and Excise because of some smuggling activity. The sole reason for this deduction was that is what they do in Spain. Why he should insist on this reason I have no idea. But he repeated the same story when, after finding out that this '...*unofficial alternative path by the side of the river...*' was, in fact, a dead end and we had to pass the boat, again, as we headed back to the A259. "We 'aven't left Rye yet an' we're 'eadin' up the wrong path."

Strange window display

But once back on the main road it is a steady walk towards the left-hand turn which leads to Rye Harbour. But before we reach this turning Ron and Sally spot a strange thing in a shop window. What it is made of or why it should be in a shop window I have no idea. But Sally loved it!

Sally the 'tourist'

My boats bigger than Mally's chopper

Camber Castle

We turn left, heading towards Rye Harbour and cross the River Brede. "Wasn't this the River Tillingham, back up the road in Rye?" I ask. "It was," replies Ron, "and it's also a tributary to the Rother," he continues as we cross the lock and turn right, down a drive to the side of the river Tillingham/Brede/Rother. "But how come," I plead, "can it be the River Tillingham up the road and just a few hundred yards down the road it turns into the Brede?" But all Ron would say was "complicated ain't it?" Sally is now standing above the lock doing her touristy bit by taking photographs. She has a new digital camera and insists on taking as many photo's as she can so that she can show her husband Rob when she gets home.

Here, again, our instructions seem a little off. As we walk down this lane the river, whatever it's called, is on our right-hand side. In front of us the driveway veers to the right of some houses. But the path goes to the left. Our instructions tell us to veer right. But if we veer right we are walking up someone's driveway. We are to pass through a gate and continue along the river bank. But where we veer right the pathway, as Lee pointed out, is to the left not the right. It seemed that, unknown to me a decision had been made by the other three members of our group, because as I wandered along someone's drive, looking for a gate, everyone else held back. Thankfully a gate was found and everyone then rushed up behind me and followed me through.

In the distance can be seen the remains of Camber Castle. Not the most formidable of castles, in fact Ron described it as being three Martello Towers stuck together, but when it was built in the 1500's by Henry VIII for the defence of our coastline I'm sure it serve d its purpose, until, of course the sea receded and the castle was abandoned. Our instruction book advises us that extensive repairs have been carried out over a large number of years and now, at last, Camber Castle is safe enough to be open to the public but only at the

View across Brede

weekend. As Sally was an overseas visitor many pictures were taken of the Castle so that she could show her friends back home. Lee spent some time wandering around, looking into the castle and managed to find out from various information boards that the castle was secured by a total of 42 men. Which seem a very few men to guard against the whole of the French invasion force? No wonder the French succeeded.

We now need to find a path that is a few yards short of the main entrance to the castle and head towards Castle Farm. It is now that Sally decides that she needs the ladies room and insists that we all walk ahead and she'll catch us up. "Good job we didn't stop at The Mermaid," says Ron, "could 'ave been stop an' start all the way ter Winchelsea. But," he says with a little smile, "we will be stoppin' fer a drink somewhere, won't we?" "I thought we'd stop when we got back to Rye, that way the walk is completed and we will know how long it's going to take to get back home," I tell Ron. "Oh! Not stoppin' till then, then." It's obvious that he's disappointed. Eventually, after just a few minutes, Sally manages to catch us up.

From Castle Farm we head up the drive until we come, again, to the A259. We turn left here and walk along the road, over the Royal Military Canal and head for a steep climb up into Winchelsea. Unfortunately, before we get as far as Winchelsea, we have to pass yet two more Inns. I notice a little unrest but both Lee and I ignore it.

When we reach Winchelsea we head straight for the church, which is a magnificent building. Both Ron and I have visited here before but for Lee and Sally it was the first time and I think they were impressed, Sally even more so when Ron told her that the churchyard was the last resting place for one of her heroes, 'Spike' Milligan. Terence Allen (Spike) Milligan died in 2002. There can't be any reader who doesn't recognise the name 'Spike' Milligan but if you have any doubts as to his fame just look up 'The Goon Show' on Google. I will say no more, other than that his humour was a little strange and not

Winchelsea Church

Sally 'with' Spike

The New Inn, Winchelsea

The remains of the windmill

really my type, if I'm honest. We did manage to find his stone and the last line on his headstone reads, in Gaelic, 'I told you I was ill'.

But inside this fabulous church is true atmosphere and history. Both Ron and I sat. The feeling of calmness and serenity is indescribable. It has to be one of the most atmospheric churches we have ever visited. A truly delightful place. But all things must come to an end and we had to drag ourselves back to reality.

We leave the church and head towards the New Inn. Both Lee and I head towards the next turning before I get the feeling that we are not being followed. I turn round to see both Sally and Ron standing by the pub door. "You can't be serious about not getting a drink until we get back to Rye," pleads Sally. What can I say? I look at Lee, he just shrugs so we head back to the New Inn. "I thought Ron was bloody joking, when he said we wouldn't stop for a pint," says Sally. I try to explain that getting back to Rye and having a drink in The Mermaid was planned because both Ron and I have to get home so that we can take my wife out for a meal this evening. But nothing was going to stop Ron and Sally having a pint at this pub. We settle down in the bar, each have a pint of Speckled Hen, I have a cup of coffee. "That was bloody expensive," says Sally, "most expensive pint I've had since I left Canada. But it ain't bad, is it?" We chat for a while about this and that, before collecting our things and head for the door. "How much is your pint of Speckled Hen?" Sally asks the barmaid, "I'm not sure," she replies, "I think it's £2.90 a pint." Lee, Ron and me have got out the door as mentally Sally works out that three pints at £2.90 comes to £8.70. "But hang on," she says, "You charged my friend over £10. I thought that was bloody expensive." "That's right," says the bar maid, "three pints of Speckled Hen and a cup of coffee." "Christ, I forgot the bloody coffee, sorry." And she's out the door. Unfortunately I left my thumb-stick by our table and Sally left her cigarette. So, like true gentleman, when Sally offered to go back to retrieve my stick and her 'smoke' we all thanked her and said we would wait.

Only one adult swan?

Lee finds it funny

We now join part of the 1066 Country Walk by following the drive opposite the A259. This leads us to the site of a former windmill destroyed during the hurricane of 1987. Only the foundations remain but it is a stark reminder of the devastation during that storm. Strangely we tend to think of that event as being 'local' and only affecting parts around our home, but of course the damage was far more extensive. Where this windmill used to stand was once the site of the Church of St Leonards. It is remembered on the plaque being read by Lee in the picture. Also, if you look at the picture carefully you will see the view that can be gained across the River Brede. Just a few steps further on, through a gate and we could see for miles. It was fantastic.

We now follow our instructions as we head back towards Rye, which can be seen in the distance. Unfortunately, we can see it but can't get to it. All along our route are large 'stream' like ditches which criss-cross the marshland. Keeping to the instructions was a little difficult as we attempted to keep this ditch to our left, the next stream to our right. And it certainly didn't help when we needed to cross a stile into another field when there was no stile to be seen. What was a plus though was the amount of mushrooms we all managed to find as we went from one field to the next trying to cross the stream that was directly in front of us. We also witnessed a strange sight, a single swan with two young. "Something must 'ave 'appened," comments Ron, "don't normally see one adult swan with its young. Always 'as ter be the two". But this wasn't helping us get to Rye, and it was starting to get cold. In true Ron and Graham fashion we went the wrong way and had a detour of nearly a mile. We ended up by the railway line and had to head back to where we had turned, only to find that the farmer had removed the stile and replaced it with a new fence. On the ground were two breeze blocks (large grey bricks) for us to climb to get over and these were overgrown and we only just managed to see them.

From here we have to cross another field. It's Lee who spots the Bull sign first. The inevitable words come forth, "They won't 'urt yer," says Ron. How many times have I heard those words? But Sally has us all laughing with "Let me go first, I'm a Vegan!" as she strides through the gate. The laugh continues when Lee suggests that we let Sally carry the mushrooms. "When the bull sees the whites of the mushrooms, we can run in one direction whilst the bull goes after Sally!" But we all manage to get across the field without causing the bull to even raise its head.

Beautiful floral display at Winchelsea Church

We emerge from this track opposite the Tillingham/Brede/Rother and it's just a short walk back along the main road to the Railway Station Car Park. It is now that Ron notices that I have been carrying a fold up rain coat on the waist band of my trousers. "Didn't trust yer ol' mate when I say t'aint gunner rain on a Wen'sday afternoon," he says pointing to the bag. "Let's be honest, Ron," I reply, "It started to rain as we headed across that open ground back to Rye." "That wer'nt rain," he insists, "just spray off them streams an' ditches that was." "I don't know why you're having a go at Graham," interrupts Sally, "show him what you and Lee brought with you, just in case." Both Lee and Ron produce torches from their pockets. "I'd heard that you get lost a lot so I brought this torch, just in case it was dark when we got back," says Lee, "an' I know we get lost some o' the time so I brought mine as reserve, just in case we really got lost," says Ron, with that silly grin. They have no faith!!

This could have been called a 'History Walk' because of where we have been and what we saw. It was enjoyable if not a little barren in places, walking along the marshland. But Rye and Winchelsea made up for it. Rye had its very old cobbled streets and Winchelsea had its church and what was left of Camber Castle in-between. Hopefully, when Sally gets back to Canada, she will relate the walk to her husband, Rob, and very soon he'll be able to come over to England and come with us on one of our walks.

You may have noticed that this walk was written in a slightly different style than previous chapters. As I read it back to myself it doesn't sound as if we spoke to each other much, but I can assure you that conversation did go on. But those who know Sally will be aware that she can be very verbal and whilst our conversations were varied, they were also a little 'colourful' in language. We had many laughs on the way with loads of jokes and stories but I think the content of the stories would have been lost with the omission of the 'colourful language'. For obvious reasons I am not permitted to put down on paper what was actually said. But I'm sure that if you speak to Ron, Lee, and Sally or, even myself, we may let you into some of the things that were said. But then again......

Enrichment Walk

When this walk was first suggested I was a little apprehensive. From the start I didn't understand what an 'Enrichment Walk' was. Second I didn't know how to find this type of walk and a number of issues cropped up as my understanding increased. It was my daughter who suggested that this type of walk could be different from the others Ron and me had completed. So, to be honest, I sat back and let my daughter explain to me what it was that would be so different. Because 'different' it will certainly be.

As some may be aware, my daughter, Michelle, works at a school. Her job title is 'Internal Intervention Manager'. Part of her responsibilities is to co-ordinate various projects; one of these projects is for a group of children, from her school, who are regarded as 'gifted and talented'. It transpires that a young lad named Josh wants to be a photographer when he gets older. My daughter had seen some of his pictures and was impressed with his talent. A couple of other children also showed an interest in taking pictures so, my daughter thought that we could take three of these 'gifted and talented' children with us on a walk and the children could take the photographs. "So how come the walk is enrichment?" I ask. Michelle explains, "Not only will the children be taking photographs but we will be giving the children new experiences and widening their understanding, as well as introducing new skills. The children's photographs could be part of the next book and, just in case we get lost, they can also do a bit of map reading just to help you both out. The fact that they will be in a totally different environment from school, but learning at the same, time has to be enrichment." Ok, I'm sold on the idea, but a number of issues gave me some concern. Because we would be with children I would have to ensure that Ron had been checked out by the authorities (Criminal Records). As I work at a Girls School I have been checked, obviously my daughter is ok. It would also be necessary to carry out some form of Risk Assessment on the walk. This means 'doing' the walk prior to being with the children. But first I will have to find a walk that a) is not too long, b) is reasonably close to home, c) will hold the interest of school children, and d) be safe for children to carry out. What could be easier??

Some very bright wellies

The one factor that was in my favour was that this walk was to be arranged for the summer months. As we are currently approaching Christmas I have some time to locate a walk and do all the preparations. That was, until Michelle just happened to mention the idea to Josh, at school. He is now so excited that she is having a job to stop him from talking about it constantly and doesn't think he could possibly wait until the summer. "Can we do it before Christmas??" she pleads. So, it's thinking caps on and after a while I manage to find a walk that may fit the bill. It is a walk of 2¾ miles around Horam[22], starting along part of the cuckoo trail and then, performing a circular walk, ending back on the cuckoo trail. The book tells us to be on the look out for Iron ponds

---

[22] 'Kiddiwalks in East Sussex' by Len Markham published by Countryside Books – Walk 15

along our route which would indicate that the area was used for the excavation of iron ore to make cannons etc. Sounded just the job, so it is on a cold and damp Sunday morning that Michelle and I complete the walk in the interests of Health and Safety. Whilst finding our way about and over the large number of stiles on the walk we start to discuss other issues about the forthcoming walk with the children. Who else to bring with us, other than Ron and Josh? Where to collect the children or should the parents take them to school and we pick them up from there? What time should we set out? What

The Cuckoo Trail

time shall we tell the parents we will have the children home? What should the children wear? Should all the children bring cameras? Who decides on which photos go into the book? Should we make it a competition? If we leave in the morning should we take a packed lunch? If we do take a packed lunch will we have to establish any allergies? Will we need a first-aid box? What if it rains??? It is so much easier when it is just Ron and me!

But the decisions have been made. Michelle has completed the Risk Assessment. Both Michelle and I have proof of our CRB checks (Criminal Records) and that proof has been shown to the Headmaster. It has been decided that the two children to assist Josh (aged 9) with the photographs are Jessica and Reno (both aged 10). Michelle has written to the parents of the three children who will be with us to explain the 'why's and wherefores', and they are more than happy to let us take care of their loved ones for a few hours. The first aid box is stashed away in my rucksack along with sandwiches, fruit, drinks and all the necessary equipment for our enrichment experience. Let's hope it doesn't rain!

Although I am not taking the photographs for this chapter I have my camera inside the rucksack with some spare batteries, just in case. At the allotted time I head off

Clever photography from the children

to the Kings Head and collect Ron. Whilst I'm waiting for him in the car park I suddenly realise that I haven't spoken to Michelle this morning to see if everything is still ok and that the walk was going to be carried out. Thank God for mobile phones. When I eventually get in touch I discover that she has arranged for the children to meet her at their school and, as we spoke, two children had already arrived and one was on his way. Ron and I set off for Horam and Michelle tells me that she will meet us at the car park, near our starting point.

What is this?

Putting the sun to good use

Try, as I might, I can find very little of interest about Horam. It seems a lot went on around this place but nothing happened in it. The name Horam was first recorded, would you believe, in AD950 as 'Horham', which meant, in Saxon times, 'a dirty settlement'. This description probably came from the very muddy condition of the area often made worse in bad weather by overflowing streams. But there was a good side to this muddy existence: Horam became a major centre for the Wealden iron industry with at least eight blast furnaces and five power forges all within a four mile radius of the village.[23]

Living close by, in Clappers Wood, was a man named Jonathan Harmer (b1763c – d1849). He was buried at Heathfield on 2nd February 1849[24] and was a well-known gravestone artists. His terracotta stones can be found in a few church cemeteries in Sussex. The main period of his work was during 1806-1825. The distinctive reddish brown clay used to form his masterpieces was collected around the Horam-Heathfield area and pressed into moulds and cast in an oven. A collection of his terracotta plaques together with moulds can be seen in the Museum of Local History at Anne of Cleves House in Lewes.

The now disused 'Merrydown Wine Company' buildings originated from a tentative venture in the garage of a house called 'Merrydown'. In 1946 this venture produced 450 gallons of redcurrant wine and vintage cider. The result was for Ian Howie and Jack Ward, over the next few years to expand and they eventually became a well-known and respected exporter of wines and ciders. At its peak the company had a turnover of over 5 million pounds and had gained something of a worldwide reputation for quality[25]. Unfortunately the company has now finished trading and the buildings are no longer used.

As I said earlier, this walk is Walk 15 in 'Kiddiewalks in East Sussex' and, as I have completed the walk with Michelle already I am sure that finding our way round is going to be easy. We park in the car park (free) in Hillside Drive, Horam and await the arrival of our young companions. For a small place it is noticeable how busy this car park is. Traffic is constantly coming and going as people either head into the village for a newspaper or start walking their dogs along the cuckoo walk.

---

[23] 'Sussex Place-Names' by Judith Glover, Published by Countryside Books, Page 114
[24] PoHS83, East Sussex Records Office
[25] 'Hailsham and its Environs' by Charles Robertson, Published by Phillimore Page 188

Reno, Jess and Josh

We don't have to wait too long before Michelle arrives with Jessica, who prefers to be called Jess, Reno and Josh. After introductions are carried out a short lecture on 'does and don'ts' is given to ensure that the children are aware of what is expected from them and how we, hopefully, will assist them in enjoying the next few hours. My first impressions of the children are; quietly polite, a little apprehensive, somewhat excited and Jess has to have the brightest Wellingtons on the planet.

We leave the car park and turn right and then left onto the Cuckoo Trail, heading towards Heathfield. I explain to the children that we are on what is known as Route 21 and that signs, with the number 21 painted on will be seen all the time we are on the Cuckoo Trail. Ron tells them that this part of the Cuckoo Trail used to be the railway line that ran from Heathfield to Hailsham and then, on to Eastbourne. One of Ron's proudest boasts is that he was on the last train from Hailsham to Eastbourne in 1968. The children have cameras at the ready, and start clicking away. Luckily they are digital and we have no need for film or processing. The way that the cameras were being used it could have cost a fortune to have the films developed. And we have only gone a few yards! Perhaps it is because I have not been with young children for some time but I was surprised at what they thought of as exciting. Simple things such as red berries and trees, Jess seemed to be obsessed with trees. Anyone who knows the Cuckoo Trail will be aware that it is lined with trees. In the first 100 yards Jess must have taken a photograph of every tree along our route. Once a picture had been taken one of us, either Michelle, Ron or myself had to look at the little screen to see the picture they had just taken. Ron explained to the children that there were many ways to remember things in the countryside. "My ol' mum an' dad used ter tell me what to look out for," he explains, "If you see the ash before the oak, your in fer a soak but if the oaks before the ash it'll only be a splash." "What does that mean?" chuckles Josh, "well," continues Ron, "If the ash tree 'as 'er leaf before the oak, that means it's goin' ter rain, really 'ard but if the oak 'as 'er leaf before the ash, it won't rain very hard, only get a splash, see?" Our walk has got really slow now as the children start to take a real interest in their surroundings.

Reflections in a puddle

We bear left and it's Jess that first notices the sign, "Look," she says, "the number 21 is painted on the post, just like Mr Pollard said." "And there's a sign here telling us all about the railway," says Ron as

More clever work with the camera

we pass what used to be Horam Station and head under the first bridge. It's just past this first bridge that we notice Josh is limping. "Are you ok, Josh?" asks Michelle, "not really," he replies, "I've hurt me foot. " "We've only been walking for a few minutes," says Michelle, "how can you be hurt, did you trip?" "No," replies Josh, "I was so excited about coming on the walk I forgot to put some socks on. Me feet are freezing in these wellies." What can you say? We can't go back to Eastbourne so Ron suggests that if we walk a little quicker it might help get his feet warm. So we keep heading along the Cuckoo Trail until we reach Hendalls Farm Bridge. All the time the children are snapping away with the cameras. To make it fair to the three children they swop cameras every now and again. Josh seems to be happy with one camera in particular, "Its got 14 times zoom," he explains to everyone when we look at the pictures he's taken.

"I'm bored," says Josh and my heart sunk. Oh no, I thought, they don't like it. We've only been out for less than half an hour and they're getting bored. But Reno and Jess said that they weren't bored at all and that Josh was being silly. "No I'm not," says Josh, "I thought we were going to get muddy, that's why I've got my Wellingtons. But we haven't seen any mud yet." "It won't be long now," I explain, "as soon as we come off the Cuckoo Trail we'll have to walk along a road and then cross a stile into the fields." This seemed to have the desired effect as Josh rushes of to take even more pictures of Jess and Reno lounging on one of the many seats placed along the trail.

Just a few hundred yards past Hendalls Farm Bridge we cross another iron footbridge before turning right on to Tubwell Lane. This Lane leads us up towards Maynards Green School and a very busy main road. Thankfully the children were very well behaved, although Reno was trying to take more photographs and started to back into the road before Michelle managed to grab his arm and stop him. Once over the road we headed down a narrow country lane called Sicklehatch Lane. We turn right, over a stile, and head across fields towards the corner.

We try some map reading

Again I have to marvel about things that come into children's heads. Before we started this walk it was decided that as the children would not be in a classroom environment we would, at times, 'let them go'. Just let the three be together, without an adult looking over them, give them space and let them interact with each other. It was during one of these 'let them go' periods that I

The fascination with trees

noticed, in the distance to my left a young bullock. But before I could say anything Jess was getting quite animated about mole hills. Her camera was clicking away as she headed down a slippery path. "Are any of you worried about animals?" I manage to ask, Ron straight away says, "They won't 'urt yer, just don't show 'em yer scared." But straight away the three children run to catch us up and Josh asks, "Do they pooh?" Now I assumed that he was asking if the cows smell. But I am corrected by Jess who, quite correctly pointed out, that all animals have to pooh because that's where we get manure from. Reno, then starts to tell us the do's and don'ts of animal pooh. "I watched it on TV," he says, "Llama pooh is the best pooh you can have for your garden." He then explains to us about the living habits of Llama's and why their pooh is so good for the garden. Everyone just stopped and listened. It was fascinating to hear a young lad talking in this way. Even Josh had stopped sliding in the mud that led us down to the gate.

Once through the gate and away from the animals we head into a small wood. Because of the amount of rain over the last few days the small streams in this wood were running quite freely. We detour from the track and let the children explore the area. Ron explains to them that this is where men used to dig for Iron ore, many years ago, to make cannons used in the many wars between England and France. He showed them where the water had turned orange as it ran through the ground indicating iron ore deposits. It was nice to see Ron interacting with the children and they were taking notice of all he said. I really think Ron was enjoying himself. I looked at some of the children's photography here and was pleasantly surprised at the clarity and imaginative effects that were being produced from them all.

We now cross over a wooden bridge before we head uphill and a stile which we all climb over. Just to the right of the stile is a sliding gate which can be pulled up. "That's so you can come 'ere with yer dog and rather than lift 'im over the stile yer lifts the gate an' 'e just walks through." All the children thought 'that was neat!' The instructions now tell us to keep to the woods edge but as both Michelle and I were here last week we know that we need to cross the centre of this field to get to the next stile. This stile is very narrow but we manage to get the children over without difficulty, although Josh seemed a little worried about the stiles safety. Once over this stile we head for the far corner of the field and pass between two ponds. Again the

A panoramic view

children didn't miss the photographic opportunity. Josh again tells everyone about his 14 times zoom. We now climb more stiles, with what Jess described as cat flaps because 'they aren't big enough for dogs' and head, uphill towards a vineyard. As the path levels out, to our left, is a paddock with a couple of horses, one small Shetland pony and another larger horse. Cameras start clicking away as we try to get towards a picnic area so that we can stop for a bite to eat. It is now that we discover that Josh doesn't like hard cheese. "What is hard cheese?" asks Michelle. "You know, Miss Pollard," says Josh, "cheese that you can't spread. You have to cut it off a big chunk." "You never mentioned this when I asked you what you would like in your sandwiches," says Michelle, "In fact all of you said that you just didn't like jam and peanut butter." "I'm not that keen on tomato or cucumber either," continues Josh, "but if I have to have a cheese and cucumber sandwich I'll eat the cheese if you take the cucumber out." What actually happened was that he ate very little of his sandwich but managed to get through his

Root formation

apple, his crisps and a carton of juice. Reno decided that he might be out for longer than first thought so he decided to save his apple for later. He called this his 'contingency plan' (his words not mine). He informed me that he also had a 'Plan B', which meant that he would 'nick' Jess's apple if he could.

We sat, idly chatting for a few minutes before we all decided that it was getting a bit chilly and we needed to get back. Past the picnic area is a small path which leads us out across more paddocks, we pass between two houses, climb yet another stile and head out towards a road. Again we take great care to ensure the children cross the road safely as we approach a cottage and a stile, with a direction marker to The Cuckoo Trail. But Josh and Reno have noticed a little table outside the cottage gate. On the table is a box of 6 eggs. "Why would anyone leave a box of eggs by the side of the road?" asks Josh. Ron explains that the eggs come from free-range chicken and are for sale to anyone who passes by. There is now some discussion as to what 'free-range' means. "Look," I offer, "if we head down this path you'll see the

chickens and then it will be clear what the term 'free-range' really means." We all climb over the stile and head down the narrow path. On our right is a pen containing eight or nine chickens and one cockerel. "That's free-range," says Ron, "there not cooped up in a 'en 'ouse. They run loose. An' the one with the big plume of a tail is the male chicken. He's called a cockerel" "I've seen one of them before," says Josh. "'ave yer?" asks Ron. "Yes," answers Josh with a big grin on his face. "On the telly on the Cornflakes advert!"

Ron shows us how to make a thumb-stick

Our instructions tell us to keep to this path as we cross yet more stiles. The path is very muddy, Josh and Jess love it but it isn't until now that I notice Reno is wearing trainers and they are filthy. "That'll be all right, I'll just dry them off when we get home." At the end of the path we climb a few steps and we are back on the Cuckoo Trail and heading back to the car. But before we get to the car, Ron and I had a chat and we decided to try and find some sticks, thum b sticks to be exact, that the children could take home. It wasn't long before we were heading off the trail into the woods, cutting down small branches so that we could make thumb sticks. Photographs were taken of Ron cutting and trimming sticks as I looked out for the next possibility. At the end of the Cuckoo Trail each of the children had their very own thumb stick.

Back at the car the children thanked us for the day and wanted to come with us again next week. We tried to explain that we couldn't do that but they were more than welcome to come with us again when we completed the Family Walk or the Kiddies Walk. They decided that they could choose the photographs for the chapter when they got back to school on Monday and I promised to have this chapter written as soon as I could so that they could match the pictures to the story.

All in all, the walk was very pleasant. I know Ron enjoyed it immensely. Our instruction book describes the walk as taking 2½ hours; well it took us over 4 hours. We did stop a number of times but that's what you do when your with children, isn't it? The fact that the children enjoyed it and wanted to come with us again made it all worth while to me although I would have preferred some more historical places to see.

A few days after the walk I met with Michelle and she informs me that both Reno and Jess fell asleep on the way back to Eastbourne and Josh just couldn't stop talking about the day. One of the objects of the walk was for the children to take pictures and some of those pictures would be included in this chapter and that is exactly what they have done. How they managed to reduce the numbers from the 573 pictures they actually took to the few that I have reproduced on these pages is a mystery to me. But they did it somehow. And the children should be congratulated on not only the quality and clarity of the actual pictures but also the variety of subject matter.

We have very nearly reached Christmas but before we do, Ron and I have just one more walk to complete before we hang up our thumb sticks for a little break, and would you believe, we are completing this walk tomorrow.

The walk is completed (picture taken by Michelle)

Sponsored Walk

When it comes to children we are all suckers unless, of course you're Scrooge. But most of us love children, especially at Christmas. Whilst driving the school bus the radio has to be tuned to Southern FM. Not my preference but the girls like it. If anyone listens, regularly, to this station you will be aware of the vast amount of time and effort put in by the station on charity work. One of their favourite charities is 'Help a Local Child' whose patron, Sir Richard Attenborough, started the ball rolling back in 1976 with 'Help a London Child'. Southern FM have been involved with 'Help a Local Child' since 2003 and have managed to raise over ½ a million pound to give to well deserved organisations in Sussex. They work with organisations such as The Chestnut Tree House, a children's hospice in Arundel. They managed to raise £55,000 when they organised a charity abseil down the side of Arundel Castle. 'Jack the Lad' (morning D J) walked the length of Sussex raising over £27,000 for the charity. They also gave The Royal Alexander Hospital £60,000 to buy equipment for the children. They have assisted with the East Sussex Foster Care Association with money to take children on trips and the Inspiration Project, run by this association, helps children reach their personal goals in life. Another project they are involved with is one that I, personally, didn't know existed. It's called 'The Dragonflies Project' and assists young children to cope with bereavement of a loved one. I found out about this project by watching the video on Southern FM's website[26]. The little girl on the video, called Lucie, made me cry.

So, as I was saying, the radio was on and they were asking for volunteers to carry out a charity walk. Not a long walk, just 3 miles. It was to be carried out on 7th December 2008 along Eastbourne sea-front and all the walkers had to be dressed as Father Christmas. It was just made for Ron and me. So without asking Ron I enrolled us into it. The event is being organised by the Myasthenia Gravis Association with Southern FM. Again I had never heard of Myasthenia Gravis (I even have a problem pronouncing it). But have since found out that Myasthenia Gravis (MG) is a chronic autoimmune disorder that results in progressive skeletal muscle weakness. Skeletal muscles are primarily muscle fibres that contain bands or striations (striated muscles) that are connected to bone. MG causes rapid fatigue (fatigability) and loss of strength upon exertion that improves after rest. In early stages, myasthenia gravis primarily affects muscles that control eye movement and those that control facial expression, chewing, and swallowing. If untreated, the disorder may affect muscles that control breathing (respiration), causing acute respiratory failure.[27] Which ever way you look at it, it doesn't sound nice. So we now have a number of reasons for completing our walk. But at the end of the day it is about raising money for some very worthy causes.

Just before our warm up

For obvious reasons I am unable to capture the event on film so the accompanying pictures have been taken by my daughter, Michelle, as we make our way from the start of our walk, The Sovereign Swimming Complex, towards Hollywell, at the

---

[26] http://www.southernfm.co.uk – visited 22/11/2008
[27] http://www.mgauk.org/ - visited 22/11/08

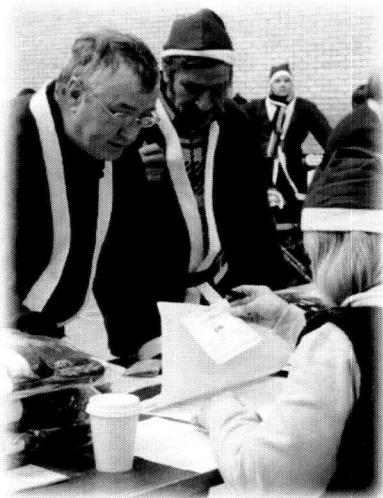

We sign in and hand over money

other end of Eastbourne sea-front. But before we start we need to perform some vehicular manoeuvres. If any of you are aware of Eastbourne town you will know that The Sovereign complex is at one end of the town and Hollywell is at the other. So I collect Ron in my car (from you know where) and I'm followed by Michelle and my wife, in Michelle's car. I drive to Hollywell, park my car on the sea-front (which we now have to pay for) and Michelle collects me and Ron, resplendent in our Santa outfits, and transports us back along the seafront, to the Sovereign complex, where she parks her car. The idea is that we walk from the complex, leaving Michelle's car in the car park, to Hollywell and the end of our sponsored walk. Once completed, we all jump in my car and head back to the Sovereign complex where Michelle and my wife will collect Michelle's car and we can all head home. Simple isn't it? And I have to say that all went to plan.

That was until we went in to register. This was to be carried out in the gymnasium alongside the swimming complex. We found our way in easily but we then had to queue up in surname order depending on which letter your surname started with. A-E, F-K, L-R, S-Z. "We should line up in the eff ter kay line," says Ron, "How come?" I ask, "Your name starts with a see and my name starts with a pee." "So it might," says Ron, "But the eff ter kay queue ain't so long, an' most ov' our money is comin' from the Kings 'ead. So it starts with a kay!"

First we warm up

I must explain that when we entered into this walk we were sent sponsor forms to fill in and were presented with a Santa

That's us on the left of the picture

outfit (one size fits all?) What I didn't realise and, to be honest, I thought it was a bit off; we had to ask our sponsors for the money 'up front'. Surely the idea is for us to complete the walk and then ask for the money. But the organisers, presumably, wanted to establish how much money they were getting so that they could tell the radio on the day, I don't know. But what Ron and I did was to leave a sponsorship form behind the bar at The Kings Head and a couple of posters hung in the bars asking for people to sponsor us. The landlord and landlady gladly took the money for us and presented the amount on the Friday

The Mayor says a few words

before the walk. Both Ron and I had also collected names on our forms but the majority of cash came from the pub . So, technically, Ron was right but we had entered under our own surnames so we decided that although the money was a collective thing we would register first on the pee queue, explaining to the lady that we were together and then register again in the see queue. Why do things have to be so complicated?

I have never seen so many Santa's in one place, all shapes and sizes. It was obvious that some were going to take this seriously. Ron had noticed a few people with cut off Santa trousers. These same people wore trainers yet others, like Ron and me were here to have some fun. There were children, dressed up, even dogs had on a Santa suit and everyone seemed to be happy. But first we needed to be warmed up. Ron had noticed some scantily dressed young ladies standing in a corner of the gym. "What do yer think they're 'ere for?" ask Ron, wearing that silly grin. "If anyone o'them fillies would like ter put me through me paces I'll 'ave ter sit down fer days afterwards just ter get me breathe back". But warm us up they did.

We jumped, we marched on the spot, we jumped again then we swayed to the right then swayed to the left. All in time to music. I'm knackered before we start. Ron's behind me so I'm not sure exactly what he's up to but I can imagine a big smile as the girls dance and gyrate in front of us. Soon the time comes for us to start the walk. We are marched outside, onto the promenade and there we wait. And wait. It's freezing cold but, apparently we need to wait for the mayor to say a few words before we are let loose on the unsuspecting people of Eastbourne. In the picture, above with the Mayor, can you spot Ron?

But soon we're off. Some shoot off like a bullet but we had decided, right from the start that we would be taking it easy, so easy it was.

The weather couldn't be better, not too warm but when you got moving things started to warm up. We also

The belt's the first to go

noticed that part of our Santa suits had started to disintegrate. The first to go was the belt, and whilst walking it was obvious that other people had the same problem. Bits of belt were strewn over the ground or placed in rubbish bins.

Now I'm going to get on my soapbox a bit here. I'm sorry if I upset anyone who was a spectator on this walk but aren't Eastbourne people miserable. You can always tell an Eastbournonian. They don't acknowledge you when you speak to them. I'll be honest when I say that Ron and me will talk to anyone. In fact Ron does talk to everyone and anyone. And this walk was to be no different. Here we are, two Sussex gents, dressed up to the nines like Santa Claus, both strolling down Eastbourne promenarde on a chilly but sunny day what are we likely to say to people sitting and watching. But of course the odd 'Ho, Ho, Ho!" or the ocassional 'Merry Christmas' I even asked someone if they had

Michelle shows her photographic skills

seen some reindeer wandering about because we had lost ours. And what did we get back, nothing. Not a word. Yet if we said the same thing to any non-Eastbournonians you always got a witty reply in a non-Sussex accent. Why is that? Many years ago, when I first got married to Emelia we lived in Eastbourne for a few months and hated it. Not the town, we both love Eastbourne, but it's just the people. But enough said. It's beginning to make me angry and Christmas is a time for forgiving. So I apologies now.

When we were passing the Lifeboat Station I must admit to a little bit of fear. I know a volunteer from the RNLI and he promised to give Ron and me a soaking as we went past. Thankfully he was nowhere to be seen. Something else that I thought would be a nice touch was to throw the children a sweet or two but, because of Health and Safety, this is a definite no,no. "Could 'ave some kiddies eye out," says Ron, so I'll have to find someone else to give £10 of chocolates to.

All along the route we are directed by military type people, I'm sorry for not being more specific but to be honest I didn't look to see if they were Army, Air Force or Naval but they were very efficient, directing us along to the left or the right of any obstacle. At one point we are directed away from the prom and find ourselves walking opposite some of the hotels on the seafront. I saw them first and hoped that Ron hadn't spotted them but it was too late. Some holiday-makers from across the waters had appeared and were relaxing on the steps of the hotel. That's enough for Ron. He starts. For obvious reasons I am unable to print what he said or thought but, needless to say, if he was overheard he could be spending some time with the authorities. "That's the bloody trouble with this country," he rants, "they can call us all the names under the sun an' we can't do a thing. We call them something and it's against their 'uman bloody rights." I manage to get him past the hotel before we both get arrested.

This really is Eastbourne

But back to our walk, it is surprising the views that can be seen, just walking along the seafront at Eastbourne. Some of the pictures taken by Michelle are really very good and I have to admit I asked her if they were actually taken somewhere else but she insists that they are all Eastbourne.

I was going to elaborate on certain aspects of Eastbourne. Things like its history and culture but I thought, just for once, I would leave it all out and just walk. Again I am not taking photographs, I have no need of a map, even Ron and me can't get too lost on a three mile straight line! At the end of the day we are doing this for charity and it will be the children who benefit. And that's what it's all about.

At the Pier

All along the route we have attempted to speak or have some fun with anyone who looks as if they are taking an interest. Some people suggested that we should be walking with buckets to collect a little bit of extra cash but if I can't throw sweets at them I'm dammed if people are going to throw money at me, could have my eye out. As I said, others just totally ignored us so it was a pleasant surprise when a cheery voice called out to us. Apparently the Yorkies had been waiting for us since one thirty, hoping to catch a glimpse of us as we flashed past. They were about to give up, thinking they must have blinked and missed us running past(?), when, in the distance, they could see some stragglers (or strugglers) heading in their direction so sat back down, with their fish and chips and waited. But it was nice of them; they walked to the end with us and chatted all the way.

You see, they don't come from Eastbourne but are from up Barnsley way.

T he finish line was a piece of green tinsel held in place by a couple of extremely attractive young ladies. We 'dashed' through the finishing line to be presented with our medal and advised that a hot drink and mince pie were our just rewards for completing the 'run'.

But it was fun, in a strange way. Bits had been falling off the suit most of the way round but we managed it. After all it was only three miles. With the help of the regulars at The Kings Head and all the people who sponsored us we managed to raise just over £300. Which was a fantastic achievement and we would like to thank you all for your generosity.

Unknown to Ron and me, there is a prize for the people who collected the most money. Today, 5 days after the walk/run I received in the post, two complimentary tickets to this year's pantomime in Eastbourne for being one of the '…..biggest fundraisers on the day.'

So thanks to you all, the organisers and Michelle and Emelia and everyone else who made this a nice, easy stroll for the two of us? Were now off to the Panto. XX

A couple of friendly faces

We both received a medal

Snow Walk

Today is the 2nd February 2009 and the country has come to a standstill. Before I went to bed last night it had been snowing. Not a lot but it had started to settle. As you know I work for a private girl's school, driving the minibus from Eastbourne to Hastings and back. I got up a little earlier today, just in case the snow had got worse. And it had. At 6 o'clock in the morning the snow was 4 inches thick (that's 100mm to our younger readers!) and it was still snowing. It took a while to brush the snow off the car so that I could see to drive to Eastbourne but I was determined that a 'little snow' wasn't going to stop me from earning a crust. The road off of the estate was treacherous because the 'gritters' don't come onto estates, which is strange when I think about it. I pay my Wealden Council tax, which pays for the 'grit lorries', but East Sussex County Council only grit main roads so that people, not living in the East Sussex area can pass through, whilst us on the estates are stuck in our driveways?

But I am drifting off the reason for writing. On the way to work I thought just to make sure I am up to date with the weather conditions, I'd listen to the radio. Southern FM is tuned and the presenters, Jack, Danny and Lindsey, are advising everyone, but everyone, to stay at home. Now I'm driving down the A22 towards Eastbourne. The road is wet, not too slushy at all considering the amount of snowfall and, of course, the gritters have been out all night on this one stretch of road. On the side of the road is a 'smuttering' of snow. Not as deep as at Hailsham but there was a 'smuttering'. And the radio is telling me not to go out? I drive into Eastbourne without mishap. The roads into Eastbourne are fine. Perhaps Eastbourne Council permit 'gritters' onto the minor roads but I have no problems getting to the school. Still the radio is telling me to stay at home. As I pull into the school parking area my mobile phone rings. The boss tells me that as the road conditions are so bad (?) none of the buses will collect children and I must phone all the parents to let them know. None of the other drivers have ventured into work. I spend the next ½ an hour trying to explain to parents that the bus isn't running because of the weather. Out of the 12 I phoned, one couldn't accept my explanation, one hadn't looked out of the window so had no idea what I was talking about, two asked if I had any suggestions what they could do with their children, four asked if the school was opening at all today and two accepted my apologies and the last two didn't answer the phone. So I drove home, made my wife a cup of coffee (she's still in bed and didn't realise I'd actually been to work and come home again). Both my children telephoned to say that they wouldn't be going to work, my wife's customers phoned to cancel appointments and I have now been told that the school that I work for has been closed due to the weather. The country has come to a standstill over four inches of snow. So I decided to make the most of it, and go for a walk. At least that was the idea, but things change, don't they? My conscience made me phone the school to ask if I was needed to complete my maintenance work. "If you can get in ok then it would be appreciated, we're all here," says the boss. So it's back to Eastbourne I go. When I arrive there are five of us.

St. Mary's Church, Hailsham

All the other office staff had been sent home or just didn't arrive. Out of all the staff present four, including myself, had driven from Hailsham, the other member of staff was from Eastbourne but had walked in because he'd heard, on the radio, that the roads were bad (?) "I'll swing fer that 'Jack the Lad'," he complains, "telling everyone that things are that bad we should all stay off the roads and sit in doors. At least some of us made the effort." But his rant didn't help. The school remained closed for the day and the only ones who appeared to be enjoying the snow were the few Asian girls who ventured outside to have a snowball fight. It was decided that we should carry out repairs that were required, keep an eye on the weather and if it got worse to head home before we got stuck in Eastbourne. And worse it got. So bad was the snow that at 12 o'clock I called it a day. I explained to the boss what I had managed to complete and headed home.

Tesco arrives in Hailsham

I tried to get in touch with Ron to see if he would be prepared to come for a little stroll around the Town we call home but he wasn't about, so I decided to have a stroll on my own. Those who know the Town will also be aware of the vast difference that has occurred over the recent years. Others may not remember as far back as I can. Vicarage Field was once a field. A large oak tree stood at the front of the field, near the road, and the field was used for fairground rides every year. Old houses lined North Street, Holts the Solicitor used to own a large property there, the Post Office (now Royal Mail Sorting Office) was always busy, and White House School was built and later destroyed for Tesco's. All the streets were two-way, none of this one-way street nonsense. I can also remember being able to park in the High Street, but that was before taxi ranks and double yellow lines. But in my younger days, if you saw a double yellow line you didn't park on it. The traffic Warden, yes we used to have two wardens, would give you a parking ticket. These days you can park wherever you like, double yellow lines, on roundabouts, bus laybyes, on pavements it's a free-for-all because we can no longer afford traffic wardens and the council provides free parking all round the town yet the Police turn a blind eye to any violations (unless, of course, it effects there 'solve rate' whatever that is).

Cricket Pavilion

But it is a walk that I have arranged to do and a walk is what I need. I actually live at the Horsebridge end of town so a slippery walk into town is needed. First I must get to the Doctors Surgery in Western Road so that I can renew a prescription. Due to my diabetes I have to check my blood sugar levels regularly. My granddaughter, Chloe, likes to help. I'd hoped it was because she's looking after her granddad's health but truth is she knows the needle sometimes hurts and she likes the sight of my blood. Unfortunately, over this weekend the results were not too good, I'm either about to lapse into a diabetic coma or the test strips are faulty. So I've got to get some more test strips, hence the walk to the Surgery which, as I said, means a walk to Western Road.

To get to the Surgery I have to walk down Summerheath Road. This road has seen some real changes. Firstly I can remember one of the towns' largest industries was located in Summerheath Road, that of George Green, sometimes known simply as 'Greens', 'Green Brothers' and later as 'Geebro'. Now it is an estate called Beauzeville with its privately owned houses. But originally George Green, a spinner from Staffordshire, agreed to spin yarn for Thomas Burfield (formerly in South Road) until, due to hard work and business acumen George decided to break away from Burfield and set up his own works in 1830, (some believe this split was due to a disagreement with Thomas Burfield[28]). Both businesses seemed to flourish and expanded with time and many workers were employed by both factories. In the 1871 census over 100 people are listed as either 'twine spinners' or 'twine makers', 'hemp dressers' or 'sack makers', 'rope makers' or 'weavers'. But it is difficult to estimate the number of clerks, packers and labourers that may have been employed in either of the factories but certainly a large number of the working population of Hailsham were engaged in the industry, including boys aged under 13 years.[29]. Soon Hailsham became known as String Town with some of its notable ropes being used by the hangman at executions.

Just past here is the Recreation Ground, technically in Western Road and not Summerheath Road, and it hasn't changed in years. My memory here is not only the numerous cricket and football matches I have watched or the times I have used the 'Rec' as a short-cut to get home after school, but also the very large roller, used by the grounds men. Many events occurred around, in or on that roller and, should it be able to tell all it would fill a book by itself!

Hailsham Railway Station

(photo taken from the bridge looking towards Polegate ?)

I have now reached our beloved surgery and the happy smiling faces of the doctors' receptionists who appear to have been put on this earth for one purpose only, to make seeing a doctor one of the most difficult things that you are ever likely to do in your lifetime. They ask such questions as '..do you really need to see a doctor?' or '..what's the matter with you?' and '..is this repeat prescription really necessary?' or '..can't you get to the surgery?' but today I'm in luck and the smiling face behind the counter recognises me as not being a malingerer and is only too happy to take my repeat prescription with the comment '..I'll get the doctor to see to it as soon as I can, Graham.' Which means it'll be ready in two days time. And they call it progress! My prescription is ready and all I need now is to get to Boots the chemist to get it filled.

---

[28] 'Hailsham and its Environs' by Charles A Robertson , Published by Phillimore - Page 149
[29] 'The String Town: Hailsham 1870-1914' edited by Brian Short ISBN 0904242137 – University of Sussex

Out of the Surgery I turn left, pass The Congregational Church and head left over the railway bridge. For those unsure, there did use to be a railway station in Hailsham. The line used to run under this bridge towards Heathfield until Lord Beecham decided that the line didn't pay and closed the line and station. The station was opened on the 15th May 1848 and closed to passengers on the 9th September 1968[30]. Ron will tell all who are prepared to listen his story about '..bein' one o'the last passengers ter use the train'. The only way to get about now is by car, taxi or bus. I have heard a rumour that consideration is being given to a possible return of the railway. But I don't think this will be in my time?

Hailsham Pavilion

I now risk life and limb by attempting to get across the road at the junction of North Street, George Street and South Road. At the lights just opposite The Terminus. You need eyes up your '£%se' to get across here. Traffic coming towards you, down George Street (still one-way) splits and turns either left, into South Road (two-way traffic) or right, up North Street (two- way traffic). At the same time you've got traffic going into and out of Station Road (two-way traffic) as well as traffic going into and out of Sturton Place. In the mean time you're waiting, expectantly, for the little 'green man' to let you know that it's safe to cross. You just hope he's got it right or you could get hit by cars going in every direction!

Busy (?) shopping walk

George Street has aways been George Street. My memory is of 'Deer Paddock', now the Police Station (unmanned after dark!!) previously owned by Southern Water (?). Opposite used to house Wealden Council Offices and, of course, there is The George Hotel, recently refurbished after a fire which destroyed the roof. If memory serves me well this was not only one of the many Inns in Hailsham but also doubled up as a court house. I'm sure there must be someone out there that can tell us a story or two? I can also remember a little shop in George Street owned and run by, again if memory serves, the Chetwyn (?) sisters. An old haberdashery shop where everything was a complete mess but the sisters could lay their hands on anything you asked for. Old Miss Chetwyn (?) used to ride around Hailsham on an old pedal cycle. Thinking of cycles, does anyone remember Charlie Riggs? He used to drink in The Terminus with his wife, I forget her name, or was it Evelyn? Charlie was another Hailsham character that went everywhere on his old bike. He was a very gifted model engineer who would often be seen showing off his latest

---

[30]www.subbrit.org.uk visited 13/02/09

hand-made engineering masterpiece at the bar of his favourite Inn. He was a very clever man who worked for Greens/Burfields and was often asked to make, from scratch, a piece of machinery that had broken at the factory.

Further along George Street used to be Jon Aupers, the ladies hairdresser. This is where my wife worked as an apprentice many years ago. Further along the road is the Pavilion, originally a picture house, then a bingo hall, then left derelict for a number of years before being beautifully restored by volunteers to it's original state. Hailsham Pavilion Cinema was erected as a purpose built 'Picture Palace' in 1921. It's first film was 'The Kid' starring Charlie Chaplin and the place was packed. It is now a very popular place of entertainment of all types, not just films but live shows, bands, groups as well as school children have all performed at the new Hailsham Pavilion.

Next we come to Market Square. Again, due to the 'strange' layout of the junction you take life into your hands getting across the giveway signs and a round-a-bout. On the corner, what is now a hairdressers, was my first real place of employment. Southern Rentals rented out televisions for a monthly fee. I was originally employed as an aerial riggers mate, working with Brian Sleight, erecting aerials around Sussex. I spent more than two happy years with Brian before I was asked if I wished to try my hand at repairing televisions. I took the chance and never regretted it, although I was a little disappointed, when Brian became self-employed, he didn't call his very own aerial business 'Sleight Erections'.

So far I have only covered a small area of the town. These are just my recollections of part of my home. Later in the book I am joined by Ron for a 'proper' town walk where he will, I'm sure, part with some of his own stories, told in only the way Ron can.

Until then I'll make my way back home in the snow and reflect on things gone by and reminisce on the changes I've seen over my 57 years in Hailsham. But of all the changes I have seen, one seems to remain the same – The Common Pond. And I bet that could tell a few stories??

The Common Pond

Teashop Walk

Some may think me strange but one of the things I just can't seem to like is a good ol' British cup o' tea. I've tried bags, I've tried leaves, and I've tried various makes, Ceylon, Tetley and Darjeeling to name but a few. I've also tried all manner of herbal teas and I can honestly say I have hated them all. My dislike of tea goes back to when I was a young child. Perhaps I had a bad experience, I really can't explain why but it is so bad now that just the smell of brewing tea makes me feel sick. So, you may ask, why am I doing a Teashop Walk? To be honest Ron has brought me a new book full of these 'teashop walks'[31] and Ron is a great lover of tea and thinks he can convert me. We'll see.

Pulborough Church

The problem I have is deciding which, out of the twenty walks in the book, is the one to complete? After much deliberation I narrow the choice down to two. Both have my favourite place to visit, a church, but one has a church and my other favourite place, water, namely the Rivers Arun and Chilt. So, it is to the west of the county we head today, to Pulborough, once called pōle beorg 'the mound near the pools' (1086). By the first half of the 13th century its spelling had altered to Pollebergh and Pulbergh. The 'pools' referred to were probably the bends in the river.[32]

Sometime ago I had read somewhere about the 'seven good things of Sussex' and had often wondered what, where or who the 'seven good things' were. With the wonders of modern technology, the Internet, I have managed to find that it is a title of a famous poem, written many, many years ago. The writer is unknown or should I say 'anon'?

Of a score of good things found outside heaven
The land of Sussex was granted seven
The choicest of those I often feel
Is the oily, glutinous Pulborough eel
Though the Selsea cockle would be the best
The Chichester lobster's the lordliest dish
The herring of Rye is the tastiest dish
The mullet of Arundel would have my vote
If I could but forget the Amberley trout
The wheatear of Bourne whenever it's about.[33]

Not my idea for a little ditty but who am I to trifle with experts. But as both Ron and I have been to Amberley, Rye, Selsea, Arundel and Chichester it's time we went to Pulborough and, perhaps, find a walk near Bourne, wherever that is?

---

[31] 'Sussex Teashop Walks' by Jean Patefield - Published by Countryside Books - ISBN 1853066230
[32] 'Sussex Place Names' by Judith Glover – Published by Countryside Books – ISBN 185306484X
[33] http://www.bbc.co.uk/pressoffice visited 15/02/2009

Windy Miller

Worzel Gummidge

Water in the distance!

So, on a Monday morning in February I collect Ron from The Kings Head at 9 o'clock and drive towards a lay-by at the Pulborough United Reformed Church, which should, according to Ron take us about one hour. The walk we are to complete isn't too long, the book tells me that it's 3½ miles so all things being considered we should be back in Hailsham by 1:30pm. We drive down the A22, towards Polegate. Flowers have been placed at the spot of a very nasty road accident which happened Friday night. Reports say that it was fatal and the road was completely closed for many hours. Our thoughts are with the families.

But we need to look on the bright side. I have two days off from the school, its half term, so we are going to enjoy it. Neither Ron nor I have been for a walk in a few weeks so we have some lost time to make up. We should have been walking with Alan today and we were supposed to be heading for his home area, Medway, but unfortunately he isn't too well and has ended up in hospital. It's getting morbid again! Let's change the subject. Darts is one of Ron's favourite past times and he's a little gutted that his partner in tonight's game, Arthur, has had to back out because, you won't believe this, his wife is also in hospital. What is happening to everyone? On a lighter note about darts, Ron has made the newspapers. Not as a champion or as a runner up but the comment is '..as a South Road living legend.' The article[34] also goes on to describe Ron as '..a cross between Windy Miller from Camberwick Green and Worzel Gummidge! He even talks like him – Yarp he do!' Personally I don't think the comments are very fair, but I have to say that, don't I?

Eventually we arrive at Pulborough and find, easily, the lay-by where we need to park the car, get our walking boots on and head for the teashop at Pulborough Brook. " 'ang on a minute," says Ron, "Did you just say Brook?" he asks, "Yes," I reply, "the teashop is run by the RSPB, and it's at the Pulborough Brooks Nature Reserve." "But we passed that over a mile back up the road," he says, "yes, but, we will be walking round the reserve before we get to the teashop." I explain, "you'll see," I continue, "it'll be great." "You do realise that if it's a bird reserve, and it's on a brook, that means a 'ell ov a lot a water?" I didn't realise what could go wrong I ask. "Just you look down that road, opposite," continues Ron, "that's

---

[34] Sussex Express, Friday Jan 23rd 2009, Page 40, Column 4, Heading 'Diary Of A Darts Player' by Andy Relf

Path between 21 and 22

Caught on camera

There's no crossing here

one 'ell ov a lot o'water!" From the picture of 'Water in the Distance' I see his point. Let's hope it's all going to be ok. But oh, how wrong can I be??

The walk is, as I said, taken from the book 'Sussex Teashop Walks' and is walk number 6 on page 31. We start off by heading along the busy A283, heading towards the town. We pass the first turning on our left for Rivermead, with Rectory Lane on our right. We have to take the next left turn, which is where Rivermead completes a 'u' shape and ends back on the main road. Once we turn left we have to find a path between numbers 21 and 22. This is a marked footpath and is easy to see.

"Look at this," says Ron, pointing to the ground, "right next to the sign telling us not ter let dogs foul the path, a great big.." "We're in West Sussex," I interrupt, "'tis to be expected." But what wasn't expected was the sight that met us at the end of this path. Complete open space. Acre upon acre of nothing but soggy, wet, smelly, boggy grass. "Told yer it'd be wet," says Ron. Right now I'd wished I'd worn the wellies! So, just to make sure we don't get our trousers soaked, it's time to look like a chav, and roll our trouser legs up.

You can see from the photograph that the finger post is pointing us in a right-hand direction. This wasn't exactly correct, although that was the direction we headed. All the time we were walking we could see a mass of water on our left-hand side. But when we reached the other side of this boggy grass we needed to get over the river and we couldn't see any way of getting across. "Nothin' changes," says Ron, "not walked fer weeks an' we still get it wrong." "That sign must be pointing in the wrong direction," I offer, "if you look down river there's a footbridge with what looks like another river." A look at the map shows us that we should be crossing where the rivers Arun and Chilt meet. So we head towards the footbridge, all the time we are very conscious of the enormous mass of water nearby.

The footbridge over the River Chilt

The River Arun wasn't always called the Arun. Many, many years ago it was known as the *Tarrant*. As early as 150AD it was known as *Trisantonis* which, in Early Briton, meant 'the trespasser', indicating the river's tendency to flood land near to the river[35]. I must just add here that I'm learning all this *after* the walk. If I'd have known it prior to the walk, we wouldn't be here at all. It is very muddy and very wet under foot; even walking along the bank of the Arun we can still hear our squelchy footsteps as we head towards the massive expanse of floodwater. It is obvious that the water level, although still high, is starting to recede. The debris along the river bank is well above the current water level, indicating just how high the water was before we came along. All the time we are walking along the bank, the massive flooded area is getting closer to us. "Not lookin' too good, ahead," says Ron, "must be over a 1,000 acres o'land just covered in water. Let's 'ope we don't need to get over it!" But you've guessed already. Our instructions tell us to continue along the bank of the Arun until we meet a footpath sign, where we have to turn left. And there is no chance of us doing that. I have no idea how deep the water is but I can't swim and it would be plain stupid to even try to wade across. We can see the gate we need to get to on the opposite side but the only thing to do is to retrace our steps, back to the car and attempt to get to the 'Reserve' by completing the walk in the opposite direction. " 'ow many miles is this walk supposed ter be?" asks Ron. "3½," is all I say, "supposing were halfway round," continues Ron, "we now have ter walk back to the car, so that'll be 3½ miles we've walked already. Then we'll have to walk another 3½ miles to get to the reserve and back to the car again. That makes a 3½ mile walk seven bloody miles." I don't know what to say so I say nothing as we turn round and head back

There's no way to cross the water

the way we came. Most of the way back is in silence. But as we I look in the distance I can see what I assume to be Pulborough church, standing high on a hill. "We could just go and look at the church and call it a day," I offer and although I have no idea how to get to the church from where we are Ron agrees to the suggestion with a "well, 'tis a nice day, might as well make the most of it." So, rather than head back to the car we continue along the bank of the Arun. As we approach one of the bends a young fisherman, laden with rods and nets is heading towards us. Remembering the poem I assumed that the

---

[35] http://en.wikipedia.org/wiki/River_Arun visited 17/02/09

fisherman would be looking for the 'glutinous Pulborough eel'. "Doin' a bit o' pike fishin' then?" asks Ron. "Yes," comes the reply, "have you seen any about?" he asks. "No," is Ron's reply, "but you could strike lucky further along the river." "I hope to continue my luck," says the lad, "I managed to find a £1 coin along the path so I thought it might be an omen." "Best of luck," says Ron as we continue along the river bank. "How did you know he wasn't fishing for Pulborough eels?" I ask. "Obvious," replies Ron, "'e wasn't carryin' the right gear fer eel fishin'. 'Ad keep nets and I saw 'e was usin' mackerel fer bait."

We head back to the start

"You saw all of that in just a few seconds? I'm impressed," I tell Ron. "Not only that," Ron continues, "but the lucky sod 'as found a quid. I've not found anything since we started." We continue along the bank until we come to a dead end. Here we follow the path to the right, around what looks like a playing field. The path goes round to the left and eventually comes out at a concrete path leading up to the main road, presumably the A283. The same road we parked the car on nearly two hours ago. At the main road we turn left and head towards, we hope, the Parish Church of St Mary, Pulborough.

As we walk along the road we can see the church to our right but can't find access to it. There was a path but as Ron pointed out, "there must be a road ter the church, can't 'ave bride stompin up a public footpath to 'er weddin'. There must be access to vehicles somewhere." But we seemed to walk for ages before the church disappeared from view. We came to a mini round-a-bout. Instinct told us to turn right. In front of us now is a large restaurant come hotel offering all day breakfasts, all manner of evening meals and a bed for the night at £65 per person. "Blimey," says Ron, "I'd rather sleep under the stars than 'ave ter pay sixty five bloody quid for a bed fer the night."

"That's £130 if you have someone with you," I say. "Now 'oo do I know that I would like ter spend the night with, that was worth all that money?" A smile has come to his face and I have a shrewd idea who he's thinking about.

The church is just past and opposite this hotel. The climb up is a bit steep but the churchyard itself is worth the effort. In fact it was the only thing that was worth it, because the church was closed to the public until April. That was a real shame because if the churchyard was anything to go by, the inside must be stunning. The website[36] advises us that the present church is 12th century and that a very informative booklet is available inside the church. It's just a shame that no-one is permitted to buy the booklet in the winter? I hear Ron mutter, 'all this way an' we can't get in!' but when I look at him he's smiling.

The church in the distance

---

[36] http://www.stmaryspulborough.org.uk/ visited 17/02/09

The magnificent Shire Horse

Rather than head back the way we came we decide to stroll back to the car using a bridleway we had seen opposite the church. "As long as we go in a straight line and not turn off we must, eventually, arrive at somewhere near the car, shouldn't we?" I ask Ron as we stride down the bridleway. "Don't rightly know," he replies, "but we'll ask this young gentleman, that's walkin' towards us, with 'is little dog." This 'young gentleman' looked old enough to be Ron's dad. But he did point us in the right direction as we continue down the bridlepath we will come out at Rectory Lane (do you remember at the start?) and then it'll be a case of turning left and back to the car.

But Ron surprises me. "Seems a shame we ain't goin' ter the teashop," he says, "we can't call this a teashop walk if we ain't been ter the teashop, can we?" He has a point. "But that would mean we'd have to follow the instructions in reverse order," I tell him, "we're dangerous following instructions the right way, you know what could happen if we do a walk backwards." "But we got all day, an' it's a nice day. We could get back ter the car an' leave these coats an' 'ead fer the teashop." So it's agreed. We will do another 3½ miles for a cup of tea?

The instructions in the book are numbered 1 to 10. From the start we had completed 1 to 4. It was at instruction number 4 that the flooded area stopped us getting to number 5, so we were now about to venture from number 10 to 5. I have to remember that all rights would be lefts and that I would need to read the whole instruction before we tackled it, in reverse. Easy!!

We get rid of our coats in the car and head, now away from Pulborough, to look for a road on our right. We pass a field with a couple of beautiful shire horses. They looked like youngsters but we had to stop and

Ron repairs the sign

admire their style and strength of character, really great animals. Just round the bend we come to a lane, not a road, on our right. There is a bridleway sign but the book doesn't mention this. Instruction number 10 says '*Turn right to a road. Turn left back to the start.*' So, reading that in reverse means; from the finish, turn right into a road and then turn left. Or does it mean 'Turn right and then left, onto a road? I'm confused already! I'm afraid to admit it to Ron who heads along the bridleway like a man on a mission. "This is the right way, look," he says, "It's 'ere that we turn left," and he's onto a public footpath. I only hope we're going the right way. "Must be right," insists Ron. "Keep the edge o' the water in sight an' we'll soon be drinkin' a nice cuppa!" I can't wait.

We find our way, at last

We seem to be following the instructions ok, but in reverse order. We see a cottage, according to our instructions, on our right, where we have to turn right. It's on our left and we turn left so that must be right, isn't it? We cross a few stiles on this stretch and one needs a bit of tender loving care. Ron drops his thumb stick, delves into his plastic bag and emerges with bits of wood, plastic ties and a hammer. "Soon 'ave this sign lookin' as good as new," he says and proceeds to ensure that the finger is pointing in the right direction before hammering home a wedge to keep it in place. Now a funny thing happened. After leaving the post, all repaired and looking as good as new, we cross a lane, and head into a field. Our instructions tell us that we need to cross three fields, the first of which is covered in primroses. Now as we are reading this backwards we still need to cross three fields but it will be the third one that is covered in primroses. Are you getting the idea yet? All of a sudden Ron says, "Oh bloody 'ell!" "What's the matter?" I ask, "I've left me thumb stick somewhere," he replies. "Where did you leave it?" I ask, "It must 'ave been when I repaired that signpost, I'll 'ave ter get it on the way back." "But what if we don't go back the same way?" I ask, "I'll go back and get it now then," says Ron, "Stay there, I'll be back shortly." And off he goes, back along the field to retrieve his stick. With nothing better to do I just sit on the stile and wait. It's funny but while I'm sat there I start thinking of the amount of times I've left my stick and thought 'why didn't somebody say something before we walked too far?' but I hadn't realised that Ron had been walking for the last few minutes without his stick. Then it struck me. I'm sat on a stile, in the middle of nowhere. All I can hear are the songs of birds. It was bliss, the sun was shining, birds singing and in the distance was the sound of running water, all I needed to make it complete was a glass of amber nectar and a young….. "Why 'ave yer got that silly smile on yer face?" asks Ron as he approaches with his thumbstick held high. "Just thinking," I reply and we head off towards what is described in our instructions as '*a tiny*

Enormous Highland (?) cattle

12th century church, dwarfed by the adjacent rectory.' And what a little gem of place this is. The original church was built here around 1230, built by the landowner for himself and his tenants. Thankfully the church is open to the public and when you step inside you step back in time. It is a wonderfully preserved piece of history that has that smell, that certain something that just is England. The small burial ground has only a few headstones, the most recent being 2003. Yet in the little booklet purchased at the church it states that in the 18th century there were so many marriages by special licence in Wiggonholt that it was being suggested that Wiggonholt was a kind of Sussex 'Gretna Green'. The area is extremely well-kept and I would like to say that it is a credit to the village, but looking around there only seems to be a couple of houses. But the place is a real joy and a must go and see place if you are in the area.

It is only a short walk through a fenced path to the Pulborough Brooks Nature Reserve and I will be very honest and say that I chickened out at having a cup of tea. Thankfully Ron didn't push it and we settled for a coffee for me and a pot of tea for Ron. We sat in the garden and enjoyed a relaxing few minutes taking in the surroundings. Considering it was early February it was surprising how many people are here. "Did yer see the price ov' a cheese sandwich?" whispers Ron, "No," I reply, "but I'm thinking of getting some of that Sussex Spice Chutney." "I'd 'ave 'ad a cheese sandwich only I didn't bring me gold card with me," he continues, "be cheaper ter ave a meal than a cheese sandwich. 'Tis bloody pricey, although the tea an' coffee were pretty cheap."

Wiggonholt Church

That's the trouble with places like this, they tend to put the price up a bit but they can't be doing much wrong, by the amount of people in the teashop. Of course there is a gift shop attached and all manner of goods can be purchased with the funds going to the Royal Society for the Protection of Birds. A very worthy cause indeed.

But now is the time that we head back to the car. Obviously we now retrace our steps. Should you visit the reserve and would like to visit the lovely church, as you leave the door to the Reserve there is a little sign which simply says 'To the Church' on a pathway on the left, please go and see, you will not be disappointed.

But it is really strange because although we have only just walked from the car to the Reserve and we are now simply walking in the same places to get from the

Inside the church

Reserve back to the car, it is amazing at the things we didn't see on the way here that we did see on the way back.

Just round the corner of the stile where I waited for Ron are enormous Highland cattle, just grazing in a field. And on the path just past the post, recently repaired by Ron you can see the extent of the flooding. There is an enormous amount of water here and it struck home the message I read at the Reserve when it said that the flooding was good for swans, ducks and heron but other birds couldn't cope with these conditions. It just goes to prove how the correct balance is so difficult to get and sometimes, just sometimes, nature gets it wrong, or does it?

This was a very tiring walk due not only to the mud and slush but also the 3½ miles that has, by now, turned into nearly 10 miles. But it was worth it. Although my legs now ache and my feet feel alight it was enjoyable. I'm not sure where we'll be heading next, or even when, but if we manage to find just a little of what we saw today, it will be worth it.

When it floods, it REALLY floods

Village Walk (West Sussex)

The Cricketers, Duncton

It was very difficult to decide on which village should be honoured with our presence and it was after much searching through books, maps and the Internet before I decided on the village of Duncton. We could have picked a number of villages in the West of our county, as they all deserve a mention, but a decision had to be made and it was the connection that Duncton has with the well-known English game of cricket that became the decider.

As you must be aware, Ron loves his cricket. He can talk all day of his past achievements at one of his favourite sports. I, personally, can't stand the game. Possibly because I don't understand the rules or, more than probably, I can't see the point of it. But just in case it was the former I decided to try and educate myself and looked up the rules of the game and came up with the following:

- *You have two sides, known as teams.*
- *Each side (team) consists of eleven men.*
- *There is another man (known as the 12th man) but he only plays when one of the eleven men can't.*
- *One side (team) is out in the field and the other is in.*
- *Each man that's in the side that goes in goes out and when he's out he comes in, and the next man goes in until he's out.*
- *When they are all out, the side that's out comes in, and the side that's been in, goes out and tries to get those coming in out.*
- *When both sides have been in and out including not outs, that's the end of the game.*

You see? Basically it's pretty simple stuff. But the rules also insist, apparently, that they don't play in the rain or snow or if it gets a little dark. Lots of games lasting on average five days end in a draw. So what's the point of playing the game, you may ask? I'm sure Ron will tell us as we walk round this beautiful little village, made famous by cricketing legends Jem Broadbridge and Jemmy Dean. And no, I hadn't heard of them either. But I mentioned the two names to Ron and he instantly recognised them as Sussex and England players of the 19th century. Such were their notoriety I think a brief history of the two gentlemen is called for.

Jem Broadbridge

James 'Jem' Broadbridge was born in Duncton on the 25th June 1795. He died in Duncton on the 12th February 1843.

Mainly playing for Sussex, he was a significant English cricketer in the 1820s and 1830s. He was arguably the outstanding all-rounder of his time. The right-handed bowler and batter, played for Sussex at the same time as William Lillywhite and their bowling enabled Sussex to become hailed as the Champion County in the 1820s.

Broadbridge and Lillywhite were innovators who did much to have roundarm bowling legalised. His known career in major cricket spanned the 1814 to 1840 English seasons. In 102 matches, he scored 2671 runs with a highest score of 135. He took 51 catches and 324 wickets.[37]

Jemmy Dean

James 'Jemmy' Dean was born in Duncton on the 4th January 1816 and died in Duncton on Christmas Day 1881.

He became famous as an English cricketer playing for Sussex CCC in the mid 19th century. Credited with 305 1st class appearances his cricketing career spanned the 1835 to 1861 English seasons. He was a right-handed batsman and fast roundarm bowler, occasionally keeping wicket.[38]

Bus shelter

I hope that any cricketing fans reading this are pleased with my little bit of historical research and we can now get on with the walk which is taken from the book titled 'Village Walks in West Sussex'.[39] There are two walks in the book for Duncton, one is 2½miles and the other is 3¾miles. We have decided on the longer of the two, and for anyone who is unsure exactly where Duncton is I am assured that it is situated on the A285 near Petworth. I hope we can find it. But, just in case we have problems, I've taken time off work so that we have a whole day to get lost in.

Ron has asked if it would be ok to have some company for the walk. Alan (from electric fence fame[40]) would like to join us and Marian (mobile phone fame[41]) has some time on her hands as she convalescences after a little back problem. All is agreed but I am a little worried about Marian. Although the walk is only 3¾ miles our instructions include a mention of Duncton Hill. Marian assures us that she'll be ok and all is agreed, but when I go to pick them all up in my little Fiat I thought it would be best, if she didn't mind, that she drove her car to Duncton as it would be more comfortable. The fact that I'm not driving and would, eventually, be able to have a little drink at The Cricketers never came into my mind! Honest.

It's surprising how many pubs you pass on the way to Duncton, and Ron, Alan and Marian seem to know most of them. "What's the food like in that one?" asks Alan, "Bloody awful," replies Ron as

Holy Trinity Church, Duncton

---

[37] http://www.gravelroots.net/duncton/2.html#cricket - visited 28/03/09
[38] Ibid
[39] 'Village Walks in West Sussex' by Douglas Lasseter - published by Countryside Books - Walk 6, Page 29
[40] 'Are We There Yet, Ron' by Graham Pollard - Chapter 10 – Page 72
[41] 'Are We There Yet, Ron' by Graham Pollard – Chapter 23 – Page 161

Path to Roman Catholic Church

we head along the A27 towards Lewes. "Food was cold, an' the meat arrived 10 minutes before the vegetables. The puddin' was cold an' when we asked fer it ter be warmed up it came back with the custard stuck ter the side o' the bowl." For those unaware, should you run a restaurant of any kind in Sussex and see between two and six people arriving around Sunday lunchtime and one of them is Ron, you are about to be tested by 'The Sad Sod's Sunday Lunch Club'. They visit local eateries, have a meal, and then score marks on the quality of the place. One of the major foul ups that really annoys one of the Club members is that when the plates arrive at the table they are cold. So be warned. A few little jokes are passed amongst us as we take a really scenic route to Duncton, along the A27, through Worthing etc. and we arrive at the village and park the car in The Cricketers car park. "I've got to go for a wee," Marian informs us all and she's off, running towards the pub doorway like she's an alcoholic needing a fix. (Only joking, Marian!!). And today is wonderful, a little cold, after all it's only April, but the sun is out and it's dry so I manage to encourage Marian to leave her coat in the car with an assuring "you won't get cold today!" (Mistake number one)

If you remember Alan is a very good reader of a compass which is a little reassuring because our first instruction tells us to '...*walk north from the pub and cross the road continuing on the pavement on the west side.*' And I just happen to have brought a compass with me, but before I can show my skills at orienteering my three companions start walking away from the pub. "Hang on," I shout holding my compass aloft, "we haven't looked at the compass yet, where are you going?" "We're heading north," says Alan "an' then we cross the road so's we'll be on the west side," adds Ron, "you don't need a bloody compass ter tell yer that, surely." No I don't, but that's because I've got a map in front of me. I slip the compass in my pocket and run to catch up.

Our next instruction is to pass the Police House. Naturally we didn't see one but I noticed that the first house we passed was called Copse House. Someone had a nice sense of humour. "Look at the size o' that bus shelter," exclaims Ron, "they must 'ave some tall buggers livin' 'ere." The shelter is over seven feet tall with glass windows on three sides. "Never stand a chance in 'ailsham would that," continues Ron, "be smashed ter buggery before the putty 'ad dried." In front of us is the church, to be precise, the Holy Trinity Church, Duncton. Thankfully the church is open so we all manage to step inside and have a look round. The church is not that old, being built in the 1860's when this part of Duncton Village was built. The original village was in today's Upper Duncton which is at the foot of Duncton Hill. By 1086 the original Duncton had a small church built.

20 Tombstones all in a row

Victorian Kissing Gate

Alan looks for a snack

Alan was warned

This saved the parishioners a long walk to Petworth, their parish church until 1692. This old church was demolished in 1876. Its bell, reputed to be the second oldest bell in Britain, was cast in Normandy in 1369 and now resides in the tower at Holy Trinity Church[42]. This is a very pretty church and is obviously well used by the local people. Walking around the gravestones we were hoping for a glimpse of the famous cricketers, but we were unable to find them. Perhaps they were not buried here. We did find the large grey granite column by the grave of Robert de Fonblanque who died in 1932. His wife, Florence Gertrude was a leading supporter of 'Votes for Women' and led their 1912 march from Edinburgh to London. Near the flag pole is another notable stone, that of Jane Rapson who was born in 1878 and died in 1978 aged 100.

We exit the churchyard onto a lane and turn right, looking out for an old schoolhouse. No problem here but our next instructions are a little confusing. Standing by the schoolhouse we need to cross the road to the pavement on the east side. (I haven't ventured to get the compass out.) We then need to bear right with a cluster of cottages on our left. We can't see 'a cluster of cottages'. "Perhaps these houses behind us are a cluster of cottages?" offers Marian. "But even if they are a cluster of cottages," chips in Alan, "we can't bear right 'cause there isn't a right to bear." Good point, Alan, I thought. "So 'as anyone any idea where these cottages are?" asks Ron. "We'll just have to walk up the road, away from the school house, and see if we can find a turning," is the only offering I can make as I look at my map. "Another thing to look out for is a church, because the Roman Catholic Church should be close by," I advise the group. "What like that one over there?" says Ron pointing s lightly to the right of where we are now standing? Sure enough, behind the trees to our right is the spire of a church and the path we need to get us to this church is just around the corner, opposite a cluster of cottages.

Unfortunately this church is locked so we were unable to have a look around the inside, but what I did find, and I'll have to do a little bit of research, are 20 tombstones, in a perfect straight line, of priests and they are all from, according to the inscription on the stones, the Society of Jesus? The picture shows the line of stones very

---

[42] 'A Brief Guide to Holy Trinity Church, DUNCTON' by Jeremy Godwin (1997) purchased at the church

Burton Church, Diocese of Chichester

'Grans' organ?

clearly and if you look closely you may be able to see another stone opposite, at the end of the path. This stone has the following inscription:

Pray for the Soul
of
Hugh Bertie Cambell
Pollard
Soldier and Writer
Died on March 17th 1966
aged 78 years
RIP
And his loving wife
Ruth Marie Pollard
August 1972

I shall have to delve into my family history but I'm sure that Hugh is no relation but I vaguely remember a Ruth Pollard, from Chalvington who I am unable to locate. You never know I may have stumbled onto something? And Hugh seems to have had a strange occupation being a Soldier and a Writer. Normally soldiers, if buried at old age, have a rank of some kind written on the stone. And as far as know none of my family converted to the Catholic faith. But who knows? We must continue our walk.

We exit the churchyard and turn left, heading towards a three-way sign near a Victorian kissing gate. Unfortunately it looks as if the last time this gate was used was in the Victorian times and it may not be too long before it disappears into a heap of rust. Thankfully the path we need is very clear and we all manage to walk along the field path with ease. Some of our regular readers will be aware that one of companions today, Alan, is a bit of a connoisseur on all things rural. It is now that he decides to inform us on all things Rural and promptly goes into raptures about what you can and can't eat from the hedgerow. But try as he might he didn't convince the rest of us to try his 'tasty morsel'. But I'm sure most will remember Alan for his mishap with an electric fence when he walked with us at High Hurstwood.[43] For those not familiar I will just say that he needed to relieve himself and didn't realise that an electric fence

Looking towards Duncton Hill

---

[43] 'Are We There Yet, Ron' by Graham Pollard - Chapter 10 – Page 72

A gentle climb??

was within his range. It must have been very painful but I'll admit it was one of the funniest things that both Ron and I have witnessed. Today we had to warn Alan to keep away from the electric fences. Once bitten, twice could be dangerous. We now head down the slope towards the buildings of St Michaels Burton Park and Burton church. From the distance the church looks like a tiny unobtrusive little building. But when we reached it I was astounded. The little church is so full of character and has to be one of the loveliest little churches in Sussex (also one of the smallest and it's full of treasures). Built, would you believe, in 1075 the church is not dedicated. Its next door neighbour is the mansion of Burton Park built, originally by the Courtauld family. It appears that the Mansion used to be owned by an Anne Goring who married Richard Biddulph. Eventually it was passed to a cousin from Essex named Wright who added the name Biddulph to his own when he inherited the mansion. One of the stones in Burton church is in memory of a John Gerke who was once the old butler to Wright-Biddulph.[44] Since 1950 the mansion has been used as a girl's boarding school, but what it is used for now I have no idea. But it looks very impressive.

But it's the church that really took my breath away. There are monuments dating to pre-1553 and all manner of inscriptions and wall paintings. But what really took me by surprise was the organ. I couldn't believe my eyes. In front of me was an organ exactly like the one my old grandmother used to play. I can remember sitting between my gran's legs and pumping those pedals for all I was worth so she could practice her hymns. It even had the bits of string that held the sustain pedal near the knees and all the stops that changed the keys to other notes and sounds. I was really blown away and it brought back so many memories of me and my grandparents. I just stopped and stared for a while. In my own space. It was fantastic. As I said the church original dedication has long been

Even Des couldn't get this going

forgotten but in 2003 the church was named after Sir Richard of Chichester to mark the 750th anniversary of his death. I hope that the church remains as it is, a beautiful place for anyone to visit, at anytime.

From the church we head up the drive, passing the entrance to the mansion. It is about now that Marian lets everyone know that she's getting cold. If you remember it was me who advised her that she wouldn't need her coat. Marian wasn't going to let me forget it. The fact that she had left her thumbstick at the car and would need to 'borrow' someone else's is not mentioned

---

[44] http://www.barbsweb.co.uk/history/burton.htm visited 02/04/09

"Where we 'eading' for now?" asks Ron. "We need to head towards Duncton Hill, which is just in front of us, and we should come across Duncton Mill and its streams." This comment seemed to be a cue for a song because suddenly Alan burst into his rendition of 'There's an old mill by the stream, Nellie Dean' at the top of his voice which seemed to break the seriousness of the past few minutes and we all started to unwind a bit.

The climb up Duncton Hill was a little strenuous, to say the least. I had another look at the instructions and read that *the going is all very good, firm paths and tracks, there is one gentle climb....* ' but this was a bit more than gentle, or are we really not fit? As I said, Marian was getting over a back problem and I was worried that this climb could have aggravated the problem but a little sit down at the top of the climb and she was ready to get going again. But as Marian said, sometimes going downhill can be just as bad as going up. What with Marian and her bad back, me with a dodgy ticker, Ron with a jippy tummy and Alan having to use his inhaler we should be heading towards an old people's home instead of a pint at the pub. Thankfully the downhill stretch was completed in comfort and without further problems. A few derelict pieces of metal were discovered and we did see our first bluebells which reminded me that one of our next walks is to involve some of these lovely flowers. "Hyacinthoides non-scripta," says Alan, "did you know that Landowners are prohibited from removing bluebells on their land for sale and it is a criminal offence to remove the bulbs of wild bluebells." "Are you serious?" I ask, "I certainly am. It became an Act of Parliament in the 80's, so it did." The old saying, you learn something new every day comes to mind because I never knew that. At the end of the path we need to turn right and head downhill again to reach

Large trout pond

Duncton Mill. Ahead of us we can see the mill ponds where we hope to see some large rainbow trout. But what caught our eyes first was the group of people gathered on one of the lawns. The group, both male and female, seemed to be giggling childishly about something as they formed a circle on the lawn. "Don't you worry about us," shouts Ron, "we won't disturb yer," he continues. The group has now joined hands and they are all facing the middle of the circle. "What the 'ell are they doin'?" I hear him whisper to Marian as we continue down the lane, "How the hell do I know," whispers Marian. Some strange music has now started and the group starts walking in a circle. "Are you practicing Morris Dancing?" asks Ron in all innocence. "Certainly not!" comes a haughty reply from an elder member of the group, "we are a religious group performing meditation exercises." You can imagine what Ron tried to say before we all managed to drag him off down the road. But once we got to the pond we were all amazed at not only the size of the trout but the numbers. We estimated that there were in the region of 250 to 300 trout in the pond. Alan suggested that the biggest must weigh in at about 20lbs and they were gorgeous. We spent some time here, watching and encouraging the fish to come towards us. Obviously it is not possible to fish here and it was just as obvious that both Alan and Ron wanted a rod and line, just for a few minutes. In the background we could hear chanting and the clapping of hands. The religious group were getting into a frenzy. Our instructions tell us that the old mill wheel can be seen over the fence opposite the pond but, unfortunately it is no longer there. Unless, of course I was looking over the wrong fence. I have since found out the Duncton Mill is advertised as 'A Centre for Wellbeing and Excellence' and was voted first in the top ten of worldwide healthy retreats in the The Guardian in 2007. Which probably makes it very expensive. Even so, listening to the chanting and clapping coming from the group they seem to be enjoying themselves. Let's hope Ron doesn't burst into the giggles when we have to walk past them on the way back up the hill. Desperately trying to keep a straight face we passed the group without comment and made it to the end of the drive, where we turn right and head along a clear field path.

At the end of the path we turn right and walk along the outside wall of Manor Farm. There used to be a Roman military bathhouse here and a fair few jokes passed between us about the size of the Roman army (?) and how much soap they would use. All silly stuff really but hilarious at the time.

Trout swimming in clear water

As an aside, I think it was on our wheelchair walk with Mally that we noticed a large amount of Mistletoe in the trees[45]. As we head back towards The Cricketers we pass a number of trees laden with Mistletoe. Makes you wonder if it's going to be a good year for kissing?

We find the wooden bridge over a running stream where Ron drops a coin and makes his customary wish. All that's left is to climb the stile and we are back at The Cricketers and a well-earned pint (or two). The Cricketers used to be known as The Swan until 1867 when it was bought by John Wisden publisher of the famous yellow covered *Cricketers Almanac*.[46] He installed, as his tenant, none other than the father of the same James Dean mentioned at the start of the chapter.

People who know me may be aware that I only drink lager. The reasons that I only drink lager are that I prefer cold beer, I enjoy a refreshing drink but more importantly you can go into any pub and the lager is, usually, of the same quality, full of chemicals and as gassy as hell. Ron, on the other hand loves real ale. But there's real ale and then there's real ale. I've heard Ron say that some ale he'd just tried was off or it tasted malty, sometimes it's flat, some are too warm. Apparently it's all to do with the way the cellar is kept. But lager is, usually, ok. Today, for some reason I suggested that Ron could convert me and he suggested a pint of Betty Scroggs. I

Fast flowing stream

---

[45] This title – Page 15

[46] West Sussex Inns by Brigid Chapman - published by Countryside Books – Page 49

believe he tried this when we were with Mally. To his surprise I agreed and I will admit it was really nice and not what I expected. We also decided to have a meal at the pub. Both Ron and I had liver and bacon, which was delicious, and Alan had haddock and chips. The size of his fish was enormous but he managed to get through it ok. Marian just had soup of the day, chicken and coriander. As we had two founder members of the Sad Sods Sunday Lunch Club with us I was interested in what they had to say about the meal. Ron thought it was good value, although the liver was very tender it was, in his opinion, slightly undercooked. Marian wasn't too impressed with her soup, suggesting it was chicken put through a blender with herbs and milk. She also said that my plate was cold when it arrived. Alan was just amazed that haddock came that big and me, well I thought it was great. The whole day was just so enjoyable and I can't wait to talk somebody else into doing the driving to our next walk…..

Just a few years older than Ron??

Riverside Walk

As we approach Easter I was considering a little walk with the kiddies and at the end supplying each youngster with an Easter egg. But in todays politically correct environment this may be considered bribery at the least and exploitation of the young at worst. I then thought that a bluebell walk would make a pleasant change. After all my seeds in the greenhouse have started to germinate so it must be getting warmer and the time is right for these beautiful flowers to be in bloom. But I've come up against a couple of problems. One is that the only walk I can find where we are guaranteed bluebells is around Arlington, and everyone knows that it's a place we have already visited. Problem number two is, according to Ron, "tis too early, better ter leave it fer at least another week." So another walk is to be found and whilst pondering over our predicament on a Monday evening, sampling the amber nectar at our local hostelry, purely for medicinal purposes obviously, our esteemed landlady asked if her parents, who were visiting from Hull over the Easter holidays, could walk with Ron and me. "Somewhere not too far," suggests Helen, "and on the level, with not too many stiles and also near a little pub somewhere, with an old church, possibly in the Rye to Hastings area." Narrows the field a little does that but I have come up with a little walk that's not

St Mary's Church, Slaugham

too far being only 3½miles (one point to me) it's nearly all on the level (two points to me) there aren't too many stiles (three points) there is a pub called The Chequers (four points) and the church dates from the 1200's (five points) unfortunately it's nowhere near Rye or Hastings but it's at Slaugham (pronounced Slaffham). But five out of six isn't that bad, is it?

As usual I've delved into all matters 'Sussex' and found out a couple of interesting facts about Slaugham. The Covert family lived there and were great Sussex landowners. Rumour has it that they could travel from London to the sea without leaving their own manorial land. In 1494 William Covert bequeathed 6s 8d (about 33 pence) to every poor priest or clerk within five miles of Slaugham who wished to go to University. Sir Walter Covert built Slaugham Place in 1600 but the family fell upon poor times and soon died out[47]. And finally, according to Kelly's Post Office Directory 1867 the population in Slaugham in 1861 was 1,518[48]. At the same time, according to Kelly's, there were 5 public houses, The Black Swan, Old White Horse, The Red Lion, The Half Moon and The Fountain. Ron is getting quite excited. But I believe that not all of the Inn's were located in Slaugham but were located in the surrounding areas. Ron's calmed down now! I've also found out that a sister of someone of note is buried in the church at Slaugham[49] so we'll have to keep our eyes open for that. I can remember reading somewhere that the telephone box in the centre of the village was painted white, under

---

[47] 'People of Hidden Sussex' by Swinfen & Arscott – pub. by BBC Radio Sussex Page 131
[48] http://steve.pickthall.users.btopenworld.com/ssx1867/slaugham1867.html - visited 9/04/09
[49] 'Hidden Sussex' by Swinfen & Arscott – pub. by BBC Radio Sussex Page 124

instructions from the Lord of the Manor and if memory serves me right it is one of only three such telephone boxes in Britain.

This walk is taken from the Internet[50] and is issued by the Sussex Ouse Conservation Society. I have printed off the instructions as well as a map of the walk so all should be ok. But.......and there's always a 'but'. I thought Slaugham was near Lewes, funnily enough so did Ron. It wasn't until I printed off a map of the area that I found Slaugham is just off the A23, near Pease Pottage. Of course we won't tell our new companions of our lack of geographical knowledge. After all we don't want them to think we don't know where we're going. Do we? And then I receive an apologetic text from Helen saying that her parents will not be visiting after all as her dad had hurt his foot and can't drive. So it will be down to just me and Ron, like the old times, when we first started our strolls, oh so many miles ago.

Do chickens keep dogs?

The Matcham Vault

So, on Good Friday 2009, I collect Ron and we head, again, for West Sussex and attempt to find Slaugham (Slaffham). As a personal note I have often wondered the significance of 'Good Friday'. I appreciate it is also known as Black Friday, Holy Friday and Great Friday[51] depending on your affiliation, but the term 'Good' has always seemed inappropriate to me. Because, I believe, it is a religious holiday observed, primarily by Christians to commemorate the crucifixion of Jesus and his death.

Supposedly if he hadn't been 'killed' then He couldn't have 'risen' again and then we wouldn't have Easter. So without Easter to celebrate what would Cadbury do with all that chocolate??

But seriously, my first decision is whether to go the pretty way to Slaugham, via Haywards Heath and Ansty or the more direct but longer (?) route and head straight for the A23. Ron doesn't mind which way we go, "just s'long az we gets there." So I decide on the pretty way and head for Haywards Heath etc. Our discussion on the way to Slaugham involves the popularity of 'our' local. It was once said, by an outgoing tenant, that the pub trade was dying and that the new landlord and landlady would only last six months. So how, when I visited the pub the other night, could I not park in the car park – it was full, I couldn't sit at the bar – it was full nor could I sit at a table – they were full and that was just the public bar. The saloon bar was also full to the brim, and this person insisted that the new

---

[50] www.sussex-ouse.org.uk/walks/walks5.htm - visited 07/04/09
[51] http://en.wikipedia.org/wiki/Good_Friday - visited Good Friday 10/04/09

tenants wouldn't last six months yet they've been there over a couple of years so they must be doing something right.

Back to our walk, I will admit to having a map, as supplied by the Sussex Ouse Conservation Society and I will use this map as the reason for not being able to find the start of the walk. Because the map clearly shows two ponds. Not just two ponds but two big ponds. I could only find one. We spent the next few minutes trying to find the 'other' pond but had no luck. So it was decided to go to the church, start the walk from there and see how we get on. Just to help matters, as we approach the church of St. Mary's the skies open up and it is teeming it down. But we are Sussex men, stout, hardy and brave, and a little rain isn't going to thwart us in our quest to bring our followers the facts. We've also got macs and, would you believe, Ron has brought along a pair of leggings, the wus.

Unkempt graves

So our first point of call in Slaugham is St. Mary's Church and I have to admit that, internally, this was a bitter disappointment. The booklet purchased at the church[52] describes some of the recent work thus *'...and with other refinements this much loved church of St Mary's has been modernized, retaining and enhancing its ancient beauty.'* I'm sorry but, and this is only mine and Ron's opinion, it looks awful. The Victorian pews have been removed and replaced with *'...wood and fabric chairs',* the new lighting makes it look like a stage production and there is absolutely no atmosphere. Again this is only our opinion but it has to be one of the worst churches we have visited. I'm sorry people of Slaugham but we are being brutally honest and we couldn't get outside into the rain quick enough.

Once outside we hastily started looking for a piece of real English history, The Matcham Vault, which we found on one of the walls to the rear of the church. Catherine Matcham was the youngest and favourite sister of none other than Vice Admiral Horatio Nelson, 1st Viscount Nelson, and 1st Duke of Bronté. Catherine was married to Squire George Matcham – they had many children. But, again we were both very disappointed with what we saw. The vault is cracked and in desperate need of some form of renovation and the very long inscription is hardly readable in places. The remainder of the graveyard was just as disappointing as we head out of the churchyard towards Slaugham Mill pond.

WWII Tank trap

As we approach the pond we can hear running water, lots of running water and it's about now that I wish I hadn't had that last cup of coffee before I left home. Nature called, actually she shouted, and I had to leave the footpath for a while to do what comes naturally. "Don't affect me, like that," comments Ron, as I head back along the path to join him. "I can listen ter runnin' water all day an' it don't affect me. Mind you," he continues, "let me 'ave a few

[52] Visitor Guide St Mary's Church Slaugham – priced £2

pints o'that 'arvey's an' I could pee fer England, so I could." But I wonder why it does affect some people like that?

Just as we turn left to walk around the outside edge of the pond we pass a couple of WW II concrete tank traps. These concrete structures were built as anti-tank defences should there be an invasion. From our instructions the cascading water we can hear is water running out of this pond into a lower pond to our left. This is the point at which the River Ouse exits the pond.

We continue along the path and pass what can only be described as a very desirable residence on our left. This is a converted corn mill and was built to replace an earlier mill that was destroyed by fire in 1795[53]. The pond, however, was originally

Slaugham Mill Pond

No fence to the right of the stile?

created for the iron industry which was established many years before the corn mill business started. The views across this pond are exceptional. As you all know I love water scenes and a lot of pictures were taken as we strolled around this beautiful area of unspoilt countryside. The picture above is taken from the start of our walk around the pond and we eventually end up at the far side of the pond, just to the right of centre, in the picture and it was fantastic.

"Can you imagine," says Ron as we

---

[53] Sussex Ouse Conservation Society, Riverside Walk instructions

pass a clearing, obviously used by a fisherman to gain access to the water, "just sittin' ere', beer in one 'and, fishin' rod in t'other. Summers day. The cricket on the wireless. God, I'd think I've died an' gone ter 'eaven." We stopped a while and took it all in.

At the end of the path around the pond we come to a stile. Crossing the stile we now head, uphill, across a field towards a double set of stiles. Once over these we then head, across another field, towards Old Park Farm with its posh clock tower and weather vane. The path continues between two barns and we follow a rail fence to the end. We need to keep following the footpath signs keeping the stream to our left. To be honest I didn't see a stream but Ron assures me that there is one there. But what we did see was another case of a stile without a fence attached. It looked really odd and we both wondered why it should be the way it was but never mind. We keep following the signs, as always in West Sussex they are well maintained and easy to find. I will now tell you of another thing that is easily found in West Sussex. Those that have followed our walks around Sussex are aware of our pet hates. One of mine is rusty machinery being left out in fields but one that really annoys Ron is dog pooh! And West Sussex is the worst place to find it in its most annoying form, wrapped up in a plastic bag and left in the hedgerow or, even worse, on the ground. Over our past walks in this part of the County I haven't mentioned it in any of the chapters. It's been present but I thought not to mention it. After all I would be repeating the same information. But, again, we've witnessed it. And it's getting beyond a joke. Why would anyone place their dog pooh in a blue plastic bag and not take it home? No, they would rather just leave it on the ground. What is

West Sussex litter

it with you West Sussex dog walkers? It can only be a little minority that do it. But Ron has suggested that it's the same person just ahead of us on each of our walks? But that's not possible, is it?

At the end of the path we come to a kissing gate. Through the gate we turn right and head along the road. "Did yer notice?" asks Ron, "we walked through all o'them fields an' 'aven't seen a single animal." "No," I reply," I hadn't noticed and I'm not complaining either." "No," continues Ron, "but don't yer think it strange, all them fields, the big barns full ov'ay and not a single animal ter eat it? Seems funny ter me" I hadn't thought about it at all really and I can't say I'm not sorry that we didn't come across some large cattle or bulls, or sheep, although, now Ron's mentioned it I suppose it doesn't seem right.

Once away from the countryside and all things rural Ron

Hardy fisherman in the distance

To keep the children in?

starts talking about other things. People who know Ron will be aware of his very strong opinions about the state of the Country and events that happen and are highlighted in the National Press. Ron only speaks about these things when walking along a road or if someone in the pub mentions it. If he's in the countryside he rarely mentions things like this. I suppose that Ron becomes 'politically incorrect' because of today's soft 'mamby pamby' ideas. But what is strange, is that most of what he says is basically true, but the rest of us are too afraid to say out loud. I believe, like Ron, that we should bring back capital punishment or devise some deterrent for committing some crimes, the birch worked reasonably well in its time; I also believe that as a parent I can and should be held responsible for my children's actions. I also believe, like Ron, that if I am out of work I should not be entitled to everything free and I should earn my 'dole' money and not be handed it as a right. I'm not sure that I would go as far as Ron where illegitimate children are concerned and some of his solutions to our ethnic minority problems are somewhat barbaric but when a single mother has five children by as many different fathers surely questions should be asked before that family are given even more money and another brand new house to live in whilst others are struggling to pay a mortgage. All of these subjects were commented on as we strolled up this road. In fact it all started as we walked past the primary school at Warninglid with its wire perimeter fencing and padlocked gates. All I said to Ron was what's the wire for, to keep the children in or the adults out? From then on I couldn't stop him. And when he

Ron checks the flow of the Ouse

started talking about the two lads aged 10 and 11 who had been arrested and charged with attempted murder in Yorkshire I can't repeat what he would do to them and their mother.

Gradually I manage to calm him down, with the help of the River Ouse as it passes under the road. There are another couple of WWII tank traps here and the water flow is very fast. It was just past here that I had a little bit of luck? Ron, always on the look-out for the odd coin has got me into the habit of not looking where I'm going but I now tend to look at the ground. Whilst walking along the road I spotted not money but a small electric motor. Now why would I think this to be a great find I hear you ask? I have just joined a Radio Controlled Model Boat Club and these small electric motors are ideal for model boats. All I have to do now is see if it works. I'm happy, Ron thinks I've lost the plot.

The rain hasn't stopped and we have started to sweat under our macs. I think I'm wetter inside the mac than outside but, thankfully, we are nearing the end of our 3½ miles and we approach the very first pond we found at the start of the walk. Sitting there, under the trees and a brolly is a fisherman. It's strange but if you see a fisherman on a river bank or by a pond the first question you feel you have to ask is "any luck yet?" and today was going to be no different. Whilst I wonder round trying to get a picture Ron asks the inevitable question. It appears that our intrepid fisherman hasn't caught anything. He explains to Ron what bait he's using and Ron suggests he uses bread crust. "I usually only fish competitions," says the fisherman, "and you aren't allowed to use bread so I don't use it at any other times." Seems a good reason but I wonder why they

can't use bread? We leave the pond and follow the instructions towards a concrete way-sign which should be ½mile up the road. "We turn right 'ere," says Ron. "Are you sure we've walked ½mile?" I ask, "Only this sign says WSCC (West Sussex County Council) and is not a directional sign," I point out. "Must be this way," insists Ron, "'cause the next instruction says we should 'ead fer the wood." "But if we turn right now, we are already in the wood, we should be crossing a field, looking down over the village of Slaugham," I argue. But Ron will not be swayed. He heads off in to the woods with me following. We arrive at

Home-made camp

what looks like a camp made by local youngsters out of twigs and mud. I'm still not convinced we are in the right place. I turn left, to see if I can find the concrete way-sign and Ron turns right to see where the path leads. Of all the walks we have completed together I think there was only one other time that I didn't agree with Ron, which is pretty remarkable after all the miles we've walked together. But as I am the one who usually gets us lost I thought I'd let Ron do it this time. Because when we eventually continue on Ron's path we come out at a road. "So what now?" I ask, "do we turn 'Left or Right, Ron?'" "Lets 'ave a look at that map," he says, "we must 'ave ter turn left," he continues, "'cause it's down 'ill, and we 'ave ter cross a river. Water don't run up 'ill so if we turn left that'll bring us ter the pub." And of course he was right. Down the bottom of the hill was a little stream and we climb back up to the top to find the car, the church and more importantly for Ron, The Chequers pub.

We strip off our wet clothing, change shoes and head for The Chequers. But before we venture inside we notice a great photo opportunity, the white telephone box. Ron is directed to stand in front but as he got to the box he says, "'ang on a minute." He opens the door to the telephone box, bends down and comes out with that silly grin, "only found 25 pence, on the floor," he says, "made my day that 'as." Inside the pub looks like a typical country pub, nice furnishings, open fireplace, books on shelves for those who wish to read. The lady behind the bar was pleasant and took our order whilst I looked around. The prices looked a bit steep to me and I was wondering if Ron wanted a bite to eat here. As I'm walking round a fellow walker came in with a very wet and muddy Spaniel. "You look as if you've 'ad a lovely long walk," says Ron, bending down and making a fuss of the dog. The 'owner' doesn't say a word. Ron continues to make a fuss of the dog and is totally ignored by the man holding the lead. Ron walks to the table

I've sat at. "Miserable bast*&d," whispers Ron. "Do you fancy a sausage sandwich?" I ask, and all I got was a funny look. "'Ave you seen the price ov a bloody sausage sandwich?" he asks, "It's bloody six quid!" "That's nothing," I said, "if you fancy a beef burger and a few chips that'll set you back £12," I show Ron the menu for Good Friday. ""Liver an' bubble an' squeaks £15," stammer Ron, "an look at the price fer fish an' chips." I notice that at the bottom of the menu are the words '*A discretionary 10% service charge will be added to parties of 6 or more people*' I didn't mention that to Ron as we finished our drinks and left. As we headed back to the car, towards the church, an elderly lady with an old greyhound was wandering towards us. Ron stops to speak and the reaction is so different to the 'pompous little ……' inside the Chequers.

This walk was pleasant. Why it is called a 'Riverside Walk' I'm not really sure. We crossed the Ouse twice but never walked along the side of any river throughout the 3½ miles. The main disappointments were the church, The Chequers and the 'pompous little….' at the bar, but the old lady with the greyhound, towards the church, was a joy. We eventually found a place to eat on the way home, The Piltdown Man. Now that is a real pub and the food was delicious, hot and plenty of it. It was also reasonably priced. We both managed to have a meal for the price The Chequers were asking for just one plate of Fish and Chips!

Three white boxes in Britain but there's only one Ron

Bluebell Walk

As you all know both Ron and I find lots of our walks from the various books on the subject. Today we are going to attempt something a little bit different. I noticed a couple of adverts in our local Friday Ad involving walks. The first advertisement read:

BLUEBELL WALK, *Saturday 25th April, Carters Corner Farm, Cowbeech, BN27 4AJ. Enjoy the beautiful walk via the Bluebell covered woods at Carters Corner Farm. Plus: Cakes, refreshments, book and gift stall, in aid of St Wilfrid's Hospice – Entry: suggested donation of £2.[54]*

The second advertisement was for a ghost walk. Now I'm a sceptic. I'm not sure on the validity of some claims about spiritual sightings but I also like to think that I have an open mind and am prepared to listen to other's points of view. This advert read:

GHOSTWALK, PEVENSEY, *Saturday 25th April 7.30pm Castle Car Park. Just turn up 90 minute guided walk by Lanternlight now in 15th year! Adults £6/£3U14 contact…….*

Both are intriguing and we must carry out both walks. We could perform them both this weekend but it was decided to 'do' the Bluebell Walk first and get in touch with the organiser of the Ghost Walk to make sure he had no objections to me writing about his guided tour. So today it is to be the Bluebell Walk.

"A lovely little walk," says Ron, "beautiful flowers, walking through the woods, and we get cakes an' refreshments fer only 2 quid. Can't beat that, can yer?" "We may have to pay extra for the refreshments, Ron," I explain, "but it's got to be worth a try, just so that we can donate to St. Wilfrid's. A very, worthy cause indeed." So we are all prepared for a little wander through the bluebells. Let's hope the weather stays nice, although the forecast is rain. Finding the place should be fun as well. Ron thinks it's on the road to Herstmonceux and I think it's the other side of Cowbeech, past The Merry Harriers heading for an area known as Foul Mile, (I'll let your own imagination fathom out why it's called that) But, if memory serves me right, Carters Corner Place used to be owned by Lord Hailsham, and is closer to Magham Down than what I know as Carters Corner (?)

Carters Corner Farm

I feel I should just give a little mention to the St. Wilfrid's Hospice, just in case anyone has never heard of it (?) I will quote from their literature as I couldn't have put it better myself: *St Wilfrid's Hospice is a local charity providing skilled and compassionate care and treatment for all patients and their families with complex needs*

---

[54] Friday Ad – 17th April 2009 – What's On Section – Page 36

as they near the end of life.[55] What a fantastic way to describe the work carried out by this Hospice. And it is run solely on public donations.

It has rained all night but the morning looks ok, if not just a little bit overcast as we head towards Carters Corner Farm. From his usual 'pick up point' our route takes us through part of Hailsham Town, into Battle Road and past Hailsham Community College. Just past 'the college' on the right-hand side was a very nice display of daffodils. I say 'was' because at some time over the past few hours someone (?)

The little pond by the back door

has vandalised the flowers. All of the flowers have been kicked from their stems and left lying on the ground. Now it doesn't take much to get Ron going but this was just too much! Apart from castratin' the b$5st**ds or 'bringin' back the birch' I am unable to print exactly what Ron thinks should happen to the perpetrators of this crime. But he is angry. He is very angry. "The flowers were doing no 'arm", he stutters, "yet mindless,

Well-placed signs

The entrance to the wood

bloody morons thinks it's funny ter do that. The little *+se 'oles 'ave even damaged some o' the trees round our Common Pond." Ron is in full voice now and nothing I say will stop him. I just let him run out of steam, agreeing with him every now and again in the hope that I'm nodding in the right places. Eventually calm is restored as we head towards a very well-signed Carters Corner Farm. Well that's not strictly true. The actual truth is that the Bluebell Walk signs were very evident along the road towards Cowbeech. We passed the house once owned by Lord Hailsham. I believe his name was Quintin Hogg, and the saying, at the time was, 'Hogg by name hog by nature'. If I'm wrong I'm sure a reader will let me know (?) Anyway, we kept passing signs saying 'Bluebell Walk↑' so we knew we were heading in the right direction. Before we knew it we'd passed Carters Corner Farm, which is actually halfway up Cowbeech Hill, before you get to the turning to Herstmonceux, which is where Ron thought the place was. If you remember I thought it was much further up the road, past Cowbeech. So we were both wrong. We turn the car round and enter the drive to the farm and we're greeted by Gerry ('that's Jerry

---

[55] http://www.st-wilfrids.co.uk/ visited 23/04/2009

Do 'edge'ogs climb trees?

with a gee,' Ron informs me). We park the car in the allocated place, change footwear, just in case it does start to rain, and for some reason, I decide not to take my stick.

Gerry (with the 'gee') invites us to walk along the path and wishes us a good walk. "'Oo do we 'ave ter pay?" asks Ron, "I'll take your cash if you wish," answers Gerry, "Payment is purely by donation," he continues. Ron obliges by handing Gerry £4, "that's fer the two ov' us, then." Gerry thanks us and guides us towards the start of the walk.

I'm not sure if we were early (it's now 10:15) but things don't look very ready and people are rushing to and fro around the garden, it all looked a little hectic. Volunteers from The Hospice were still putting up awnings and laying tables. We noticed a man putting out signs so decided our best approach would be to follow him. Again the sign was clear and as we pass the gentleman he advises that "the route is well-signed from 'ere'. So's you can't go wrong." He, obviously, never heard about me and Ron? And you've guessed it; we missed the next post and end up going in the wrong direction. It wasn't until I heard, in the distance, someone hollering at us that we eventually found the correct signs to follow. Once you see these signposts it does seem very silly how we managed to miss them because they are so very obvious. But what wasn't so obvious, to me anyway, was the beauty that unfolded before me. I have never smelt such a beautiful fragrance as that that hit me as we approached the wood. I have never seen so many Bluebells, in one place in my life. It was stunning.

Broken & Old

(the tree, not Ron)

This is only a very small wooded area but it is covered in flowers. The fragrance is something that can't be described and words cannot explain the beauty and the silence that is within this wooded area. In fact there are no words to describe this, you have to come here and experience it for yourselves. Both Ron and I walked along the signed path and didn't say a word. Both of us just couldn't take it all in. If you stopped and just listened, the birds in song, the sheep bleating and not a single sound of car or lorry. "This 'as got ter be what 'eavens like," says Ron as he stops and looks around. Of all the walks we have carried out over the past three years this has to be one of the prettiest spots we've seen and as Ron puts it "it's all natural, wot a real wood should look like, untouched an' unspoilt, smashin' it is!"

I'm afraid (?) the camera came into a lot of use on this walk and I took many photographs, but whichever way you look at it they all seem the same, thousands upon thousands of Bluebells. So what I have tried to do is give here as many pictures as I can without boring you all to death and hope that in some small way you can appreciate what this place is like. Basically I will let the pictures do the talking.

Hanging Ivy

We follow the path

White Bluebells?

At the end of the walk, which is only about ½mile long we come to what can only be described as a Sussex gate. It has bolts on both sides so there is no excuse not to close the gate behind you. But Ron suggests that a Sussex gate is the wrong title because 'there ain't no string ter 'old it all t'gether."

We both loved this little walk. The problem I had with it was that I was so busy taking photographs that I felt that I had missed out on the actual walk. "Let's do it agin, then," suggests Ron, and that is exactly what we did. This time I paid Gerry the £4, "but you don't have to pay again," he protested, "Keep the money," says Ron as we pass him and head for the start again, "worth every, bloody penny." We now have the company of a couple of sheep dogs who insisted on keeping us entertained all the way round. And this time I did notice a lot more. Like the little stream running through the wood that appeared to flow in one direction and then, a little further into the wood, was flowing in a different direction (?) Ron found some different plants but was unsure of what they were but someone, reading this must be able to give us the name?

This time, when we got back, we decided to have a cuppa. All the proceeds would be going to the Hospice and, by now, the tables had been set up and it looked as if they were ready for people. Apparently over 500 people attended the event last year and everyone was hoping the weather was going to stay bright and the rain would stay away. We both had a cuppa, I was tempted, as always, towards the homemade chu tney and Ron, always the betting man, had a couple of quid on the Tombola, his luck as usual, wasn't with him. "I 'ope ter 'ave a bit more luck with the gee gee's this afternoon," say's Ron. And, for now, we decide to head for home.

As I said, only a very short walk but it was a very enjoyable stroll, and should you find yourself at a loose end this time next year and fancy a little walk, head for Carters Corner Farm. Not just for the walk but also, to see the animals and spend some time in good company, and perhaps spend a little money to help a very good cause, St Wilfrid's Hospice. You never know, you may need their help one day.

Ghost Walk

As I said in the previous chapter I have written to the organiser of this ghost walk to ensure that he was ok with Ron and me tagging along on one of his Saturday evening walks around Pevensey. As long as we don't use any of our guides' material verbatim, we will be welcome to join him. I looked on the Internet about ghosts and was amazed at the number of sites available that dedicate themselves to this phenomenon. Would you believe there are over 32,000,000 sites, on the Internet, listing all manner of ghostly things, including pictures, stories and ghostly music? Thankfully I didn't look at any of these sites on my own or in the dark. Call me a coward but some things just can't be explained. Just writing this has made the hairs on the back of neck prickle and I have to check that there's no-one behind me. The more I read the more I'm beginning to regret mentioning the idea to Ron, but he seems very keen and I don't want to let him down, sooooooooooooooo.........

I've finally plucked up courage to do this one!! As I said I'm not sure that I believe in real (?) ghosts but I am prepared to see and learn for myself. I have an open mind, I can do this. After all, what's the worst that can happen? It isn't until I pick Ron up that I find out that he feels just as apprehensive as me, although he does admit to seeing 'The Grey Lady' from Michelham Priory. "Just appeared, she did, right by the bridge, just before the entrance, scared the s$*t out 'o me an' me mates. I'll never forget it!" For anyone unsure of who (what?) the 'grey lady' is she is reputed to be a member of the Sackville family whose child drowned in the moat many years ago. She is sometimes seen staring into the moat and has also been known to '…peer mournfully into the faces of sleeping guests and then drift away into the walls.[56] But is it just a story or will I be convinced, and, after this walk, be able to say that I am a believer. We'll see.

The advertisement from the Friday Ad tells me to park in the Castle car park. Now straight away I'm a little confused. Is there a pub called 'The Castle' by the castle or do I park in the castle car park at Pevensey Castle? The only pub I know that is called 'The Castle' is in Pevensey Bay so it can't be there because that is a fair walk to the castle so, after much discussion and argument over a pint of amber nectar we decide to park at the car park next to the castle. Of course, it was the correct decision.

St. Nicholas Church, Pevensey

How many people reading this have driven, walked or passed through the village of Westham (apparently pronounced Westum?) and seen the church with the sign 'built by the Romans in 1080'? I have seen this church hundreds of times and assumed that it was the only church in the area? But in the next village, even prettier Pevensey, is the Church dedicated to St. Nicholas. This church is reached by a little lane, leading from the car park beside the castle. I had no idea that Pevensey had its own church but unfortunately we were unable to look inside because the door was locked, but just to find this church really surprised me and the setting is really pretty.

---

[56] http://www.darkencounters.co.uk/michelham-priory/casebook-michelham-priory.html visited 03/05/2009

Ron looks uncertain?

But back to the car park we find our guide, Robert, and introduce ourselves. Again Robert asks us not to use his material in this book and I will endeavour to keep to his wishes. The fee for this 90 minute 'Walk by Lantern Light' is £6 each. "How many people do you get fer the walk?" asks Ron. "It really depends, on Halloween night I had 110 people," replies Robert, "but my smallest walk was with only two people. It depends on what else is going on, because this Saturday is at the start of a Bank Holiday, I may not get many people. We'll just have to wait and see." Ron, being Ron, has already worked out how much over 100 people would have paid for a 90 minute walk as he turns to me and whispers, "do you know 'ow much money 'e took fer that one 90 minute walk. Why don't we do something like that? Could make a bl%8dy fortune." "Yes Ron, but only on a good night, what about the nights when only two people turn up?" I ask. "Tis still just under £12 an hour," he hisses. "But it might only be £12 a week, if this is all he does." I reply, but I have been considering a little venture like this but, at the moment, it's just an idea. I'll have to see how things work out but some guided tours around our beautiful county does appeal to me.

Part of the inner wall

We set off on our walk through the East Gate of Pevensey Castle. Our party totals 9 "That's fifty four quid," Ron whispers, "fer 90 minutes work!" Robert, our guide, warns us that we may not see any ghosts this evening but, of course, he couldn't guarantee this. As a personal note I hope we don't! At the middle of the castle grounds Robert

Robert tries to light the lantern, again

stops and tells us stories about the castle itself, being two castles built at different periods in history. We then hear of some 'ghostly' happenings and sightings from the very spot we are standing including a nice story about how the village of Burwash became to be called Burwash. Robert also advises us that some ghosts are never seen, but can be heard. Now I've not only got to keep my eyes open but my ears as well!! I'm not sure if it's where I am or what Robert is telling me but my senses seem to have perked up 100%. Or am I being paranoid?

From the middle of the castle grounds Robert leads us up to the drawbridge and continues his tales of events that have been reported or seen at this location and about a certain 'White Lady'. Again, I cannot explain, but I have this feeling that I didn't want to be at the back of the group as I hear of a camping trip by youngsters who 'see things' that eventually disappear. Did I hear something behind me? As Robert continues to talk I have to keep looking over my shoulder. Throughout the first few minutes of our guided walk I can feel the adrenalin still rising, I keep hearing strange noises, or am I being stupid? Robert certainly has a way to communicate his subject. All Ron says to me is "spooky, init?"

From the drawbridge Robert now guides us to the West Gate where, again, he revels in stories of events, including a lovely story about 'job sharing drummer boy ghosts' who can be heard at most castles along the coast. There is also a story of the massacre that happened on the very spot we are standing, where originally, a small village was destroyed and all the inhabitants were slain. Robert really tells it in a way that makes it feel as if you are there.

Old man shuffles towards the gates

From the West Gate we head for the church dedicated to St. Mary the Virgin reportedly built, originally, by the Normans in 1080. This is the church everyone sees as they approach or leave the castle. It is a wonderful structure from the front but we are escorted to the rear of the church, which isn't quite as pretty. However, we're not here to admire the view but find out about such things as the Plague. One of the things I find difficult to understand (perhaps that's not the right word?) is that Pevensey used to be a large port. The sea used to lap up along the walls of the castle and goods and produce from all over the world used to land here.

Robert explains all this very clearly, along with some really unwanted goods, i.e. rats. These were the rats that spread the 'black death' and the spot where Robert has positioned us is, would you believe, the exact spot where all the bodies from the area that had died from the plague would have been buried en masse. I and a couple of other people in the group took at least two steps back. But that is not where Roberts' stories stop. After showing us what he describes as, one of the earliest timepieces in the whole

of England, he leads us to the front of the church and tells a story of the ghost of an old man seen shuffling along the path away from the church doors. Robert is in full flow now has he tells more stories of 'funny' events around this church. The story of a young girl, in the house next to the church, who wanders along the passage. One of the stories, I can't remember if it was around now or not, was about tapping people on the shoulder. Now if that happened to me right now I'd pass out but strangely I have this sudden urge, as we walk away from the church back towards the castle, to tap the shoulder of the lady in front of me just to see the reaction. But I manage to control the urge. It's starting to get darker now and Robert is having problems keeping the lantern alight. "Per'aps it's runnin' out o' white 'spirit'" chuckles Ron, "No," says Robert, "It's paraffin." We both look at each

The goal at Pevensey

other and Ron whispers, "I don't think 'e got the 'spirit' joke." It is now getting a little cold. Didn't Robert say that just before a ghost appears the temperature drops? My senses are on 'red alert'!

Back at the castle Robert explains about a 'grey or pale lady' who appears on the battlements of the castle. Some believe this lady to be Lady Joan Pelham whose husband took over the castle in 1394. Her husband was called away to fight a battle in the north of England and Lady Joan was left in charge of the castle. With most of the soldiers gone, the unprotected castle was besieged by an invading army who demanded its surrender in the name of King Richard II. She managed to hold on until her husband returned, pacing the parapet every day, but she suffered such mental torture under the pressure that it is believed her troubled spirit still walks the battlements. But others believe that it is the ghost of Queen Joan of Navarre, the wife of Henry IV. Falsely charged with witchcraft by Friar Randolph she was put in the custody of Sir John Pelham at Pevensey Castle in 1419. She was let out several years later when Henry V reprieved her from her deathbed, apparently feeling remorse for the ill-treatment of his step-mother.[57]

We now head out of the East Gate where yet more tales are told before heading down the little lane, past St. Nicholas Church and we stop at the back gate of somebody's house. Here, we are told, was recently seen a ghost, who walks across the gardens, through the walls, and disappears into thin air. It's now getting dark as well as cold. I'm listening to Ron talk to one of the people in our walk, "If yer like churches an' 'istory," Ron tells the man, "yer must go ter 'erstmoceux church an' Ninfield Church. Beautiful places they both are. An' the yew tree…..," "I know the Yew Tree," interrupts the man, "nice pub." "T'aint a pub," corrects Ron, "tis a yew tree, in the grounds o' the church. Be'ind that tree is Standard 'ill where the troops of William rested before the Battle of 'astins." I'm giggling as we turn left and head down a twitten towards the main road. We turn left and head back towards the castle. I must admit that I was surprised not to stop at the jail and hear of more grizzly events but Robert had saved the best to last. Outside the Rose and Crown, opposite the East Gate to the castle, he tells of the horrific events that happened around 1586 in what is now known as 'The Haunted Chamber'. It certainly had the hairs on the back of my head standing up.

Robert explains the theory

I've never experienced a quicker 90 minutes than that of tonight. I'm still not totally convinced about ghosts but I will admit to having a worrying few minutes whilst I developed the pictures for this walk. Gladly, or sadly, no funny images appeared from the camera. But I really did enjoy this walk. It was very informative and light-hearted in places. Yes, there were a couple of moments that had me thinking long and hard about the phenomena but, as the saying goes, seeing is believing, and although I didn't see anything this evening, I have experienced things, in the past, that I can't explain. Especially since the death of my parents. So, I'm still of an open mind, I'm still not a firm believer in ghosts although Robert was very convincing.

---

[57] www.timetravel-britain.com/articles/castles/pevensey2.shtml - visited 02/05/2009

If you want to go on this walk don't be shy, it's worth every penny. Just turn up, on a Saturday evening at 7:30. Park in the Castle car park (it's free!!) and wait for Robert. He'll be there and you won't be disappointed. If it's chilly, take something warm to wear, if it's not chilly take something to keep you warm, especially if you're a bit on the nervous side as some of the stories are a bit spooky. Robert also does a 'murder evening' by request as well as a ghost walk in Alfriston on some Fridays. If you want to get in touch with Robert he can be contacted at www.sussexguidedwalks.co.uk. Both Ron and I loved this walk around Pevensey so much that we might try the murder evening next. My nerves might not be able to take another ghost walk!

Where the ghost of a girl wandered the passageway

Battlefield Walk (in Kent)

This walk could be called a friends walk because it has been suggested by Alan who used to reside in Kent. It was actually taken from a book of walks and is described as a Battlefield Walk[58]. It could also be called an overseas walk because Ron thinks anything outside Sussex is foreign. But Alan wanted to show us around his 'neck of the woods'. As he says, both Ron and I have bleated on about how nice Sussex is so it's about time we broadened our outlook and we experience a different area. Ron still isn't convinced that they even speak the same language as his Sussex brethren and he's adamant that they're no good at cricket. "Tis obvious," comments Ron, "Sussex must be better 'cause Sussex 'r in the 1st division o' the County Championship an' Kent could only just make the 2nd. Proves it, does that!" Ron downs another mouthful of Harvey's Bitter and challenges anyone to argue the point, but nobody does.

On a more personal point, now is the time of year when we remember Sean Snee, one of our closest friends. Every year, since his sad and sudden death, our local pub has organised a Charity Pool competition in his memory. Ron is gutted. "I'm not even in the first round," he moans whilst looking at 'the draw' hanging on the notice board at the King's Head. "You must be," I say, "you've paid your money." "So I might 'ave done," he moans, "but I've got ter play a preliminary first an' then, if I win that, I've only got ter play bloody 'Frenchie'! I'll 'ave no chance against 'im. That'll be the third year runnin' I 'aven't got past the bloody first round!" "You never know, Ron," I offer, "perhaps Colin ('Frenchie) will have a bad day?" "Yeh, some 'ope o'that," he continues, "still, at least I've 'ad a go. 'elped the charity a bit an' I've started sellin' raffle tickets. That reminds me. Better go an' see if I can sell a few t'night." And he's off, with raffle tickets in hand and a pint glass to collect the cash.

Roman legionary

As I said at the start I have taken this walk from the book 'Battlefield Walks Kent & Sussex' and the walk we will be carrying out is Walk 2 from the book and is titled 'Medway AD43'. I like my history but I get a bit confused when we talk about the AD bits. Don't get me wrong, I'm more than happy to accept that things happened during this very early period in history but the names always seem to confuse me. Caratacus, Trinovantes, Cassio Dio, Aulus Plautius, Verica are all, I presume, very popular names from the period but they're not too easy to remember, are they? Not like Ron and Graham. So I hope I don't have to get too involved in the AD history bit whilst we are walking, but I'm sure it will pop up now and again.

Another personal bit about this Saturday is that Gillingham, a football team supported by Alan, is playing at Wembley in the final of the divisional play-offs. If Gillingham wins they will be promoted to League 1 in the football league and Alan, possibly, may not be in a fit state to walk due to his celebrations. But if they loose, it will be black armbands and 'better luck' next season? As we are walking on a Monday we are

---

[58] Battlefield Walks Kent & Sussex by Rupert Matthews published by Frances Lincoln ISBN 9780711228269

Memorial to the 3 men who lost their lives in the Kent Air Ambulance in 1998

hoping, whatever the outcome of the match, Alan will have got over the whole episode, either way.

First we have to get to a place called Burham and I have absolutely no idea where it is. "It'll take an hour and thirty minutes max," Alan informs us. All I've got to do, apparently, is head for Heathfield, Cross-in-hand, Mayfield and then on to Tonbridge and follow the signs for Maidstone. "You'll see signs for Burham," Alan informs me "That's a silly way to go," offers the pub 'know-it-all' (every pub has one!) "Why not go up the A22 and across to Crowborough, Be quicker that way." Alan must know the way, because he does the trip once a fortnight so we let the 'know-it-all' have his say and then agree to ignore him. I decide to put the address into my ever reliable SatNav and, would you believe, it's telling me to head for Heathfield etc.

But before we head north or is it north-east (?) I, obviously, have very few books on Kent. But I need a little information on Burham that I can pass on to you all. So, I have had to resort to the good old Internet. And after looking at the website[59] I just know Ron will be looking forward to this walk. I have to say that the website was very impressive. A couple of things worry me after reading the latest Parish Magazine (available on-line[60] or I have a printed copy if you wish to have a look) but with a population of only 1,300 it has no less than five pubs! Now I know that Ron is interested.

The history of the village of Burham can be traced back to Roman times. AD43 saw the Battle of the Medway at the crossing point on the River Medway where Burham is now situated, when the invading Roman legions, advancing west across Kent, were confronted by a massed army of the ancient British Tribes. The Roman victory altered the course of history in Britain, and the remains of Roman buildings have been found in Burham and the neighbouring village of Eccles[61]. Obviously this was years ago but a more recent event here needs a little mention: on Sunday 26th July 1998 the Kent Air Ambulance helicopter crashed on a remote hillside within the boundaries of the village while returning to its base at Rochester airfield. Three crewmembers lost their lives that day and a memorial stone has been placed at the Bluebell Hill picnic site close to the scene of the tragedy.[62]

'Alan's' Team colours

Image from
http://newsimg.bbc.co.uk/media/images/

We will carry out this walk on a Bank Holiday Monday. Typically the weekend has been glorious with blue skies and hot sun. On Sunday I

---

[59] http://www.burhamvillage.com/HomeFrames.html visited 20/05/09
[60] Ibid – follow the link on the village home page
[61] Ibid – extract taken from web site
[62] Ibid

The start of the North Downs

took my wife to Eastbourne and we ended up sitting on the beach eating fish and chips (I know it's against my diet, but they tasted fantastic!). We watched the sunbathers and children playing in the water . But when I got up on Monday the grey clouds were overhead and, as I write this, the rain has started and I can hear thunder in the distance. All-in-all, a typical British Bank Holiday Monday. But Alan is waiting for us in the 'back waters' of Kent expecting Ron and me to turn up at 10.30. We have found out that Gillingham (The Gills) actually beat Shrewsbury one nil at Wembley so his team are promoted to Division One of the Football League. Both Ron and I have decided not to mention the game when we meet him and see how long it takes before he tells us about the game.

But still the rain belts down and I'm having my doubts about this walk. According to Alan (and SatNav) the drive will take 1½hours, perhaps the rain and thunder will have stopped by the time we get there? So, with as much wet weather gear as I can carry I go to collect Ron at 9 o'clock and we head for Burham.

Not only are Gillingham in play-off contention but this weekend is the deciding games on who goes down from the Premiership. I watched the game between Newcastle United and Aston Villa. All Newcastle had to do was not concede a goal to remain in the Premiership and they lost one nil. Now women everywhere know that all men are experts in the noble game and both Ron and I believe that the current Newcastle United players, from one of the biggest and best supported clubs in the country couldn't beat Eastbourne. They were pathetic but what makes it worse is that in a few weeks time all the players from that terrible team will be playing in another premiership team next year. They should be made to honour their contract and stay with the club they all destroyed!! But enough, I hear you say, what about the walk.

We arrive at Burham in just under 1½ hours. Only one little diversion when Jane seemed to lose her way but we managed to get to Church Street. The rain has stopped. All we need now is Alan. We drive up and down Church Street, can't find him. "Call 'im up on the phone," suggests Ron after our third trip up and down. Alan tells me he's at the Post Office, in Church Street. "Can't remember seein' no Post Office", says Ron and neither do I but, just in case we did miss it, we go up and down Church Street again. Still no Post Office and then I suddenly remembered a shop on the main road and head back up Rochester Road, away from Church Street and there is the Post Office with Alan, changing his shoes, outside. "What took yer?" asks Alan. "We ain't in Church Street," offers Ron in way of an explanation, "Church Street's up the road, on the left,"

Ron spots some Fungi

I explain, "and we need to start the walk opposite Church Street," Alan agrees to follow us to where I think we can park the cars. It's a little side street, just before one of the pubs in Burham, The Windmill. "May 'ave ter try out the Windmill at the end ov the walk," chuckles Ron, "Did yer notice," he continues, "not a mention ov Gillingham? But it's early, let's wait ter see how far along the walk we gets." Just in case the weather turns against us I've decided to wear my fluorescent coat. It's bright yellow so the theory is that I'll be seen in all weathers but I'll also be dry. Ron has a coat and Alan is wearing his waterproof golf jacket. We set off and our first instruction is to head up towards Bluebell Hill. "There's a ghost up Bluebell 'ill," Alan informs us, as we head up towards a five-bar-gate. "Only see 'er when it's really wet and windy. She sits by a bus stop, soaked ter the skin. People stop ter give 'er a lift, 'cause they feel sorry for 'er and when they turns around she's gone. Just vanishes into thin air. She's well-known in these parts

The Robin Hood - but where?

The route of the Batavian army

an' she's in every ghost book you can find. Me mum used ter tell me about 'er" Ron and I look at each other as we struggle up the very steep hill. It is incredibly steep and Alan hasn't stopped talking. If you don't know him, I'll let you know that Alan could win gold medals for talking. But he still hasn't mentioned Gillingham. Until, that is, I have to stop to get my breath. I have to admit that I struggled up this hill, part of the North Downs. My calf muscles are pleading with me to stop and not continue but Alan is determined that we should hear about Gillingham's mighty victory. And tell us he does. He kept silent about it for just over 200 yards. Tina, his wife, reckoned we wouldn't get out of the car but we listened as he told his story, including the bad burger, how his team were magnificent, how sick he was after half-time, only just managed to see the goal, felt ill all the way home, went to bed early, the best team won etc. etc. etc. But his pain seemed to make mine more bearable. We eventually arrive at the top of the North Downs. I'm knackered and all Ron says is "Don't recommend that fer a bloody wheelchair walk."

At the top of this very steep climb is a lane and on the far side is a pub sign for the Robin Hood. That's all we could see, the pub sign. The pub, Alan informs us, is at the end of the lane to the right of the sign. "Bit out ov the way up 'ere," says Ron, "can't 'ave any local trade at all. 'ow can they make a go ov' a pub in the middle of nowhere? Seems odd ter me that a pub like that can survive, a village the size of Burham with only 1,300 people 'as 5 pubs, all makin' a go ov it yet 'ailsham with over 10,000 people can't cope with 4?"

....*In AD43 the Roman emperor Claudius ordered an invasion of Britain and he gave command of this invasion to Aulus Plautius a seasoned commander. It was from this very position* (the Robin Hood sign probably wasn't here then!) *that Plautius looked down onto the British position, led by King Caratacus, on level ground on the far bank of the river Medway. There used to be a small bridge over the river, opposite a church, but it had been broken up by the British. The bulk of the Roman forces were marched down the hill, from this point, to face the Britons across the Medway. This force consisted of three legions (approx. 14,000 men).*

Tastes just like sugar?

Sheep with teeth problems??

The expedition also included the 2nd Augusta commanded by the future emperor Vespasion. This gave Plautius around 20,000 legionnaries for his invasion.

Plautius wanted to launch a diversionary attack, to the north of the British forces, so he used men recruited from Batavia, now part of the Netherlands. These men were drawn from the land of swamps and marshes and were especially trained to be able to swim carrying both armour and weapons. It is the route taken by the Batavians that we will now follow......[63]

Facing the sign for the Robin Hood we turn left and proceed down a narrow country lane. We need to look out for a farm, Burham Hill Farm, where we will then turn left again. But before we get there Ron has wondered into the hedgerow and reappears with a large, wet, leaf. After walking with Ron all these years you'd think that I would realise what he does and not worry about it, but right now I think he's lost it! First he's looking at this leaf like it's a long lost friend, silly grin, twinkle in his eye, and then he starts licking it! I kid you not. From base to tip, he's giving this leaf a good lick. Alan is just as surprised as me when he asks, "What the 'ell are you doin', Ron?" "'Tis lovely, is this," replies Ron, "tastes just like sugar. All yer 'ave ter do is lick the moisture spots, from the rain. Real sweet it is." He passes the leaf to me. "Go on, give it a try." I decline the offer with the excuse that since my diabetes I don't take sugar. It was the only excuse I could think of at the time. Luckily Alan managed to change the subject when he pointed out that most of the sheep in the next field were lying down and eating. "That's 'cause the sheep 'ave bad teeth," explains Ron. "Probably been lickin' too many o' them bloody leaves," chuckles Alan, but I don't think Ron got the joke.

We find the farm without any problems and now turn left and head downhill, which is just as steep as the uphill we encountered at the very start of the walk. "Can you imagine," says Alan, "marching down this hill, then having to swim across the Medway in full armour and then, after all that, stand and fight for your life. Couldn't have been easy." As we end up slipping and sliding down some of the steeper slopes we can't imagine how difficult it must have been for these men. In places it is very steep. So much so, that at one point, it looked as if the path disappeared. But slowly we managed to get

---

[63] 'Battlefield Walks Kent & Sussex' by Rupert Matthews – Walk 2 Page 30

Where's the path gone?

to the bottom of the hill without mishap. As Ron said earlier this is definitely not a walk for a wheelchair or, come to that, if you have any walking disabilities. It is very tiring.

But once at the bottom of the hill we come to a lane. Here we turn right and, still following the route of the Batavians, make our way towards the northern end of the battle area.

It's now time for a little moan. In most of the books where we have followed routes it is very uncommon to give a name of a road. Why this is we do not know. But the map we are following clearly shows one road on our left. Our instructions are to '...continue along the lane for over half a mile, ignoring the first turn to the left, but take the second.'[64] The first turning, on the left, is 'Scarborough Lane' so why not call it that. We should then see a road on our right. We didn't. The next road, on our left, was Knowle Road. But our map shows this as a 'Y' junction but our instructions don't. They say '...the main road bears to the right..' so if we turn left here, is it the right road? It doesn't look like the right road but it is the second road on our left. It would have been so much easier if the writer put down the name of the road. So we turned left. We are now heading towards a village called Wouldham. But our instructions don't tell us that! No wonder we get lost! At a junction the instructions then tell us to follow a lane. But which lane? There is a lane on our left, called Hall Road which is a continuation of the High Street. So

Kent - The Garden of England

we turn left into Hall Road ....*The Batavians wouldn't have*

Thankfully in the next field

turned left here but carried straight on, across the marshy ground, and swam across the river. No sooner were they ashore when they were spotted by some British scouts. British chariots came racing north to meet the threat but the Batavians surprised the British by throwing javelins at the chariot ponies. The British drew back and tried to keep the Batavians pinned down while they awaited reinforcements from the British infantry. Unfortunately the infantry couldn't move as they were facing up to the main Roman force as it approached the river....[65]

---

[64] 'Battlefield Walks Kent & Sussex' by Rupert Matthews – Walk 2 Page 33

We approach the church

We walk along the lane for some time but I keep looking at the map and thinking that something's not right. "We should be able to see the river Medway," I explain, "and our instructions tell us that industrial units should be visible and we are in a wilderness." All around us is barren, open wasteland and fenced off areas. We decide to turn back and look for a path leading us back towards the Medway, but all we could find was a car park. So we head back up the lane. "At least we must be heading in the right direction," offers Alan, "I could see a church in the distance and the map shows a church." Thankfully we do arrive at the bend in the Medway that is described in our book as the place where the main Battle of Medway took place.

We follow the river round in an arc and come to the stone that has been placed in memory of the battle. It is here that we stop and admire the achievements of the armies of AD43. "Didn't need that SatNav thing ter find this place," offers Ron. "And they managed to swim, in full armour, across the Medway," says Alan. "Can you imagine asking some o' the youngsters' ov today ter do that?" asks Ron. "be too frightened ov getting' their trainers dirty." And all who know Ron will be aware of how the next few minutes went!!

The monument to commemorate the Battle of Medway (that's the stone in the middle)

---

[65] 'Battlefield Walks Kent & Sussex' by Rupert Matthews – Walk 2 Page 34

This doesn't look right

Sweet corn, nothing but sweet corn

We now have a little bit of controversy regarding events that happened here. Right next to the monument is an information board describing the events of the Battle of Medway and on this board it states that the Batavians crept up to the British and 'hamstrung' the horses. There is no mention of the Batavians being held to the north of the British position. But what is in no doubt is that us Brits got a bit of a hiding. ......*Watching from his vantage point (remember Bluebell Hill?) Plautius saw that Caratacus' forces divide as some infantry moved off north. Plautius thought that Caratacus had his attention divided between the main Roman army to his front and the Batavians to his left. It was now time for the 2nd Augusta and Vespasian to move into action.....*[66]

From the monument we now walk along the river bank towards Burham Court with its church. Before we reach the church Ron notices the animals long before me. Thankfully they were in the next field. They were only young but still looked menacing. Alan thought they were ' right chav' cows because they had earings in (ID tags really) but the big bull looked tough and ugly.

We arrive at Burham Court Church to discover that it isn't used on a regular basis. "Probably the parishioners are too busy supportin' the five pubs ter come ter church," chuckles Ron and although the graveyard is kept in a reasonable condition there was something about the church that isn't right. Inside is very bare. The pews, the few remaining, are mostly painted white and the plaster all round the outer walls, up to four feet from the ground, has been removed. "Look what some berks written in the book," says Ron as he thumbs through the visitors' book. Somebody obviously thought they were being funny. Such a shame that a part of our history, built so close to a real historical event should be allowed to deteriorate in this way for everyone to see. But, as they say, perhaps that's progress.

.....It was from this point that Vespasian led the 2nd Augusta as they turned west to reach the ford that, then, lay across the Medway. By late afternoon they quickly came under attack from the British but by the time this initial rush of Britons had been driven off it was dusk and fighting came to a halt. Vespasian thought that he had driven off the British but was surprised to find, when he awoke the next day that almost the entire British army were bearing down on him. From his vantage point (remember Bluebell Hill?) Plautius saw the danger and ordered that two more legions cross the ford in support of Vespasian. The men arrived just in time and a large battle took place. Eventually as more and more Romans got over the ford they gradually came to gain an

---

[66] 'Battlefield Walks Kent & Sussex' by Rupert Matthews – Walk 2 Page 37

advantage. The British began to retreat falling back northwards down the left bank of the Medway[67] *……. The rest, as they say, is history.*

We now follow the road back towards Burham. Again the name of the road isn't mentioned but it's Old Church Street. We turn left, where the road bears to the right and head across open fields of sweet corn before arriving back at Church Street and the car.

Now all we have to do is find somewhere to eat. "Can't be too difficult," says Ron, "we've got five pubs ter choose from." Alan recommended the Fleur de Lys so that's where we head for. It's only a few yards down the road and we are there in minutes. The Fleur de Lys Inn was built in the 16th Century and is thought to have been the Wine House frequented by the household of J.H.Rosney, the French Ambassador to the court of Queen Elizabeth I from 1597 to 1604. He is said to have stayed at Culand Farm, Burham to be near his good friend Sir Walter Raleigh who lived for a time at the Friary in Aylesford.[68]

The Fleur de Lys, Burham

We are warmly welcomed by the manager when we arrived at the pub. Although it was turned two o'clock when we arrived he was more than happy to supply us with a varied menu which proved, not only very nourishing but also very reasonably priced. If you're in the area give this lovely family pub a try, you will not be disappointed. As Ron say's, "a real pub!"

This was a nice walk, very hard in places but worth the effort. The history of the battle has made the chapter a bit on the long side but I hope I haven't bored you all. It was a real shame about the church but we can't have it all. Kent isn't such a bad place really and as Ron was very quick to point out, "People look the same 'ere as they does in Sussex." So Ron's happy. Before we go and discuss our next exploit take a look at the last photograph. It was taken at the church. Ron found it hanging from the wall. Any ideas as to what it was used for?

Possibly used in a mill?

---

[67] 'Battlefield Walks Kent & Sussex' by Rupert Matthews – Walk 2 Pages 37 & 38
[68] http://www.burhamvillage.com/pubthefleurdelys.htm visited 26/05/2009

A Good Walk Spoilt

Everyone must have heard of Samuel Clemens, haven't they? Just in case you haven't I can hear a resounding, "Who the hell is Samuel Clemens?" Well, I'll tell you. He wrote under the name of Mark Twain and, amongst other sayings, his famous line about the game of golf is that '...it was a good walk spoilt.' Another one of his sayings is that '...he would never let schooling get in the way of his education' and, one of my personal favourites, '...you can have heaven; I'd rather go to Bermuda.' But it is the golf quotation that will be proven, or not, on this lovely Saturday morning in June. Today we are going to write about something different. Some explanation is called for......

When I was a young lad, attending Secondary School, I was a member of various sports teams, Football, Rugby, Cross Country, Scottish Dancing (I'm not kidding!) to name but a few. As a team we were not very good. In fact we lost a lot more games than we won and another old saying 'It's not the winning; it's the taking part that counts', really rings true to me. But, as we all know, some people get really upset if they lose. Personally, it doesn't bother me because I'm not too good at most sports (I'm going for the sympathy vote here!) so I've got used to not winning. But I will have a go at most games. In my experience, it is the people who are really good at a particular sport who get upset if the likes of me have a good day and beat them. But, let's be honest, everyone can have a bad day. Ron is an exception to even this rule because he **was** very good at football, cricket, stoolball and darts but if he lost he was upset, of course, but he would accept the defeat and it didn't eat away at him like some we know. Both Ron and I are the same. We like to take part, we like to be invited to play but we won't get that upset if we don't win. So, what I've done is I've persuaded Ron to be my caddie at a game of golf. This will be the second time that Ron has been my personal caddie. (And he's very good at it, whatever he says!!)

One ball + one little hole

I will admit now that I used to play golf. Not well, but I could hit a ball in a straight line. After my first heart attack I decided, foolishly, that I needed to get out and get some exercise so I joined a golf club. I say foolishly because I thought that playing golf would help me get fit. Well it didn't! I now realise that to play golf you need to be fit first, because it is a long way to walk, a long way to hit a ball and it can be one of the most frustrating games on earth as you feel the blood pressure rise when it all goes wrong. Not an ideal situation for someone in my condition. But I persevered. That was over 15 years ago but due to financial issues I decided that eating was more important than playing a silly game and I left the golf club and hung up my putter. Until last year, that is, when both Ron and I got talked into a game of golf at Horam. Ron, on this occasion agreed to be my caddie, insisting on a payment of 10% of any winnings and I had to use whichever club he told me, without question. I won £5. Ron accepted his 50p like a true gent but the prize money hasn't changed us.

Like I said, Ron and I have been invited, by Alan, for a 'friendly' game of golf at the golf club I used to be a member at, Welshurst Golf and Country Club. For the technically minded the course is open to the public and is eighteen holes, 6,084 yards par 70. It is always best to book, especially at weekends and green fees are payable before you tee off. The current (2009) full membership, for golf only, is £705 (7 day membership) there is also a 'standard joining fee' of £200 per person. When I was a member at Welshurst there were also gymnasium facilities, at an extra cost, but I'm unable to find any information on the website[69], perhaps it no longer exists. For non-members the green fees, currently, are; £20 for eighteen holes Mon-Fri which rises to £26 for 18 holes at the weekend. By the time you have a couple of drinks at the 19th hole I'm not expecting a lot of change from £40. (Don't tell the wife!) Now you might understand why eating became more important than golf: it ain't cheap.

A deserted Golf Course

So at the pre-arranged time, on a slightly damp Saturday morning, I collect Ron and we head for the golf course. It was decided that we would use the trolley for the golf clubs. This saves having to carry the complete set around the course. And it makes life a little easier, especially for Ron.

When we arrive at the car park it's empty apart from one golfer getting his clubs out of his car. Of course Ron and the golfer recognise each other and it's like the meeting of two lost brothers. We can't seem to go anywhere where Ron is not easily recognised by someone. Discussions continue with the two men ridiculing the current Hailsham Cricket Team, "bloody useless they are", the English Cricket Team; apparently they've just lost a 20-20 match against The Netherlands? And I didn't know that the Dutch had a cricket team. Of course today's footballers came in for a grilling as well because England are playing a World Cup Qualifier against a team from, as Ron puts it, "…some foreign bl%$£*in' country that ends in a ..stan. Over Russia way somewhere, even I could score a bloody goal against them," and all the time I'm getting my clubs and trolley out of the back of my car hoping that the rest of the morning is going to get better.

But, we were supposed to meet Alan at 7.30. It's now 7.45 and there is no sign of Alan. "Per'aps we're at the wrong place," suggests Ron, "should be at 'oram an' not Welshurst." Now he's put doubt in my mind, but I'm sure we're at the right place. Just in case I go to the shop and check that we are booked to play here. The man tells us that the game is booked and that we are due to tee off at 8.03. Why it's not eight o'clock or five past I have no idea but we are told that as it is very quiet we could go at any time. And quiet it is. Apart from the player Ron met in the Car Park the place is deserted. "I've never seen it so quiet," I tell Ron. When I used to be a

Heading down to the hole

[69] http://www.wellshurst.com visited 04/06/2009

99 | P a g e

member here you had to queue up to get onto the first tee. The weekends were worse, but now, it seems, that the course is all ours. Alan arrives with Den, who, we are told is the dad of Tina. I wrongly thought that Den must be Alan's father-in-law because Alan's wife is called Tina. But it's a different Tina. Den hails from Aldershot and was hoping to be able to play in the Kings Head Open but, unfortunately, he is unable to make it down to Sussex on that weekend so we invited him to play a game with us. I'm not too sure that he is aware of me going to print but he'll find out soon enough.

Alan 'chips' onto the green

To start any activity it is always best to limber up. You know the routine, stretches and the like. Well, obviously, Ron and me are pretty supple and energetic individuals so decided that all that stretching was for wimps so we didn't do any. It was decided, by the tossing of a coin that Alan would tee off first. Unfortunately he couldn't find his glove so asked Den to tee off and he would go once he found it. Den looked a little apprehensive about going first so I stepped up and took the lead.

For those unaware of the rules and etiquette of golf I will try to explain some things as we go along. I do not intend to give a blow by blow account of all eighteen holes because that would be boring so I'll just touch on certain aspects of the game in general. Anyone reading this who is aware of the rules and etiquette please bear with us. First things first. You must always ensure that before you tee off (hit the first shot) that there is nobody in the way. I look down the fairway and the coast is clear. On the tee there are coloured markers posts. You must stay behind these posts. The white posts are used when playing in competitions. The red posts are the lady's tees and the yellow posts are where all other games are played from. So we will be starting every hole behind the yellow posts. Like I said, I'm going first. Which makes me wonder why we tossed a coin in the first place. Anyway, I place my plastic tee in the ground, just behind the yellow marker posts and Ron hands me the club he wishes me to use. I get myself in position and take a mighty swing at my little white ball. Expecting it to fly off the tee into the distance I was somewhat disappointed to see it land about 10 feet away to my right. Thankfully nobody laughs, although I'm sure I heard Ron give a giggle. "Don't worry," he says, grinning, "You always play rubbish fer the first few 'oles." Den goes next and his ball goes so far I can't actually see it and Alan's ball follows Den's. And basically that is how the whole game went.

Dennis shows us how it's done

I was useless. It didn't get better, as Ron suggested, until we were at the 12th hole when Alan said, "It's because your looking for the ball, directly after you hit it. Just keep your head still. Don't look for the ball until after it's left the club head. It was the first thing I was told when I had me first lesson." And it worked. The next few holes I managed to par. I will try to explain the term 'par'. Each hole should be reached in a certain amount of shots. From the first shot towards the hole until the little white ball drops in the hole you count how many shots you take to get the ball into the hole. The golf club determine how many shots it **should** take. The shortest distance to a hole is, usually, a par 3 (it should take three strikes of the ball to get it into the hole) and the longest distance to a hole is par 5 (it should take 5 strikes of the ball to get it in the hole). There is no par 6. Simple, isn't it. But it is so frustrating as you steady yourself, line up the shot and prepare to hit it. There are so many things to remember. Keep your head still, bend the legs slightly, keep your arms straight, and don't look for the ball, slow back swing, a smooth follow through. All this and you miss the bloody ball or it doesn't go in the direction you want it to. I miss hit so many balls in this one game I lost four balls. They just disappear in the long grass to the sides of the fairways. Thankfully I'm not the only one who had problems. We all, at some time, had to head for 'the rough' to try and find the ball.

Den hunting for a lost ball – we did a lot of that

Yet every now and again everything comes together and you manage to get the little ball into the hole within the recommended number of shots (par the hole) or, even better, get the ball into the hole in less shots (1 less = a birdie) and it is these time that make the game worthwhile. Unfortunately, for me, that didn't happen too often. But it was a nice day and the course was beautifully kept. Throughout the eighteen holes Alan didn't stop talking, which was nothing unusual. Ron performed his caddying tasks with his usual accuracy but I did let him down with the way I was hitting the ball. Den, I think enjoyed it. Especially his very last shot of the game, on the eighteenth hole, when he took a shot, which was a long way from the hole and then he turned away, thinking he had missed and the ball actually trickled up to the hole and dropped in. Great shot Den.

Throughout the game, should you ever be near a golf course, you will be able to hear some of the more usual shouts and outburst that were, I fear, a part of our game today. Listed are just a few of the things heard:

- ❖ 'Fore' : normally used when the ball is heading in a dangerous direction.
- ❖ 'I don't believe that': normally used when the ball is heading in the wrong direction.
- ❖ 'Jesus, mother of God," ditto above.
- ❖ 'You f%$*&ed that up' Ron, offering advise and encouragement, as my caddie.
- ❖ 'Where's the next tee' when we're lost and not sure where to go.
- ❖ 'Pick yer bloody ball up fer christs sake' Ron's advice, as my caddie, when I've taken too many shots and I'm losing, miserably.
- ❖ 'Where the hell is that going': normally used when the ball is heading in the wrong direction, again.

These are just a few of the outbursts heard throughout the eighteen holes but, nevertheless we will go on playing another day and enjoy being outside in beautiful surroundings. Of course the 19th hole (the clubhouse) was visited at the end where a nice cool drink was taken and a sit down was enjoyed. I'm not sure how the others feel but I really should have done some stretching exercises before we set off. I'm beginning to stiffen up and it's painful to move. While sitting, having our drink, Ron is watching a player preparing to tee off. He is doing his exercises, stretching his calfs, twisting his body and generally looking like a true professional. He steps up to the tee, addresses the ball and prepares to strike it down the fairway, only to miss-hit it completely. Ron practically fell off his chair laughing, but that so could have been me, trying to hit that ball!

At the 16th hole we had to ring a bell to let people know where we were - something to do with health and safety

Pub Walk 2

Although we have actually visited a couple of pubs over the past few weeks (try and keep us out of a pub) it has been some time since we completed an actual pub walk. To be honest this one is called, and described as, a stroll and comes from a little book titled 'Pub Strolls in East Sussex'.[70] The author tells me that it is 2½ miles in length and although we have been on part of the walk before, and I'm sure regular readers will recognise that part, the remainder is new to me, as is the pub, The Star Inn at Normans Bay.

As is my usual habit I've tried to find a little bit of information about Normans Bay and I'm very surprised to find out that it was originally known as Pevensey Sluice[71]. Everyone is aware that Pevensey is a Cinque Port, by virtue of it being a non-corporate limb of Hastings[72], The granting of this status seemed to give every smuggler on the south coast immunity from prosecution should they get caught with contraband on their person. But it was at 'Pevensey Sluice', in 1833[73], that a fierce battle between the smugglers and the then newly formed customs and excise officers took place in which the smugglers took a severe beating which effectively put a stop to many, but not all smuggling operations along the Sussex coast.

I have read a number of articles about the landing of William of Normandy before that infamous battle at Senlac Hill (Battle of Hastings – 1066) and I assumed that William landed at Normans Bay, hence the name. But it would appear that history cannot actually be certain where William landed. Some would have us believe that he actually landed in Pevensey. After all, Pevensey was a busy port so the landing there could have been possible. The book 'Sussex Place Names'[74] however says that Normans Bay '...is a fairly modern name for the holiday village that's starting to develop between Pevensey Bay and Bexhill. It's only connection with the conquering Normans is that it lies a short way along the coast from their landing point in 1066.' Others want us to think that he landed further along the coast, towards Cooden, or even Rye but, when I was at school I'm sure, if memory serves me correctly, that I was told when William of Normandy landed at Pevensey he tripped and fell into the water, face down. Not wishing his men to see his 'mishap' he pretended he was kissing 'his' land as the returning King. Which, I think is a far more memorable thing, so I've convinced myself that this is the truth. I have also

William of Normandy

Image from
www.webbspages.com/William.the.conquer
or.jpg

---

[70] Pub Strolls in East Sussex by Ben Perkins – Published by Countryside Books – ISBN 1853066702
[71] http://www.smuggling.co.uk/gazetteer_se_17.html visited 10/06/09
[72] http://en.wikipedia.org/wiki/Cinque_Ports visited 11/06/09
[73] http://www.villagenet.co.uk/history/1300-smugglers.html - visited 10/06/09
[74] Sussex Place-Names by Judith Glover – Published by Countryside Books – ISBN 185306484X

The Star Inn

found that part of the beach between Normans Bay and Cooden is part of an unofficial naturist beach[75]. Now Ron is definitely interested and he's suggested, for the first time this year that we really should take some binoculars with us?

But today, hopefully, our walk will be enjoyable although, from the map it will be a little desolate, but as I've heard a lot of good things about the Star Inn I'm sure that a little liquid refreshment will be sampled. To help us along our way we have Sally (from Friends Walk) who is to join us again. She's over here from her home in Canada and needs some fresh Sussex air in her lungs before her long flight home. The weather couldn't be better as we head towards the Star Inn, formerly known to the local shepherds as 'The Star of Bethlehem'. The sun is shining and both Sally and Ron are dressed for the bright weather. Sally informs us that she couldn't find a brolly but she has stowed some wet weather clothing in her ruck sack, just in case. "You never know," she states, "It could rain hard any second!" But there isn't a grey cloud in the sky as I park the car by the side of the pub. In fact it seems to have got warmer and The Star looks very tempting. Thankfully it isn't open until 12 o'clock and as it's only just turned 10 we have a couple of hours to walk before, hopefully, we find our way back to the car and a welcome drink. I say hopefully because things don't turn out quite the way even I expected.........

Not a stile to be seen!

The author of our book we are using today is Ben Perkins. We have followed his walks on previous occasions and had little difficulty, but today was to be the exception. The walk didn't start well. It is obvious that we managed to find the pub. Even with his eyes closed Ron can find a pub. I had passed it a couple of times but had never stopped. It was always on the way to somewhere and not somewhere to go to. Once was when the main coast road, the A259, was closed due to a road accident and I had to get the girls on my mini bus to Hastings. So, as I said, finding the pub was easy.

Our next instruction was to walk over the bridge and bear left into a lane. We then had to walk to the side of the children's play area of the pub until we reached a gate. There was no gate. We managed to find a gatepost, but no gate. Our next instructions were … '*go forward, over two stiles in quick succession and on the same direction across*

Is this an omen?

[75] http://nuff.org.uk/factfile/content/view/79/48/ visited 10/06/09

The stile to the left of the gate

pasture.' There were no stiles, the 'pasture' was an overgrown path. "Gon' a be a great year fer sloes," says Ron, look at the amount o' sloes on these bushes." All along this path are sloe bushes. Are they called bushes or trees? I'm not sure. "We should pick some and make some wine," suggests Ron. "Sally's dad, Derek, is a very good homemade wine maker," continues Ron. "I'm sure dad will give plenty of advice," says Sally. "Could write a book on it," says Ron, "could call it 'Can we drink it yet, Ron?'" Now there's an idea. Ron is now full of all the things we could make wine from including hedgerow, rose hip, elderflower, apple there's no stopping him when he gets into full flow. Just as he starts getting really excited I notice, out of the corner of my eye, my worst nightmare, animals. As you may be aware I'm not too keen on our four legged 'friends'.

Especially big, four legged friends when they head in my direction. "Oh, look," gushes Sally, "isn't she beautiful?" Now I'll accept that beauty is in the eye of the beholder but I wouldn't call a 1 ton cow that could crush me to death 'beautiful', "Oh, but she is," Sally assures me, "just look at those eyes." But I'm sorry; me and animals don't seem to get on. I'm ok once I get to know them but as a one off I'd rather keep them at a distance. But worse was yet to come...

At the end of this path, pasture, or whatever you want to call it we found a stile which, according to the instructions was '...*to the left of a gate*.' "At least e's got somethin' right," says Ron, and I'm not sure if he's talking about me or the book. But, again, our next instruction didn't seem to line up with what we can see in front of us. Because

A destroyed stile??

now we are told to bear right and walk parallel to the fence on your right. And you've guessed it; there is no fence on our right. Not only that, but the 'public footpath' sign is telling us to bear left! "P'rhaps path's been diverted," offers Ron. But, as I pointed out, there was no diversion notice. "No," says Ron, "an' we ain't seen no stiles either." Of course he's right but Ben Perkins hasn't been this wrong before? "Come on, boys!" says Sally, "make a decision, which way shall we go?" I'm still sure that we should do as Ben Perkins says in the book and bear right, Ron is just as adamant that we should follow the signs and bear left, "just in case the path 'as been diverted." But we bear right. The instructions say that we should have a ditch to our right, and a ditch we have. "All we've got to do is follow the ditch until we reach a stile," I explain as we walk along the edge of the ditch. "If you' s says so," says Ron, "but I think we'll be wrong." And we were. As we walk along side of the ditch I can see, in the distance, more cattle. For some reason, Ron and Sally think that the farmer has called them, these cattle take off, in front of us and run at full speed towards, what I think is the stile in front of us. "Did you see the size of that bull?" asks Sally. "'E certainly is a big bugger," agrees Ron. I didn't see anything other than a lot of cows running. But I can feel my pulse getting faster. Just the mention of a big bull, in the same field as me, with cows strikes terror inside me. We stop and look. The cattle have now stopped in front of us. "If the farmer has called the cattle," I whisper (?) "How come we can't see him?" I ask. Why I'm whispering I have no idea but it seemed like a good idea at the time. "He's probably over the other side of the field, by now," offers Sally, "but take a look at that bull, he don't look too happy that we're in his field." I still can't see it. If he's that big why can't I see him? Suddenly there is a loud noise coming from the ditch that scare the hell out of me as a heron takes off in front of us. I vaguely remember seing it take off and fly to our right. Both Sally and Ron are really excited about the heron but I'm still desperately trying to find the bull. And then, as if he knew I was looking for him he appeared from behind a couple of cows. He wasn't big, he was bloody enormous. I took two steps back and nearly ended up in the ditch. Sally was right, he looked angry. "So what do we do now?" I ask. "Don't think it'll be too safe to 'ead for the stile," says Ron, "that big bugger'll stand 'is ground fer sure." "How do you know?" I ask, "he may move if we walk towards him." I reason, hoping that both Ron and Sally decide to back off and head in the opposite direction, back the way we came. As if by some miracle Ron says, "I think we should go back to that stile, where we turned right and head in the direction of the arrow, this time. We

don't want to make that bull angry. Not only that but the cows have calves so they'll want ter protect their young." At least that's what I think Ron said because I was halfway back across the field before he'd finished what he was saying.

Back at the stile we follow Ron's lead and head off towards the direction of the footpath sign. I still can't understand why our directions are so wrong, but wrong they must be. But worse was yet to come......

Not something to argue with

I'm not, normally, a suspicious person but something is definitely not right with this walk. My suspicions are heightened when we come across a stile that, simply, has been demolished by someone. We are in the middle of nowhere, so it's hardly going to be vandalism is it? Yet I now notice that the fences have also been broken, or taken apart. And, surely, it can't be legal for a farmer to place enormous great big angry bulls in fields that have public footpaths? Or am I overreacting. But I keep thinking that this is a walk that could and would be completed by children; surely dangerous animals shouldn't be on public footpaths? I decide to check when we get home.

The views along this part of the walk are amazing. To our left you can see all the way to the downs. Just beyond this point is what is known to be the lost village of Northeye. Should anyone remember both Ron and I walked this part of a walk before with a Welsh friend, 'Taffy' who, throughout the walk only said 'yes, right'[76]. With the blue skies and the many birds singing this is what the countryside is all about. But, there seem to be a lot of 'buts' in this walk and we have now come across another one. Directly in front of us, just over the stile we need to get over to continue our walk is yet another herd of cattle. And you've guessed it; the cattle have young and, standing as proud as punch is a bull that, I kid you not, is bigger than the one we met earlier. This one is gigantic. "Oh, look," gushes Sally again, "doesn't he look magnificent?" "'e's got nothin' ter prove," says Ron, "standin' like that, in amongst 'is wives. 'E looks a magnificent beast, but I'm not sure that we should enter the field with 'im." You don't know how pleased I was to hear Ron say that. "If we go into the field," asks Sally, "which direction do we have to go?" "We need to get over the stile and follow the stream on the right." "So all we got between us an' that bull is the stream?" suggests Ron. I can now imagine getting caught between the bull and the river. If the bull doesn't crush me to death, I'll drown in the stream because I can't swim. I'm all for heading back. "Let's see if we can get them all to move out of our way," says Sally as she proceeds to get over the stile. "Don't do anything silly, Sal" says Ron, "Don't you worry about me," says Sally, "I'm a vegetarian, they know that I

Reflections

won't eat them so they won't eat me!" I can't believe what I'm seeing. Sally climbs over the stile. Every cow and calf in that field watches as she starts to walk towards the stream. The bull just stands his ground. Slowly the calves start walking towards Sally. "Careful," says Ron, "the calves are getting curious. If they come towards yer, the mothers will as well. Just natural that mum is there ter protect 'er young." Still the bull has not reacted. The calves are really getting brave and are only a few feet away from Sally, when, thankfully, Sally decides to head back to the stile.

"I'll tell 'em a joke," says Sally as she stands on top of the stile waving her arms to try and encourage the cattle to move away, "What's the difference between a buffalo and a bison?" she asks her audience, "you can't wash yer 'ands in a buffalo," is the reply. But still the bull and his harem do not move away. "What now?" I ask, hoping beyond hope that we don't have to enter the field. "Let's stay an' see if they move off," suggests Sally. "That bull doesn't seem too worried about us," she continues, "perhaps he'll let us through." I desperately hope that we don't have to enter the field. Ron says nothing. He's obviously weighing up the situation carefully and I am now silently begging him to say that we do not enter the field. The young calves come even closer to us.

Sally tries to encourage some movement

---

[76] 'Left or Right, Ron?' by G. Pollard – Walk 18 – Page 75

The mothers start mooing. The bull turns and stares at us. It's like he's saying, "come on then, try me!" But he stood his ground and no amount of encouragement was going to get them to move away. "Let's 'ead back," says Ron. I could have kissed him! Sally waves good-bye to her new animal friends and we retrace our steps right back to the Star Inn which, unfortunately didn't open until noon. "We've got twenty minutes to kill, what do you fancy doing?" I ask. "Let's walk up the road," suggests Ron and see if we can find where the walk would have brought us out." We head up the road, towards Cooden. For a little country road this is more a lane yet the amount of traffic on it is phenomenal. We are constantly jumping into the hedge to get out of the way of the traffic as it speeds past. We do, eventually, find where we should have joined the road at the end of the walk it is about 500 yards from the pub. As an aside, if anyone has read of our exploits you may remember some comments about cyclists. Not your everyday 'just out for a cycle ride with the family' cyclist but the ones with the drop handle bars and bums in the air, that always have to dress up in bright garish coloured shirts with matching coloured shoes and lycra shorts. Ron and I say that they looked like liquorish allsorts. As we are walking along the road a couple of the cyclists pass the three of us in what can only be described as a very bright multicoloured streak. "Christ," exclaims Sally, "looks like that last buggers' wearing a hangover." What a fantastic description. I couldn't stop laughing about it for ages.

But seriously, we headed back to the Star Inn and what a fantastic place this is. Of course both Sally and Ron had to try out the Harvey's and both agreed that it was '…a bloody good pint ov Harvey's." The inside of the pub is laid out superbly with little artefacts of smuggling laid out for all to see in the little nooks and crannies. Pictures on the walls are mainly nautical and the atmosphere was just great. The food was excellent with lots of it. Typically with any pub meal there seems to be lots on the plate. We heard a number of people exclaim that they'd never be able to eat it all. But the quality was excellent and the price very reasonable. Considering that all the trade for this pub has to be passing, there are no houses around, it got very busy very quickly and the staff seemed to be on top of the food orders. We certainly didn't have to wait too long for our meal.

Children's play area at the Star Inn

I expected the walk to be a little barren. From the start I was aware that we would not be near a church or, come to that, a village. What I was concerned about was how the signs and stiles didn't exist and the fact that possibly dangerous animals were allowed to be roaming along public footpaths. The fact that we didn't complete the actual walk was a disappointment but, at the end of the day I had a good meal, a stroll in lovely countryside and all that with great company. Sally is definitely a character. A lovely lady who loves the countryside and all that goes with it.

I'm going to take a few weeks off from walking. But we should be back, in full swing, when the girls from the school where I work break up for the end of term. I'm hoping to be able to walk on Wednesday afternoons again because as you all know by now, "It don't rain in Sussex on a Wens'day afternoon!" We'll see.

'This ain't a walk, Graham'

In the last walk we had problems with bulls and I said I'd have a look at some things when I got home. Well………. I found the following extract from the HSE (Health and Safety Executive) titled 'Cattle and Public Access in England and Wales'. I will quote it as it is written on Page 1 of the document, 2nd column, 2nd paragraph…..

The Law

- Section 59 of the Wildlife and Countryside Act 1981 bans bulls of recognised dairy breeds (eg Ayrshire, Friesian, Holstein (I thought that was a type of beer), Dairy Shorthorn, Guernsey, Jersey and Kerry) in all circumstances being at large in fields crossed by public rights of way. Bulls of all other breeds are also banned from such fields unless accompanied by cows or heifers, but there are no specific prohibitions on other cattle. 'Fields' in this legislation does not include areas such as open fell or moorland.

From this I can assume (?) that the farmer was in the wrong. Or was he? Perhaps our bull was not of the designated type but, then again, I wouldn't know the difference between a Holstein and an Ayrshire. And, come to that, who would? But further on in the document, page 2, in the 2nd column, the 1st paragraph is headed:

Precautions to minimise the risk to the public

- Wherever possible keep cattle in fields that do not have public access, especially when cattle are calving or have calves at foot.

Clearly our farmer hasn't read this part of his Health and Safety document unless, of course, the field he placed the bull with cattle and calves in was his only field, and then he had no choice? But the document continues:

- Check that fences, gates, stiles etc are safe and fit for their purpose.

On this walk around Normans Bay we found very few fences and very few stiles that could be described as '…safe and fit for their purpose.'

The document continues on page 3, the 1st paragraph is titled:

Signs

Even though you should have made every effort not to keep aggressive or potentially aggressive, animals in a field or area of public access, it is good practice to display signs informing the public when bulls, or calves with cows, are in the area.

Another source of information I have found is from the internet. The address is
http://www.ramblers.org.uk/info/britain/footpathlaw/footpathlaw2.htm#bull
This, as you can see, is from the Ramblers Association. I am sure you may be aware that both Ron and I are not too happy with Rambling Associations, but that is another story. But I found that someone has asked the same question as me –

Can a farmer keep a bull in a field crossed by a public path? And the answer, from the Rambling Association, is somewhat surprising: *A bull of up to ten months old, yes. Bulls over ten months of a recognised dairy breed (Ayrshire, British Friesian, British Holstein, Dairy Shorthorn, Guernsey, Jersey and Kerry) are banned from fields crossed by public paths under all circumstances. All other bulls over ten months are banned unless accompanied by cows or heifers. If any bulls act in a way which endangers the public, an offence may be committed under health and safety legislation.*

So, you may ask, where do we go from here? The bull we encountered was over 10 months old. It was with a number of cows who, in turn, had young calves. "If the bull was in the field with just the cows, we wouldn't 'ave a problem," assured Ron, "'tis the fact that there were young in the field at the same time that worried me." Now if Ron is worried then I'm terrified! But it just wasn't the fact that there was a damned great bull in the field. There were no warning signs, a number of fences had been destroyed and stiles had also been flattened. Perhaps we should have complained, but to who?
A few days later, in the Sussex Express[77] I read the following article written by Chris Eyte

Ramblers angry at footpath crops

Walkers have expressed fury about footpaths overgrown with crops and vegetation.
A survey showed 200 paths had been ploughed up and planted with crops at Winter time near certain farms in the South Wealden District, according to Ramblers Sussex (RS)
A RS spokesman said ….Although many landowners keep their paths open, a few cereal offenders plough up the paths on their land year after year, knowing that all they are likely to get is a slap on the wrist, if that.
A County Council spokesman said it was the landowner's duty to make sure public rights of way that had been cropped or ploughed were clear within 14 days. We look at getting as many cropped paths cleared as possible and prioritise the most urgent cases for action. Last year, just over 100 cropped and ploughed paths were reported to us. Of these 50 per cent were cleared by landowner's after we contacted them or took enforcement action.
(Which, technically, means a slap on the wrist!!)
Regular readers of ours will be well aware of the problems that farmers and landowners can cause by removing, destroying, call it what you like, footpaths. Ron and I have had many a detour due to acts of legalised vandalism, because surely this is what this is! But now we know that any ploughed or cropped field should be reinstated within 14 days and an over 10 month old bull should not be permitted to roam across a public footpath but who should we complain to? It seems that the Rambling Association could be your first port of call. They have an on-line complaints form which you fill in and send to them and they will 'do the business'. Of course you need the Internet to do this so, on the next page, I have copied the form for you and all you have to do is photocopy the page, fill in the spaces and post it to your nearest Ramblers Association. The address can be found in the Yellow Pages or your telephone directory. If you are unable to find the address then get in touch with your Library who will have the address ready for you. Both Ron and I will, I'm sure need this form very soon. We'll let you know how we get on.

---

[77] Sussex Express – Hailsham, Polegate & Herstmonceux edition Friday July 3rd 2009 Page 8

Path Problem Report Form

Local authorities are responsible for resolving path problems; the Ramblers lobbies for the fulfilment of this duty. You can help in two simple steps:
1. Use the short form below to tell us about any path problems you've encountered. We'll forward the information to a local volunteer, who will investigate and follow up.
2. Report the problem to the local authority yourself – the more people who report it the quicker it'll get sorted. Simply ask for the Rights of Way Officer at the appropriate local authority (i.e. your county council or unitary authority)

County / Unitary Authority ....

District...

Parish / Community Council ....

Path from (place name)..

Path from (grid reference)..

Path to (place name) ....

Path to (grid reference) ....

Path number (if known) ....

Location of problem (grid reference)..

Were you following a map or guide book when you found the problem? If so, which one?
....

When did you find the problem? ....

Please describe the problem in as much detail as possible:

Your Name..

Contact Email or Telephone Number ....

A Walk around Harvey's

Some time ago I tried to get a tour of Harvey's Brewery in Lewes but, for some reason, our request was denied. However, our Landlady at our favourite hostelry has managed; don't ask us how, to obtain a tour for not only Ron and me but also a few of the regulars of the Kings Head. For a nominal fee we will get coach travel to Harvey's Brewery in Lewes and back to the Kings Head as well as a guided tour around the Brewery. Ron is over the moon. For all the years he has been drinking Harvey's Best Bitter he has never seen how, or where, it was produced. Obviously we have both passed the Brewery many times over the years but we never had the privilege of walking around, inside the actual buildings. So this would be a first for us both. I then found out that the evening of the tour I was working and couldn't get someone to 'do' my school run so I suggested to Ron that he still completed the walk around the Brewery and then wrote about it himself. "But what about some pictures?" asks Ron, "Chapter won't be the same without some pictures." I suggested that someone would take a camera and all he had to do was ask if the pictures could be used in the book. And Nicola came to Ron's rescue with some stunning photographs. So, this chapter has been written by Ron, with the help of some of the other 'tourists' who needed to jog his memory of some of the events that happened during the evening, and all the pictures are from Nicola's trusted camera. I'll let Ron tell his story………..

Harvey's Brewery, Lewes

The Kings Head tour party

Tonight our Landlady, Mother Helen, has arranged for us to leave our 'church' (the Kings Head, Cacklebury) to visit the 'cathedral' of St. Harvey's of Lewes. As you can see from the picture there are a lot of experienced 'real ale' drinkers and a few who need a little educating in the finer arts of 'real ale'. For one, Sheila, drinks half pints of Guinness, so has a little experience and shouldn't need too much persuasion. But Nicola only drinks wine and coffee. Now what can you say about somebody that only drinks wine? Only, hard luck Father.

Bill 'the Hat' is the chosen one to take the disciples to the cathedral. Michael, one of the locals has been testing the Copperwheat[78] for a week. During Friday, Saturday and Sunday he was looking a little 'worse for wear' and blamed his mate, Derek, for being in this state. Derek said that with all Michael's experience he should have known better. The brewer, during our tour, must have known better because he only let Michael pass round the barley once during the whole tour. Michael went missing once and we thought we would have to organise a search party to see what

We all listen to our guide

vat he had fallen into, but he eventually turned up with that silly smile of his.

During the tour we sampled some Black Barley. I checked mine very

The room Ron wanted to get to?

carefully, just in case, but I didn't see any rodents. But you never know. At the start of the tour our guide mentioned that Harvey's started brewing in 1790 '...so no-one here would have been about then.' But some of my so-called mates all shouted 'Ron was!' and to my horror, the guide believed them, so I'm wearing well, aren't I?!!

While we were in the Barley Room our guide, Ian, talked about what different Barley was used for each brew. He mentioned one Brewery, who is supposed to take

two buckets of ice cold water into another room, put colouring in it, mix it and then barrel it. Graham, I think, will know which one he means. (not my beloved Carling, surely?? - Graham) Our Alan Baker was leaning on the machinery, (look closely at the picture above, Alan is in the background – Graham) "You work behind a bar," says our guide, "I do," he replied, as quick as a flash, "How do you know?" asks Alan. "By the position of your elbow," says the guide. It wasn't the answer our Alan expected to hear.

Our guide told us that the quicker we get round the more time we would have in the Sampling Room. Like most tours there is always someone who wants to know it all and starts asking lots of questions. Gordon was to be no exception,

---

[78] A seasonal beer brewed by Harvey's and released around June. It is 4.8% ABV using 40% Malt Wheat and 60% Malted Barley and brewed with Hallertau hops from Germany – this information gathered from http://www.harveys.org.uk visited 04/07/09

Steve and Ron

but he soon got the message when the rest of the Kings Head participants told him to shut up and it's on with the tour.

Michael is still looking in all the vats with his tongue hanging out. As of yet he hasn't dived in but that may be because Steve's got hold of his shirt tail and Derek's got hold of his arms. Slowly we get the scent of the Sampling Room in our nostrils. The disciples are moving like wildebeests when they see the river crossing. It is about now that Ian, our guide, who is the second brewer at Harvey's, advised us that we needed to learn how to get drunk. Alan French took this advice very seriously; having had seven or eight small glasses of Imperial Ale[79] whilst only advised to have one or two, as well as sampling all the other brews on show. John 'the carpet' Morris quickly noticed that if you had a drink in the Sampling Room and re-joined the queue, when your glass was empty, it would be topped up again and again. It was like winning the Lottery. Mother Helen seemed to enjoy watching us go round and round. She never left this little piece of sacred ground yet her glass always seemed to get empty and then filled up again. Steve, another stalwart drinker and possibly, single-handedly is responsible for the rapid growth in Harvey sales, bless him, fell in love with one of the barmaids at the John Harvey pub, where we had a drink of Harvey's before and after the tour. We haven't seen him since but he has pledged to master the Tom Paine[80] this year. Perhaps he now drinks over Lewes way? This was a well-organised and received pilgrimage to St Harvey's for the two new

Ron looking for Michael

disciples, St Stewart of Polegate and St Paul of the Diocese of Cacklebury who managed to convert a £2.50 voucher into a night of debauchery and alcohol. Though the giving of bread and wine was replaced by vast amounts of Harvey's and Kebab!! By the way, St. Stewart, like Alan French, took learning very seriously and was well inebriated at the end of the pilgrimage. Mother Helen was close behind. She didn't know that she'd played pool when we got back to our church but I can tell her now, she lost.

Outside the Sample Room Alan Baker got very inquisitive and turned a stopcock on and his trainers were covered in sludge. Serves him right, I'm sure he

---

[79] Harvey's Imperial Ale is rated as 9% ABV (so it's very strong)

[80] A light beer named after Thomas Paine who was one of the men who, in 1776, signed the American Declaration of Independence and once lived in Lewes - http://en.wikipedia.org/wiki/Thomas_Paine visited 05/07/09

It's too much for Maryan

was spying for a Kent brewery. In the same room Alan Stone got very excited when he saw the barrels. He banged his head, well that's the excuse he used for his hangover. Whilst in the Vat Room I saw a fly on top of the yeast. I know God works in mysterious ways but I'm sure it looked like Michael p$ss£d and happy.

'Ding Dong' Dave made the most of being able to have the time to drink more than two pints before the bell rang. His beautiful wife, Marian, couldn't stand the pace and settled down for a sleep, or had she drunk too much? Nicola and Sheila also did their fair share of sampling so we have two new recruits for real ale. We don't want too many though, Harvey's is only a small brewery so we don't want to run the risk of selling out. After all, the standard must be kept up. Proper beer for proper drinkers!

All us pilgrims would like to thank Ian, our guide. He was humorous and knowledgeable and made the evening very enjoyable. He recognised who to pick on and answered many things in a Hailsham/Sussex brogue. Of course we never answered back now would we Michael?

There was one final little panic at the end of the pilgrimage; my famous

Ron's always with the ladies

Harvey's bag went missing. We searched the John Harvey bar without luck. We rushed back to the Cathedral, but they were now closed. This bag had been on all our walks. History is irreplaceable. We ran over to where I had been twenty minutes earlier, but no bag. I went back to the coach because a phone call by Keith to Father Bill found the bag. Panic over.

In people's lives, many things are great memories. But this experience was one of the greatest moments of some of our lives, what we remember of it – of course forgetting Alan French. We have not spoken to Alan since the tour so we do not know what he remembers of it, if anything, he slept all the way home. Luckily his wife, Sue, was with him to guide him to their house and probably to bed. Alas all good things have to come to an end.

Mother Helen and Father Bill ushered their disciples off the Harvey Mobile into the Kings Head Church. The pilgrimage was over. May I thank Mother Helen for arranging the pilgrimage and, hopefully we can book Father Bill for next year.

Quote: "Ron, the writer, excelled himself in his quest to drink Harvey's" - Michael
At least I remembered!

P.S. Derek saw Alan on Tuesday, with a sore head – was it the beer or Sue with a frying pan?

So that is Ron's account of his walk around Harvey's Brewery in Lewes. It sounds as if I missed a bit of a treat, although I'm not a real ale drinker but prefer the chemical beer, known as lager. It made a pleasant change to be able to copy down someone else's writings for a change, although Ron tends to write the way he speaks and it has taken more than one effort to get to print, but I think he did a great job. As did Nicola, who took some stunning photographs and must be commended for the quality and sharpness. Should anyone wish a copy of any of the photographs I believe Helen may be able to help you out, or speak to either Ron or me when I'm next in the Kings Head.

Ron leaving the Cathedral, alone and in tears

Forest Walk

"And you are asking if I want to go for a walk and look at …..Trees?" This is the response I got from my daughter when I suggested she may like to accompany Ron and me on this, our next walk. She wasn't impressed. Even after telling her that our next walk was to involve seeing the oldest yew forest in Europe didn't persuade her either, so it was up to just Ron and me to head towards Chichester, one of the furthest points west that we have visited, to try and find Kingley Vale.

In all of the books that I've collected since we started our adventures I will admit that each and every one of them has a walk around this old forest. Some are over 8 miles, which is too long; some are only 2 to 3 miles, too short. So I've decided on a walk that is 5 miles in length and comes from one of the very first books we acquired. Those who have followed Ron and me will remember, we hope, the book '50 Walks in Sussex'[81]. This is a great little book and was our bible when we first started. So it'll be nice to return to an old faithful. The walk we are to complete is walk no. 48 on page 122 and is titled 'Views and Yews at Kingley Vale' and our starting point is the village of

An old Yew tree

Stoughton, wherever that is. Now I must explain that neither Ron nor I have a lot of experience with forests. We have, however, ventured into woods during our campaigns and we have also been known to enter the odd copse now and again but a forest is a new experience for me. I wasn't sure what to expect, trees obviously, but what else I had no idea, and to be honest, what we got I think even surprised Ron, if he were honest.

We left our favourite haunt (The Kings Head) at 9 o'clock in the morning. It had been raining but, luckily, the forecast wasn't too bad. The drive was to take over an hour and a half so Ron sat back and relaxed whilst I pointed the car along the road towards Haywards Heath and Petworth. I had looked at a map and had the choice of two routes, the A27 along the coast or the A267 commonly known as the 'pretty way'. Our chat was varied, those that know Ron will be aware that he has opinions on everything. Some I agree with, some I'm not so sure of but all the way to Stoughton he was non-stop. Don't get me wrong. We all know that Ron can moan about many things, and I'm not suggesting for one minute that he moaned all the way to Stoughton but various subjects were mentioned like the cricket. For once it would appear that our cricketers have, at last, found out how to play the game. Footballers and their wages, after all the season is about to start and overpaid actors will be prancing about the pitch falling over as soon as someone takes their ball away from them. Local hooligans and what should be done with them, apparently there's been a bit of trouble around the town. Our local pub also has become a topic of conversation. It appears that the music level increases during the evening and although many of the 'oldies' have mentioned to Ron that they can't hear themselves think it's only Ron that tells our landlord and landlady so he, therefore, feels that they think it's just him complaining but, in fact, it isn't.

---

[81] The AA 50 Walks in Sussex – published in 2001- ISBN 0749528761

I think now may be an opportune moment to describe the village we are heading for. Stoughton is situated in West Sussex and is located just over 5 miles west of Chichester. In the 2001 census 631 people lived in 255 households and there is, currently, only one pub, the Hare and Hounds[82]. "Must be a little gold mine," says Ron, "631 people an' only one boozer. Must be packed out, ev'ry day." George Brown, nicknamed 'Brown of Brighton' was born in Stoughton in 1783. He was a fast bowler and his arm was reputed to be as thick as another man's thigh. He could throw

Ron climbs one of the Devil's humps

a ball 137 yards, and was credited with having thrown a ball through a coat, killing a dog on the other side. He sired 17 children. But the most famous feature in the area is Kingley Vale, the nature reserve owned by the Sussex Trust for Nature Conservation. Yew trees are said to have grown here for 2,000 years and this is the largest forest of them in Europe. Battles were fought here between Britons and Danes, and legends and ghost stories abound. There are four large barrows known as The King's Graves or The Devils Humps. Legend has it that if you walk round them seven times, the Devil will come out.[83] Needless to say I haven't told Ron about anything spooky!

After a couple of stops to check the map we eventually arrived at the required free car park at Stoughton Down. There is not a soul about. The car park is empty. The silence is eerie. "Bit spooky 'ere, in it?" says Ron, "not a single person ter be seen, nor a 'ouse to look out of." If this was part of the village of Stoughton, where have the 250 odd houses gone? Things don't look good.

The start of our walk

A look at our instructions tells us to head away from the car park entrance and follow the bridleway which skirts some dense beech woodland. To me a tree is a tree. I wouldn't know a beech tree from an elm tree. If I'm honest about the only sure thing that I can easily recognise is a Christmas tree. Now I know what a Christmas tree looks like. But as we head along this bridleway Ron attempts to teach me the fundamental basics of tree recognition. "Yer see," explains Ron, "not a lot grows under a Yew tree 'cause it 'as a thick growth an' the ground underneath it is always in the shade an' the bark is a light grey colour." Ron continues to explain that there are different varieties of beech trees but, I'm afraid I was looking at a tree? We now have to keep right at the next fork and follow a stony path as we begin what is described in the book as '…gradual ascent beneath the boughs of beech trees.' "'Ave yer noticed 'ow much dog pooh is on this path?" asks Ron, "why do people let their dogs do that? Look at it, its right in the middle of the path." We had to mind our step in a number of places to ensure we didn't cover our shoes in the mess.

---

[82] http://en.wikipedia.org/wiki/Stoughton,_West_Sussex visited 07/08/09
[83] The West Sussex Village Book by Tony Wales ISBN 1853065811 - Page 203

Stone path under beech trees

The view through the trees

Looking towards Chichester

Our next instruction advises us that we will break cover from the trees at a major junction and sure enough that is exactly what we did. What our instructions didn't advise was that we would still be heading uphill. It was knackering to say the least. I stopped on a number of occasions just to get my breath. But the more we walked the more uphill we went. It seemed never ending. I looked at the instructions and noticed further into the walk we would reach a place known as Bow Hill. "Christ," I said to Ron, "after climbing up here we then come to a bloody hill!" "Never mind," chuckles Ron, "it looks like it levels out at the clearing up ahead." Thankfully he was right but we had to stop again to get some air into my lungs.

We now join a path as it makes its way down a slope (thank god we're going downhill!) only to rejoin the track, turn left and head back uphill towards Bow Hill. It is here that a number of conflicting stories appear. Ron believes the area is called Bow Hill because of the number of yew trees that are in this particular area and it is the yew that was used to make the famous English longbow. So Ron's thinking is on track. But I have found out that it is also the place where a battle took place and the victors used the bow to a slay their attackers[84]. I am also informed that it has pagan connections with all manner of spooky things goings on . Because it is close to this point that we find, what are known locally, as the Devil's Humps. We could only see two of these 'humps' but I am informed there are actually four. The other two are not visible because of the trees. But the actual humps are Bronze Age burial grounds. The dead would be cremated and buried, sometime in urns, in the mounds with their most valued belongings. Successive conquerers overran the south of England but no matter how dominant their reign, they feared these ancient burial sites. Even when the site could have been of military advantage they rarely built there, preferring a secondary site away from the spirits that were said to guard the burial mounds.[85]

---

[84] '10 Adventurous Walks in West Sussex' by Raymond Hugh – Page 93 – ISBN 1874476012
[85] Ibid

Comparing the leaves

What we did, in fact do, was become tourists for a while and marvelled at the views, both to the west, looking towards Chichester harbour and to the east, back towards the village of Stoughton. Unfortunately the weather was a bit inclement so the views, although spectacular were somewhat spoilt.

From the humps we head, still uphill, along a path and it is lined with some of the very old yew trees. As we look to our right the forest is practically black. No light is penetrating through the tree tops which really gives it a very spooky appearance. Again Ron tries to explain the difference between a yew tree and another. "Yer can tell by the leaf as well as the bark," Ron explains as he shows me two different types of leaf. "Yer see?" he continues, "the yew tree 'as a much darker green leaf an' it's a bit smaller." But I'm sorry, it's still a tree although his persistence is paying off. As we walk along a little further I hazard at a guess when I

Darkness behind the tree

Shady path

Downhill at last

We stop awhile

say, "So that big tree over there is a yew tree," and I point at a tree. "You got it!" says Ron, "see, I said you'd get it in the end." But, honestly, I had absolutely no idea. They are still just trees to me. But I was struck by how spooky it was. It was so still, not a sound, no birds, no traffic. I started to imagine all sorts of things that could happen to you up here and nobody would know. To be really honest I didn't like it and was only too happy to keep walking, even if it was uphill!!

Thankfully we pass by the forest reasonably quickly before we head downhill (thank god) through another area of beech woodland. As I said, the climb to the top of

Bow Hill and the Devils Hump was gradual, very long but gradual, the descent was everything but. If you weren't careful you could fly down the slope. And basically that was it. Kingley Vale. To me it was a bit of a disappointment. Yes we did see some very old trees but a tree is a tree, I'm sorry. We did learn about a little history of Bow Hill and the Devils Humps but I could have found that out at home. I didn't have to climb a bloody mountain to find out. Of course Ron and me enjoyed the walk, we always do, but it was hard and although we saw some trees we found ourselves discussing other things, like what I'd seen on TV the night before, my last holiday, Ron's love of cricket. All these things we discussed, which is unusual, we normally talk about the walk, what we see and what we hear. And then, half-way down the tricky slope, we came across a wonderful memorial to a Polish fighter pilot who was killed when his plane crashed in the field after doing battle with a German Me109. His name was Pilot Officer Boleslaw Wlasnowolski. He was a member of 213 Squadron R.A.F. Tangmere (formerly of t he Polish Airforce) and was flying a Hurricane V7221 when he crashed in the field. He was only 23 years old. His memorial read 'He died defending Britain, Poland and Freedom' We both just stood and looked across the field, now planted with sweetcorn. No words were needed.

Is this the way to remember?

Once at the bottom of the hill we turn right along the road and head for the village of Stoughton. The church of St Mary's is believed to be 11th century but has been modernised over many years. But, again I'm sorry to say, it was a disappointment. Has anyone heard of a scheme where you can 'Adopt a Grave'. I haven't and neither has Ron. But this church is obviously trying it out. There is a poster in the church porch. And when we visited the churchyard it is pretty evident that the scheme isn't working. It's a disgrace. Stones are up-rooted or broken. A number of plots cannot be identified. The weeds have taken over and are everywhere. Again I have to ask, hasn't the vicar any pride at all? All it would take is a strimmer. In the census of 2001 there were over 600 people in this Parish. If each and every one of the Parish mowed the grass once a week they would only have to do it every 11th year (600 people / 52 weeks) Not too much to ask to keep something this historical in some form of tidiness, is it? I noticed, in the churchyard, a stone dedicated to the Mayoress of Chichester. It was so overgrown I had to move the weeds to read it. Another was of a man and wife who were buried in plots next to each other. Both stones stated that they were 'loved and sadly missed by all the family' again so overgrown it was difficult to see. They died only 3 years ago?

We left the church and didn't speak for a long time. We head into the village which turns out to be a few very nice houses and a pub. In fact the pub looks more like a house. As we approach it the door is closed. "Didn't want a drink anyway," says Ron,

"Stuck up ar$ 'oles!" So we just head back to the car along one of the narrowest roads in Sussex.

Very little has been said between Ron and me about this walk since it was completed apart from the hills, and the churchyard. But be warned. It is not for the elderly or the less agile. It is hard work going up and, in places, harder coming down. We didn't see many people on the walk which may be a reflection on how hard it was. As I said a disappointment for me but our next walk will, I'm sure, make up for it. Because we have a guided tour.

Not one of the nicest places we've visited

Guided Walk

Some time ago, in fact it could be a couple of years ago now that I think about it, I met a man called Noel. It was around Christmas time (no pun intended Noel and Christmas) when I first met Noel. He played harmonica and banjo at a Christmas 'do' at our local. It was, again, some time before we ran into him again, this time he was singing songs and playing guitar with his grandson and I recognised some of the words he was singing. Anyone who hails from Sussex should be acquainted with the name Bob Copper. If your not perhaps I should give you a little history lesson. Bob was born in 1915, a member of the folk-singing Copper family who, as the stones in the church graveyard bear witness, have been farming people of Rottingdean for many centuries. The folk songs he sang have been passed from generation to generation and I believe he was awarded the MBE for 'services to folk music'. But it isn't the songs that got me interested in Bob. I love his books. My personal favourite is 'Early to Rise – A Sussex Boyhood'[86]. It tells of Bob's life in the early 1900's and is a fascinating collection of little stories rolled into one book. I was so taken with the book I kept reading bits out loud to my wife and was persuaded to buy my mother-in-law a copy and, thankfully, she loves it as well. Sadly, Bob passed away in 2004 and Noel, with his grandson, are carrying on the folk singing tradition and are sometimes found, tucked into a corner at the Kings Head, amongst other places, strumming and singing Bob Copper's songs as well as others. But what has this got to do with Ron and me going for a walk? Well I'll tell you.

The Fountain Inn, Ashurst

Ron thought it might be a good idea to have a walk in this book that was carried out by us but guided by someone else. Noel heard about our idea and was the first to offer us his knowledge and guidance. Ron told me that Noel came from a place called Ash. "Where's Ash?" I asked Ron. "'tis in West Sussex, near Steynin', I think" was the reply. As you know I like to get a little background on the places we visit and have a few books on Sussex to help me. But I could find absolutely nothing about a place called Ash. I found a few pubs called 'The Ash' but not a place. After much searching of my books and the Internet and finding nothing at all on Ash I decided to ask Noel where we were going to walk. "It's a little place called Ashurst," says Noel, "not to be confused with Ashurst Wood or Ashurst in Kent." continues Noel. "So it's not Ash then?" I ask, looking at Ron as he looks on with his silly grin. "Never heard of a place called Ash," says Noel, "p'raps I were thinkin' ov the pub, The Ash at Ashurst," says Ron, "Don't think so," says Noel, "'cause the pub at Ashurst is called The Fountain, famous it is for being mentioned in Hilaire Belloc's book 'The Four Men'[87] in about 1902, I believe but more recently, if you could call it that, it was visited by Paul McCartney, when he penned his song 'Wonderful

---

[86] The copy I have is a Book Club Associates copy but the original was published by William Heinemann Ltd in 1976 and is a much sought after book. ISBN 0434-14457-6
[87] 'The Four Men' by Hilaire Belloc – my copy published by Thomas Nelson & Son – there is no ISBN No.?

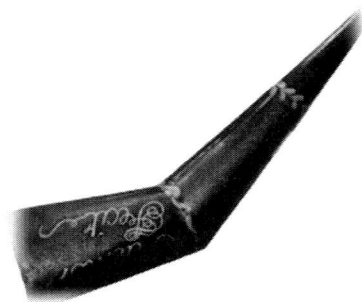

Ashurst Vamping Horn

Christmas Time'[88] in one of the little bars." It's not often that Ron is wrong but he was certainly wrong on this one. But I'm not one to gloat, I'm just pleased to be able to get back to my books and find something on the village of Ashurst in Sussex.

So, what did I find out? Noel was right when he said Ashurst was little. In the 2001 census Ashurst had just 97 houses with a population of 226 people and is part of the civil parish of Horsham[89]. The church, dedicated to St. James, is said to date from the 1100's and just inside, and opposite, the door of the church is a replica of a vamping horn, which I was lead to believe is a very old musical instrument[90].

However, the original is to be found in the Steyning museum. Apparently this vamping horn is incredibly rare because it is bent and most vamping horns are straight. Personally I've never heard of a vamping horn but I have discovered that it is more like a megaphone than a musical instrument. It was used in Ashurst Church to lead the choir. The horn is made from metal and about eight inches from the widest end there is a mesh of wires. It was invented in 1670 by Sir Samuel Moreland.

He demonstrated it to King Charles II in the Mall, who heard him clearly at 850 yards. The King ordered some for his ships and three very large ones for Deal Castle. Originally vamping horns were used as megaphones for communication at a distance over one mile and for public address such as fire alarm, parish events and the banns of marriage. Some were up to seven feet long. Vamping horns were adapted for use by church choirs but fell into disuse as organs were installed in village churches towards the end of the 19th Century[91].

Margaret Fairless Dowson

Hilaire Belloc, one of my favourite authors, praised The Fountain Inn at Ashurst in his book 'The Four Men' and Michael Fairless (who was actually a lady named Margaret Fairless Dowson 1869-1901) author of the book 'The Road Mender'[92], who died at the age of 33, is buried in the churchyard.[93] Enough of what I have managed to find.

Knowing Noel the way I do I'm sure he will be telling us a lot more about the village than I can find out in books. I just hope I can remember his stories and transfer them into print for you all to read and enjoy.

Because Noel can, and in fact did, talk. As soon as he got in the car with Ron and Lyn he didn't stop. Don't get me wrong, it was lovely to hear him speak of his life and times in Ashurst, but I'm afraid I haven't perfected the art of listening, taking notes

---

[88] A 1979 classic by Paul McCartney released as a single as well as on the album 'Now This Is Christmas'

[89] http://en.wikipedia.org/wiki/Ashurst,_West_Sussex visited 12/07/09

[90] http://www.ashurstcofe-pri.w-sussex.sch.uk/church.htm visited 12/07/09

[91] http://www.steyningmuseum.org.uk/exhibits10.htm visited 12/07/09

[92] 'The Roadmender' by Michael Fairless published in London by Duckworth & Co. (my copy dated 1908)

[93] The Radio Sussex Guide to Hidden Sussex by Swinfen and Arscott – ISBN 0950951005

Tucked in a corner

and driving, all at the same time! I'm absolutely certain that there is more to put on these pages but I simply can't remember everything. It will be different when we get to Ashurst, I'll have pencil and paper. I just hope I can write it down quick enough and I have enough paper. Damn, I didn't think of that before we left Hailsham. Let's hope that I don't need more notepaper. I did think about pencils, I've brought along three, which should be enough, shouldn't it? I vaguely remember hearing Noel talk of oil wells and drilling down over a mile only to find sea water. And there was something about a bridge that had to be widened to allow tanks across, or was it to let them get under? I couldn't get to Ashurst quick enough so that I could do 'his' stories justice and it seemed only minutes before I had parked the car in front of Ashurst Village Hall, but it was actually nearly an hour's drive. Once out of the car, Noel was in his element. Apparently the Village Hall is in desperate need of repair but it would be cheaper to replace it with a new Hall. Currently discussions are going on as to how best replace the Hall with a new one and calculations have been made on how much it's going to cost.

As we leave the car park Noel explains how the village used to survive. "There was never any reason to leave the village at all," says Noel, "because, in the old days, we had our own slaughter house." Noel points to a renovated barn across the road, "Then we also had a mill, long since gone. That was a little past The Fountain and opposite what is now called 'Mill View', pretty original isn't it. Then, further down the road was the Butchers run by the Eaton family. Next was the Post Office run by Alfred Dumbrell and his daughter Olive,

The village playing field

there was the Wheelwright, a man we called Dearie Woolvern. He was also the undertaker and my gran, Caroline Dumbrell, was the last Dumbrell to use the hand pushed bier for her funeral. "Noel was in full swing by now but I had to interrupt, "How did 'Dearie' get that name?" I asked. "He always had a cigarette in his mouth, never let it go. The ash used to just fall off but all the time he was working he'd mutter 'dearie, dear, dear, dearie. So that's what we all called him Dearie Woolvern. Never did know what his real name was." But there was no stopping Noel now, he told us of all the shops and the names of the owners in the whole village. "We even had a tallyman call once a week from Steyning. But as you see, 'tis all gone now," "Apart from the pub," points out Ron with a wicked glint in his eye. "Yes," continues Noel, "We'll come back to that a

We ignore this stile

Ashurst C. of E. School

Entrance to 'Peter 36'

St James Parish Church

little later." "Not too much later, I 'opes," I hear Ron whisper.

From here we turn right into School Lane. Noel explains that a cottage along this Lane was owned by a man who made Miles aeroplanes. Noel said it as if we were supposed to understand what he was saying but I hadn't a clue what a Miles aeroplane was. Looking on the Internet, when we got home, I managed to find information on a Miles Messenger, Magistar and Falcon, but I'm sure Noel called one a 'Cub' so perhaps I'm looking in the wrong place. Just past the cottage is a gate on our left. We squeeze through the gate and now find ourselves in the recreation ground. This is the area that some of the villagers wish to have their Village Hall. Noel takes us around the perimeter of the field explaining to us that the area beyond the huts and school used to be the army camp during the Second World War. He has a drawing of the camp that he has drawn and proudly shows us as he explains about the search lights and the huts etc. "Can remember it all as if it were yesterday," says Noel. He explains that the camp was, in fact a Search Light Unit of the Royal Artillery. "It had four lights," he continues, "three 75's and a 120. The call sign for the Camp was 'Peter 36'. Passed it, every day, on me way to school. But let's get on, I'll explain a bit more when we get there."

Noel takes us around the edge of the field; we pass an overgrown stile on our left and head towards the opposite corner of the field, passing some dilapidated huts used by Ashurst cricketers and footballers. We reach a gate leading us back out to School Lane, opposite the school where we now turn left. "It's been extended a bit over the years," says Noel, "but I was taught here, so was me mum and me gran. Head Teacher was a Mrs. Thorndyke for many years. I think she retired in 1939. Then came Mrs. Robinson and Mrs. Ridgewell, they stayed with us for most of the war. When an air raid siren went off we had to rush out the door and head for the church. We used to hide under the pews. Then the men from the village thought that it was too far for us youngsters to get to so they dug a big hole opposite the school for us to hide in. In them days we learned about nits and lice. We had no end of evacuees at our house. As many as 13 at one time, in a three bed-roomed house. Of course, with a war going on, your schooling suffered but we soon made up for that by learning how to get on with one another. But lets head towards the church," and we head off, past the school, passing a public footpath on our left, continuing along School Lane until we reach a sharp left-hand bend and a junction. The road round the bend becomes Peppers Lane and we head straight down the lane opposite which is Church Lane. This is towards, what was, the Army Camp. "I remember one night," relates Noel, "it was a really awful night. A gale blew up

The Rev. wife's seat

and the wind blew something terrible. About midnight the siren went off and the men on duty came rushing out to man the generators and search lights. Well it was lucky they did because while they were tending the lights a big tree was up-rooted in the gale and

143 years of knowledge

Noel points out the scene of the crash

crashed down on the huts that the men were sleeping in just a few minutes before." We now stop by a gate on our left. "This was the main gate into the camp," explains Noel, "opposite the gate was a path straight to The Fountain. What I used to do was, in the evening, when the warning went off, I used to run here and start one of the generators, jump on me bike and head towards The Fountain. The men 'on duty' would keep a lookout for me and if they saw me coming they'd drop their beer and rush out to meet me. The first one would grab my bike and head back to the camp to start the other generators whilst the others, with me, would run back to the camp." We move off, heading towards the church. "We should be able to go into the church," says Noel, "I've arranged for Mrs. Jesse to open up for us. But if she can't make it, I know where the key is. They were good times back then. The soldiers gave me my own helmet, knife and fork and because all mail was censured I used to sneak letters to the Post Office without going through the censure. I did lot's of things like that. As I said I went past here every day on my way to school." Before we get to the next cottage we pass over what Noel calls a 'coker' "what you in East Sussex call

The path gets worse

culvert, I believe, but basically it's a stream that runs under the road. Used to be as clear as day, the water under here. Look at it now. Never mind," he continues, "I used to tend cattle here. Got paid 2d an hour (less than 1p today) just had to make sure the cattle didn't wander off and they could eat the grass. Ah! It looks as if Mrs. Jesse has made it to the church, I can see her car."

The Church of St. James, Ashurst is in the Diocese of Chichester. The original is dated around the end of the 12th century, so it's old. It is also beautiful. Mrs Jesse made us very welcome and gave us a little bit of the history without getting too deep. She is obviously very proud of 'her' church and quite rightly so. It is as well- kept inside as the graveyard is out. I actually had to sit down. I noticed my walking partners left me to my own means during this time of reminisce for which I really appreciated the thought. "Rang the single peel here during the funeral of Laurence Olivier," says Noel, "What, the Olivier?" asks Ron. "A well- kept secret," explains Noel. "Police everywhere, there was. Took over the Village Hall they did. Just in case of trouble, but it went a smooth as anything. Mind you, I rung that bell till my hands bled. I was told to keep ringing the bell until someone told me to stop. But it was thirty minutes before I was told. It was a lovely service though. After the service his body was taken to London and his ashes deposited in Westminster Abbey." It is very obvious that Noel has very fond memories of this church. "Feels like I've come home, I used to be a choir boy here" he says. He points out the vamping horn and talks about the stain glass windows with pride. But while Lyn and Ron speak with Mrs Jesse he takes me to one side and, leading towards the altar says, "Have you noticed the front pew," and points to the pew. "It hasn't got a front board like all the other pews." Sure enough the board is missing. "Many years ago," continues Noel, "the Reverend Ashwin had a wife who had a wooden leg. She couldn't fit in the front pew so they took the board out so she could sit comfortably and they've never put the board back." We also learnt that at the back of the church is an open ladder up to the bell tower. Mrs Jesse tells us that at the last count there were 150 bats in the belfry, "and they're all protected, so we can't get rid of them even if we wanted to." The ladder, although it has been in the same place for a many number of years, has to be removed or modernised because it breaches Health and Safety standards. I had to practically drag Ron away.

Outside, the churchyard is well- kept. We found the memorial to the writer of 'The Roadmender' and Noel pointed out just a few of the 67 members of his family that are interred in this beautiful place. "And see that spot over there," says Noel, pointing to a spot between the stones, "that space is reserved for me."

We leave the churchyard back onto the road and turn right and head down what used to be known as 'Golden Lane' because of the number of glow-worms that could be seen. As I walk, with Lyn, behind Ron and Noel, it suddenly strikes me that I am walking behind 143 years of knowledge. I know Ron isn't shy of his age, being a sprightly 64, but what was surprising was, at the start of our walk, Noel admitted to being born in 1930, making him 79 years old. A very good age and a remarkable man, his knowledge of this area is outstanding and without wanting to sound belittling or patronising he is one of the most able pensioners that I have the pleasure of knowing.

Is anyone there?

But now Noel is starting to worry me. We climb over the next stile, on our left, and find ourselves on the edge of a very large cornfield. As far as you can see, towards the horizon, is corn. "If you look," says Noel pointing his stick, as we come to a rise in the field, "that house, in the distance, was where I was born, and in this field we used to put sticks in the ground to stop Jerry from landing here during the war. One night, it must have been nearer two in the morning, I was cuddled up in my mums' bed when we were woken by this funny noise, like a burring sound. I shot out of bed and looked out of the

He's heading straight at me!

window to see a German plane, in flames, coming down towards some houses in the distance. Well there was an almighty explosion and I ran out and got on my bike to see what had happened, knowing that my gran's house was near the explosion. When I got there, there was a big black hole but not one person was seriously hurt. That is except the crew from the plane and we found bits of them in my grans attic." But what worried me more was Noels next comment. "Not sure which way to go now," says Noel, "you see when I last walked here I came to it in a straight line, from mum and dad's old house straight across the road and then across this field. Perhaps we'll find a sign in the corner of the field. I like to walk where I want too, not be told where I can walk." And we continue to the field corner where we find a sign telling us to turn left. The path here is very over-grown; in fact it is so bad we had to resort to walking in the crop of sweet corn. But I have to say it got even worse, when we reached the next corner and had to turn right, the stinging nettles were taller than us, and come to that, so was the sweet corn. At times I was following sounds because I couldn't see anyone in front of me. But all the time I can hear Noel relating his stories, "During the Battle of Britain I saw 7 planes come down in one day," he says, "and, would you believe, I saw two spitfires doing victory rolls, after fighting off Jerry planes and they actually collided in mid-air. One crashed and the pilot was killed but the other managed to land at Washington, not far from here."

At the end of this field we come to a stile on our left. We cross the stile and head across an open field. In the middle of the field is a post which directs us towards a gate opposite of another stile diagonally to our right. Noel tells us to head towards the gate opposite because he is sure that after the next path we should be out onto a lane again. What he didn't tell me was that an over curious pony was standing next to the gate. And

Noel finds some machinery

of course, the pony needed some attention and it was Noel who said those immortal words, "don't worry, Graham, he wont hurt you." But you all know how I feel about animals and couldn't get out of the field and through that gate soon enough. I practically knocked Lyn over getting to the gate.

The path we need to follow is also overgrown with a tall wire fence to our left. Behind the fence is a young lady having a riding lesson. "I wonder if Noel knows 'oo she is," says Ron, "P'rhaps 'e could introduce us," he continues, rubbing his hands together, "she's certainly a nice lookin' filly."

His dreams are dashed by Lyn who has a few sharp words and gets Ron to keep moving. On the right, hidden by a lot of undergrowth is my pet hate, abandoned farm machinery. Noel explains that it looks like an elevator which was used many years ago for haymaking. After a short distance he says "I think the road is only a few hundred yards along this path," and, eventually, after overcoming holes, ruts and broken tree roots we find our way to another stile and the lane. Once onto the lane we turn left.

"This is called Honeybridge Lane. It was along here that there used to be a couple of cottages called 'Starkers' and a few yards up the road was the ruins of a house called 'Moores Mead'. When new people bought the two cottages and made them into one they didn't fancy the name 'Starkers', thought it was a bit common, I suppose, so they changed the name to Moores Mead. It was the same with the house near where we

Honeybridge Lane

parked. That used to be called 'Blocks'. Mrs. Monery and Mrs. Cartisser lived there. My dad did some bricklaying there once but as soon as new people moved in they changed the name. It's still called Blocks but its spelt different. You see when we get back. Now what we can do is a little detour, which will take us another 2 or 3 miles or, if you like we could head straight back to the village for a quick one in The Fountain." It was no contest really, was it? So we headed along Honeybridge Lane, passing some very desirable property with their electric fences and gates until Honeybridge Lane turns into School Lane and before long we are back at the car.

This has to be one of the most memorable walks completed by Ron and me. Having Noel relating his stories was fascinating, interesting, sad but also humorous. He is a great storyteller with a wealth of information. I'm absolutely certain that I have

A beautiful window from St James

missed lots that we spoke of and laughed at but as Ron said towards the end, "'Ere, Graham, you must be down to yer last pencil by know," and, to be honest I had written 7 pages of notes in my own scrawling hand, most I can read and understand but some I have no idea what the words mean. Luckily Noel has leant me some of his memories in print so I have related back to his notes on more than one occasion. But I will leave you with some advice, if you happen to see an old gent sitting in a pub, singing Sussex folk songs and strumming a banjo and there may be a young lad sitting next to him then there is a safe bet that it will be Noel and his grandson. Just stop, listen and say hello between songs, because when he starts talking you'll never stop him.

Thank you Noel.

I Don't Believe I'm Doing This Walk

A long time ago, I heard, on the radio, that there isn't a single family in the UK that has not been touched by Cancer. Now I thought long and hard about that statement and I could honestly say that I could not think of anyone, at that time, in my family ever being affected by this disease. I thought myself lucky. After all, at that time it was a killer. But now advances in medical science have come a long way since I first heard that statement and, if caught in time, medicine can do some fantastic things. But, suddenly, my family was affected by this disease. My sister, Carol, was diagnosed with stomach cancer. She fought for a long time but on the 21st of February 1996 she lost her battle. She was only 47 years old. That happened 13 years ago and I still, obviously, miss her.

Since then I have always given to cancer charities, and I was pleased to help out when our local pub, The Kings Head, decided to take part in the Race for Life which is Cancer Research UK's flagship event. With many of the females from the pub taking part they raised nearly £1,000 for the charity and it was well-supported. The event brings together thousands of women each year to walk, jog or run 5k and raise money, through sponsorship, to beat cancer. Up to this year, 2009, more than 735,000 women have taken part in Race for Life events raising nearly £60m for Cancer Research UK's life saving work[94]. You will notice that I say 735,000 women. No men. The charity is for women only. This, Ron and I thought, was a bit sexist; after all, the slogan for Race for Life is 'together we will beat cancer'.

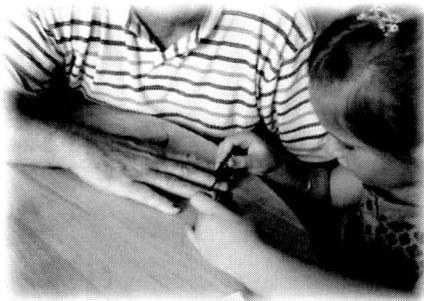

I'll paint your nails, Granddad

So on one slightly inebriated evening at our local hostelry, the conversation got round to why it should be women only. Some thought it was a 'breast cancer' charity but it is also possible for men to get breast cancer. The conversation got more and more animated as the evening went on and at the end, don't ask me why or how, I had volunteered to organise a walk, jog or run for men, over 5k. But it wasn't just any walk, jog or run over 5k it had to be carried out dressed as a woman. We were to be known as The King's Head Tarts Team and we were to raise m oney not for Cancer UK but another, I believe just cause, the Macmillan Nurses, who provide practical, medical, emotional and financial support for people affected by cancer and push for better cancer care.[95] A little organisation was called for. I put up a poster in each of the bars asking for volunteers who wished to carry out the walk and managed to get another 7 people prepared to show themselves up in aid of a good cause. Sponsor forms were handed

My helpers, Chloe & Megan

---

[94] http://www.raceforlife.org/about-us.aspx - visited 16/08/09
[95] http://www.macmillan.org.uk/About_Us/AboutUs.aspx visited 16/08/09

'Loads of colours, Granddad'

out and to ensure that we didn't hound the regulars of our pub we left one sponsorship form at the bar. Darren, our landlord, had a quick escape, when it was suggested that a barbecue could be had at the end of the walk and volunteered his services. So it was all set. Or so I thought. I was unaware, until I wrote to the Macmillan Charity informing them of our intentions that I was advised that we would need a licence from the local councils to collect money en route. My immediate reaction was who made up that silly rule and then, when you think about it anyone could go begging for a charity and then pocket the money. Oh, what a wicked world we live in. So a quick call to the Eastbourne Council requesting a licence to collect money on route was needed. Only to be told that the council release these licences on a first come first served basis and then only two every weekend. The next available date was next year. But I had organised the walk for next month! A big problem now needed to be overcome. As we needed a different licence for every council area we were to walk through the task was too much. It was decided that we would walk from Willingdon to Hailsham, via Polegate. We would not take a bucket or cans but we could take a carrier bag and leave it strategically placed. A great idea from Tim, who supplied the bags for us all to carry. "Don't yer think it'll be a good idea ter let the pubs know we're comin'?" suggests Ron. I explain to Ron what the plan was "I thought we would start at The Red Lion in Willingdon, and then walk to The British Queen in Willingdon Triangle, and then we could head for The Dinkum in Polegate High Street. So that'll only be three phone calls, although I'm not too sure what I'm going to say to them." "It's no problem," says Ron, "Just ring 'em up and say that eight men will be turnin' up dressed as tarts fer a pint on Sunday." "Ron, I don't think it'll be that simple." But in fact it was. The pubs we were due to visit were more than happy to oblige and all looked forward to seeing us on the day. But that may have been because I forgot to tell them about the 'dressing up as tarts' bit, I just said 'fancy dress'. Can you blame me?

As the day approached I was getting a little worried about the walk. It was beginning to turn into a pub crawl. Ron would now like us to go the Memorial Institute in Western Road, "they be 'avin' a little collection for us," pleads Ron, "Seem only right we call in." So I agree. But then others suggested other pubs, The Railway, The Terminus, The George, The Grenadier and The Crown but I really had to call a halt. I had told Darren that we would be back at The King's Head by 4.00 and he was more than happy to have the B-B-Q ready for that time as he had his usual Sunday activities to look after. So my plan was to try and steer

Mrs Doubtfire?

Me, Ron, John (1), John (2) and Tim

people away from too many pubs. After all, collecting for charity when you are close to the limit can be an embarrassment, and that is the last impression that both Ron and I wished to give.

My next problem was solved by someone asking a simple question, "Who is going to be taking the pictures?" asked Lyn, my proof-reader, so all of the photographs of the walk were taken by Lyn. All that was left was to obtain an outfit. And this was a little more difficult than I imagined.

Because I have no idea what size dress I would need. I'm not proud to say, but it is a simple fact, that I am not as slim as I used to be. To be honest I am carrying some excess weight. But I thought a size 12 or, at a push a size 14 should be adequate. When I suggested this to my wife she went into hysterics. "Let's get you to the shop," she says, "I think you might be in for a shock!" Well I refused to get into anything larger than a size 18. And I'll admit that even that was tight! I was having a job to breath. "Don't worry," said wifey, "by the time you've walked from Willingdon you'll have lost a bit of weight, it'll fit you a treat then."

My grandchildren (Chloe, aged 5 and Megan, aged 3) had volunteered to do my make-up, so with a pair of the wife's tights, a handbag and the bit of 'bling', on a very hot Sunday morning my son, who refuses to admit that today I am his father, drops me off at the King's Head to meet my other 'tarts'. Darren is waiting at the door with a message from Alan that he couldn't make it, he's unwell. Personally I think that it's a poor excuse but at least he managed a phone call and let us know. Ron looked fantastic, more of a Mrs Doubtfire than a tart but, nevertheless he looked great. "I decided ter come as a 'madam'," says Ron, "yer need someone like me ter keep you whippersnappers in

place, an' I'm the one 'oos gona do it!" He hitches his blown-up breast to show them off to their full potential and he has everyone in tears of laughter. When he's offered a money bag from Tim he says, "I won't need one o'them new bags, I got me 'arveys bag, as always. Anyone can drop a few bob in me 'arveys bag if I leaves it strategic like." Again we all have a good laugh. So far our group only numbers 5. Me and Ron, Tim, John (1) and John (2). We are missing two who volunteered, Mike and Steve. But we can't wait too long. I've arranged to be at The Red Lion at

At The Red Lion, Willingdon

12 o'clock and it's already ten to twelve. We only spoke to Steve on Friday so we assume he hasn't forgotten and nobody had seen Michael for a few days so anything is possible. But now we can't wait. "But what happens if they've got sponsors?" someone asks. "We can't do anything about that now. But we need to get on and I expect pictures will be needed before we set off," and I can see the cameras coming out from all the supporters who had gathered to see us off. So it's outside for a photo call.

Unfortunately the traffic towards Willingdon along the A22 was very heavy. Apparently there was some little air show going on in Eastbourne and people were heading for that, but what was quite amusing was the looks we got from the people we passed as we sat in the car giving everyone a wave.

The fact that I had phoned before we arrived certainly paid off because The Red Lion were prepared for us. Well that's not strictly true, the young man, who I believe was not from our sunny climes, on seeing me enter the bar thought, "Jesus, she's some ugly woman," and was then relieved, if that's the right word, to see the rest of us enter the bar. He obviously realised that the class of his clientele had risen somewhat when all five of us ravishing females all ordered pints. As soon as Ron (Mrs Doubtfire) walked

into the bar he was instantly recognised by one of the locals sitting at the bar. "Do you believe that?" asks John (2), "even dressed up as a woman some bugger knows him." "Probably used to seeing him in a frock," says Tim which starts everyone in the bar laughing. The landlady (?) Caroline made us feel really welcome which, in a way, was really nice because, obviously I can't speak for the others, but I did feel a little embarrassed standing at the bar, holding a pint of amber nectar, dressed to the nines like a woman. After all, which toilet would I have to head for? As I said earlier, all

At The British Queen, Willingdon

the walk photos were taken by Lyn and it wasn't until I got home and downloaded the pictures that I noticed, in every group picture Lyn took at The Red Lion, there is a little man standing behind Ron. Who he is, I do not know. But I think Ron might have 'pulled'.

It's not long before we have to say farewell to the kind people of The Red Lion and head out onto the streets and walk down The British Queen. Here we were limited to time. It was explained to me when I phoned that the pub would be only too pleased to see us on Sunday dinner time but they had some live music being played in the bar at 1.30 and would appreciate it if we could be away before the music starts.

You can only imagine the looks the five of us got as we headed out towards the A22. Some people just pretended we weren't there at all, others thought we looked hilarious and tooted and, I'm pleased to say, we got a few wolf whistles, which I'm told is now illegal because it is sexist. My God what a sad world we live in. But mainly all the banter was extremely good-hearted and we had a few 'girlie giggles' before we turned into the triangle, at Willingdon, and entered The British Queen.

Again, the phone call paid off. As the band was setting up I introduced myself to Angela behind the bar and we were all warmly welcomed. Everyone had a good laugh and a nice touch was when the landlady told us to stuff regulations and gave us permission to walk around the pub asking if her customers would like to donate a bit of cash for a good cause. I'm not sure what the band thought of us but we left them to get on with setting up their instrument and I think, secretly, they were a bit relieved to see us leave before they started.

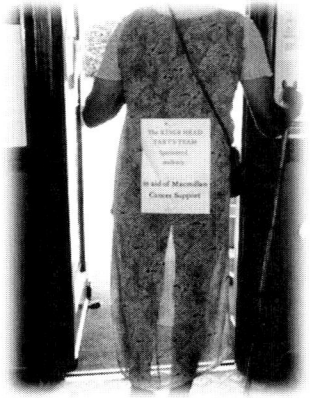

See through Ron

Our next 'port of call' was The Dinkum situated in Polegate, High Street. Those that know the area will be aware that its a little way from The Triangle to Polegate crossroads and the traffic was still streaming into Eastbourne. So it was decided to cross the road and head towards Polegate facing the oncoming traffic, thanks Tim. But the effect this had on the traffic, or more importantly, the occupiers of the traffic was amazing. Again reactions were somewhat unpredictable but what was very noticeable was the number of women that cheered, waved, tooted or whistled at us far outweighed

At The Dinkum

anyone else. Sure the odd lorry driver had a laugh and some younger lads had a good giggle and, I'm sorry to say, some of the things shouted at us were physically impossible to carry out even if we were double-jointed. But on the whole it was good clean fun and I haven't laughed like this for ages. As we approached Polegate cross roads and the traffic lights it was decided to cross the road so that when the lights turned to red we had a captive audience and we may be able to 'procure' some cash. And it worked. While people were waiting for the lights to change a number of them were more than happy to donate a few pence, but again we noticed the majority were the women.

Eventually, we arrived at The Dinkum. The landlord, Bill, is a friend of Darren so he had been forewarned of our arrival as well as my phone call. Again I am very pleased to say our welcome was fantastic. We didn't have to pay for a round of drinks here as the landlord and staff insisted on treating us all to a pint. Now I'm absolutely sure the mathematicians amongst you must have worked out by now that Graham is getting towards his limit for the consumption of alcohol, and we still have a long way to go. Now you can understand why I didn't want this to be a pub crawl. I had estimated that the walk from here to the Memorial Institute would take us about forty five minutes and I should be able to take another beer at the club before we head back to The King's Head. But Tim was having other ideas. "There are two more pubs in Polegate," he says, "I'm on a roll with me carrier; let's head for them before we go down the Cuckoo Trail." And it was down to me to be the damp squid. I say me because, originally, Alan was to be

Tim meets family along The Cuckoo

here with us and he said that he would make sure that we kept to time but he was sick, so it was down to me to be the ogre. And despite Tim's very good argument that it's all for the charity I had to steer him down the Cuckoo Trail and towards Hailsham. Tim had the last word when he said "There's still The Railway, in Hailsham, perhaps we could stop there for a pint."

To those who have read our exploits you will be well aware of the Cuckoo Trail and how Ron and I both enjoy this walk so I will not write anything about this part of the walk apart from the people of the surrounding area, whilst out for a summers walk along the trail with a loved one was suddenly accosted by five tempting 'females' who advised

walkers of such things as a 'blackberry tax' for fruit pickers, a local 'dog levy' which permitted a dog to wander along the trail 'off lead'. And of course there was the 'pretty girl tax' imposed on a couple of young ladies who were out just to enjoy themselves. But most people who passed us, usually by way of Tim's subtle manner, dropped some coinage into the bags! Even when we emerged opposite the Common Pond the local radio control boat fraternity didn't get past Tim. Apparently there is a radio frequency tax dating back to before radio frequencies were invented that needed to be paid. And, bless them, they all gave willingly.

Fun along the Cuckoo Path

Before I could stop them we were in The Railway. Now this pub didn't know we were arriving but, again, the reception was amazing. Again we didn't have to buy our drinks as a person drinking at the bar heard what we were doing and what charity we were supporting and gladly paid for our drinks and I don't think a single person didn't put something in one of the bags. Whilst we sat outside Lyn dropped another little bombshell. "You know you're all expected at The Grenadier, don't you?" I couldn't believe it. Now we still have to get to the Memorial Institute and now The Grenadier. And it's now heading towards 3 o'clock. "Well, if were heading for The Grenadier," interrupts Tim, "we might as well do The Corn Exchange, The George as well as The Terminus." "Don't forget," interrupts John (1), "Ron wants to go in the bookies, it'll be the first time he's taken money off them all year!" Now it's really getting out of hand and I'm afraid I had to try and encourage them away from these plans. After all, we only had about an hour and we were expected to be at The King's Head. So we head for The

We eventually arrive at The Railway

Memorial Institute where, yet again we are greeted warmly, although the doorman looked at us a bit funny and a couple of the more inebriated members wanted to know if we were all members of the club and if not had we signed in? Thankfully we didn't stop too long before we headed up the narrow path at the side of the club and towards The Grenadier. Malcolm, the landlord, greeted us all with pints of our favourite tipple and I am now becoming a little worse for wear. The alcohol is starting to loosen my inhibitions and I am a little worried that I might say something I may regret if the others insist on stopping at further pubs on the way back to the King's Head. Yet again people are more than happy to make small donations to our chosen charity before I herd them outside for the customary photo shoot when I confide in Lyn and Ron of my fears at getting back on time and in a reasonably sober condition. "Leave it ter me," says Ron as he heads us all of down North Street and away from the Town, but the other weren't to be swayed. Both Johns and Tim insisted that we go down the High Street and 'pop into The Corn Exchange'. "I'm not goin' in ter The Corn," insists Ron, "you go in Tim, with John, an' I'll go in the bookies, but be quick 'cause Darren is waitin' for us with the barbeque on the go an' I'm bloody starvin'" "That's a plan," says Tim and they all head off. Lyn and I walk slowly down the High Street hoping that they'll all catch us up. Thankfully, Ron is soon out of the bookies and in the distance we can see Tim and John heading in our direction. "We're just popping to the Take-away," shouts Tim, "We'll catch you up at The King's Head," and there gone.

Ron, Lyn and me head for our local, chatting and laughing at our day. It has been great. When we reach The King's Head all our followers were waiting for us and I was so pleased that we had completed it in a reasonable time. We had walked about 8 miles and although we had one or two detours we managed to get back by 4.30 so we were not too late, and the barbeque was delicious. All the walkers, including Lyn of course, were treated to a burger and a pint (yes another one) and anyone wishing to eat with us gave a donation of £2.50.

At the time of writing I am not sure how much money we raised. Darren and Helen kindly offered to keep hold of the cash until I sobered up. At least I think that's what they said. All that is left for me to do is

Finally ?? The Grenadier

to thank Darren and Helen for the barbeque, Lyn for taking over 80 (yes eighty) photographs, Pip for the loan of the wig, my two granddaughters, Chloe and Megan for making their granddad so ravishing, my wife for forcing my surplus body matter into a size 18, and, of course, my thanks and gratitude go to John 1 and John 2, Tim and, of course to Ron, yet again. Without the generosity of so many people this venture wouldn't have got off the ground. The pubs we called at are to be commended for their generosity and there friendliness and I can't thank them enough. Sadly Alan missed out on a really nice day due to illness which was a shame, and we all hope he feels better soon. It was sad that we didn't have our full number, as promised, but the ones that did complete the walk, I'm sure, had a good time, I know I did.

NOTE: After a couple of weeks collecting money from our sponsors we raised £800 for MacMillan Cancer Support – a great achievement –THANKS TO YOU ALL

The camera is always ready!

More a 'Hop' than a Walk

A few weeks back Ron, with some of the regulars from the King's Head, Cacklebury, took a walk around Harvey's Brewery, sometimes referred to as 'Lewes Cathedral'. The story of that walk can be found in these pages[96]. Since that day I have been approached by another regular of our esteemed establishment and been invited to see, at first hand, the start of the process for making our favourite tipple, the growing and processing of the humble hop.

First of all I was surprised to find out that there is a flourishing Hop Farm in Sussex. We usually assume that Kent is the place where hops are grown. I have read that the first hops ever grown in England was at a place called Little Chart in Kent[97] but Dave assures me that Woodknowle Farm, near Burwash, is a true exception to the Kentish monopoly. For our regular readers you will be aware that Ron and I visited Little Chart in our walk around Pluckley.[98]

Now although Woodknowle Farm is described as 'near Burwash' it is, in fact, within a very small hamlet called Witherenden Hill, no I've never heard of it either. But I have found out a little bit of history about the farm. In the 1851 census of Burwash the farm was owned by Thomas Beal. He was married to Ann (aged 36 born in Surrey) and,

Woodknowle Farm, Sussex

at the time of the census Thomas Beal was 50 years old and born in Hawkhurst, Kent. (Is this the Kent hop- growers' connection??) The census also lists the farm as being of 277 acres and there were a total of 14 people employed at the farm (1 man indoors, 9 men outdoors and 4 boys outdoors)[99] The census also shows a daughter, Sarah, aged 10 and born in Surrey and another female who is a servant, aged 22, called Mary Beal born in Hawkhurst, Kent. (Could she be a family member of the owner??) Unfortunately the copy of the census I received is in poor condition and, try as I may, I'm unable to reproduce it on this page. The previous census (1841) only lists the farm and owner with family and I'm unable to find anything in the 1861 or 1871 census for this address, which is a bit of a puzzle. The 1881 census tells us that the farm has lost 5 acres and is now only 272 acres and the owner, Alfred Wickens, now employs 6 men and a boy.

So, let's get back to the hops. Have you ever wondered how many varieties of the hop are grown, worldwide? No, neither have I until I started writing this piece. I will probably be proved wrong, in time, for writing this but I have only managed to locate 62 different varieties of hop[100]. Now that surprised me. I thought there would have been

---

[96] Page 111 – 'A Walk Around Harvey's'
[97] 'The Lore of the Land' by Westwood & Simpson, Page 842 - ISBN0141021039 Published by Penguin
[98] 'Left or Right Ron?' Published by LR Publishers ISBN 9780955591907 – Walk 15, Page 59
[99] HO107/1659 obtained from www.roots.co.uk visited 08/09/09 (Downloaded pay site)
[100] www.wikipedia.org/wiki/List_of_hop_varieties - visited 08/09/2009

hundreds but should anyone be interested I can supply a copy should you feel the desperate need to know the complete list of names. (You never know it may come up in a pub quiz).

If, like me, you've seen a hop farm and not known why, how or what is done to produce hops then the following pages may be of some help. But if you are aware of the goings on then the following pages may be a little boring but please bear with us. You never know, I may come up with something new.

We head down to the farm

We start our day by getting lost. That's not strictly true because we had pretty good instructions from Dave on how to get to Woodknowle Farm. Unfortunately I can't remember the bit about turning right at the church but Ron insists that we should go towards the church and turn right. "But we've just passed a sign for Witherenden Hill," I try to explain, "so we must be pretty close." We now pass a driveway with a sign telling us that they have 'Bines for sale'. "Are you sure we don't have to turn right here?" I ask.

"Dave said we turn right by the church, or was it the railway station?" says Ron, "I can't remember now, but let's keep goin'. We've plenty o'time, tis only 8.30 an' we told 'em we'd be there at 9." So we keep going. Suddenly Ron sees a sign for the railway station. "There yer go, turn right 'ere," says Ron with that smug grin. So I did. And we ended up at the railway station. "What now?" I ask. "Must a' meant the church," says Ron, "go back up road an' turn right. The church must be up the road a bit." I did as instructed and sure enough we came to the church. "Turn right just 'ere," instructs Ron.

Birds eye view of just a few hops

But we can't, there isn't a turning on the right or the left before the church or after it. "Ron, look at the name on the church, we're in Stonegate now and I'm sure Dave said turn right along a drive, halfway down Witherenden Hill. And that must have been the drive we passed over 3 miles back." We suddenly see a postman and I head towards him, "he'll know," I say but when I asked he had no idea where the farm is. "It's not on my round, sorry," is what he said. Without waiting for any more instructions from Ron I head back towards Witherenden Hill and halfway up the hill I turn left (we're now going in the opposite direction) into the drive with the sign 'Bines for sale'.

It's now 9 o'clock and as we head down the concrete drive I can see an oasthouse in the distance. "Just like Dave explained to us," I said, "at the end of the drive park by the other cars." That's exactly what we did. I got out of the car and walked round the corner and found Dave next to a tractor. "Managed ter find us ok, then?" asks Dave. Neither Ron nor I comment.

Dave takes us to Dorothy and Richard who are to guide us around the hop farm and answer any questions that we might have about the process of hop-picking.

A row of bines or bines of hops (?)

Thankfully for Ron, Dorothy assures him that all the hops that Harvey's of Lewes need have been sent. You could see the relief on Ron's face.

Unfortunately I am not permitted to take photographs around the farm or the hops, which is a real shame. But I have managed to obtain a few pictures, but they are not mine, I just hope that the written word comes over well, without an abundance of personal pictures, because both Ron and I learnt, and saw, so much. We actually saw the process in reverse order. We started at the bagging and drying area and then headed towards the fields. But if I wrote it in that order it wouldn't make sense so I'll start from what was the beginning but what was, for Ron and me, the middle. Honest, all will come clear??

On a few of our walks we have passed through or alongside of some large hop fields. Earlier I said that I was surprised to find a hop field in Sussex and now I'm telling you that we had passed others. Well, to be honest I wouldn't know a hop if it came out and hit me. The fields that we passed, which Ron now tells me were hops, I thought were grape. So I know very little about hops, or grapes come to that, so I'm really hoping that our hosts, Dorothy and Richard are going to teach me something.

As we stand next to Dave and his tractor and trailer there appears to be little action. "Machines broken down," explains Dave, "probably the 'waterfall', it's caused us some problems this year." I hear someone shout "Just 'it it with the 'ammer Alan. That worked last time," as we are ushered towards the tractor. Dave explained to us both that once the machinery is repaired by Alan, the resident mechanic, and going again we will be able to see all of the process, but in the mean time if we climbed on board his trailer he would take us to the field where the hops grow.

Dave drives between the bines

Taking life into our own hands we climb aboard Dave's trailer, a wooden two-sided trailer, and head down towards the field. Directly behind us, on the trailer, are two upright metal poles, about a foot apart and about six feet high. Dave tells us that the bines, on which the hops grow, are cut down from the strings and then laid, criss-cross fashion, around the two poles. But we'll be able to understand more when we see the action.

When we arrive at the hop field we are introduced to Tom and Nigel. Tom has been hop-picking for more years than he can remember and is only too pleased to explain, with Nigel, how the operation is carried out. But first he asks Dave why there was a hold-up. "The machines broken down again," explains Dave, "and it's not the first time this week, either." "I can remember when that machine was first put into use on the farm," says Tom, "must be all ov' 60 years ago." "Have you been working here that long?" I ask, "Yes," says Tom, "man and boy and by God I've seen some changes".

Nigel places a three-legged metal frame into the back of the trailer and climbs to the top (about 14 feet) with a very sharp hand scythe (I think they used to be called a 'swop'). "The plants will usually last about 10 years, sometimes longer," says Nigel, who has the job of cutting down the strings with the bines. "The plants are pretty strong," continues Tom, "they 'ave ter be when they've got tractors bein' driven over them. But you'll see what we mean when we get started." Tom stands by the two metal poles at the front of the trailer and gives the order for Dave to pull off. Slowly Dave manoeuvres the tractor and trailer between two rows of bines and starts driving between them. Just in front of the tractor is Michael cutting the bines at just above ground level, this leaves the bines with the hops attached hanging in mid-air. As the free bines pass either side of Tom he grabs the cut ends and puts them between the poles, each bine laying between the poles, in a different direction. As Nigel comes to a string, 14 feet or so above the ground he cuts the string and the bines, complete with the hops, fall into the trailer. What struck me, at the time, was the simplicity of the action. As one tractor and trailer came to the very end of the row of plants, another would arrive, right on time, this kept the operation on the move. But what also struck me was how large the area was. It must be one hell of a task to string up all the plants at the start of the growing season. Nigel told me that they use about 4 ton of twine. Can you imagine a 4 ton ball of string?? But it must be a daunting task to enter this field in January to February and have to tie stings to each plant. In one row there are 18 wooden posts and between each post there was up to 4 plants, that's 72 plants per row and between each of the wooden posts (21 feet apart) there are 7 rows, which makes

Nigel takes a break

504 plants between posts and I counted 31 posts before I lost count, and if each plant has up to 4 lateral shoots, or bines, it doesn't take long to use 4 ton of string, does it? As I'm standing here counting bines, rows, posts and strings the tractors are coming back and forth and it's now time for Ron and me to jump on Dave's tractor and trailer to be taken back to the oast house and have a look at the machinery. But before that it's time for a cuppa.

Heading back with a full load

I counted 14 people sitting round the oast house as Dorothy makes a big pot of tea and each and everyone gets a mug of the hot brew. Everyone chats away about things in general and it's really nice to hear good old Sussex being spoken. I notice in the middle of the table is a box marked 'top secret'. Every now and again, money is placed on the table and a sealed envelope is placed in the 'top secret' box. Richard explains that everyone has a little 'flutter' on what day and time the machinery is switched off. "You can 'ave as many goes as yer like," explains Dave, "and when the machinery is stopped, because all the hops have been gathered, the envelopes are opened, and the one who gets the right day and nearest the time, gets to keep all the money." Dorothy also explains that in one of the rooms is a barrel of Harvey's which remains corked until the machine is switched off and all the staff has a little party. The atmosphere at this time is as it's been all morning, very relaxed and everyone seems to be enjoying themselves.

Pure hops waiting to dry out

It's so different from many places I've worked where someone is standing over you to make sure everything is done. Here it's not like that. Richard explains that sometimes it does get very busy and tempers can be a bit fraught but in the main, "we're one big happy family, really."

Back at the machinery we watch as the bines are taken from the tr ailer and placed into brackets that are on a conveyor belt about 10 feet from the ground. Dave, helped by Paul, picks up the ends of the bines from between the two poles and then places them into the brackets which continuously move above the trailer. The bines then leave the trailer and pass through what I can only describe as a fast revolving rake that strips the hops with some leaves from the bine so that the hops and leaves drop onto a conveyor belt below, to be passed to another part of the m achine, and the now naked bine continues its journey through a hole in the side of the wall to outside where the bracket hits a metal pole which releases the bine to the ground so that the bine can be collected and burnt. This is a job for Julian, who has a very strange nickname. It's 'Doy',

Inspection table to bagger

what it means, if anything, I have no idea but it's a name I've not heard before. "You may have noticed," says Dorothy, "that most oast houses have a pond very close by. This is because there is a lot of very dry wood in one of these oasts and burning bines and drying hops with firewood can cause a fire to get out of hand." Personally I'd not noticed, but it certainly makes sense.

I have to say, as we watch the humble hops passing through the machinery that it is a bit loud. I'm sure both Dorothy and Richard must have thought that we didn't understand some of the things that they explained but, to be honest, I found it a little bit difficult to hear. But it was explained to us that the type of hop being gathered at the moment was called Admiral and it was an alpha hop. From my list of varieties I see that this type of hop is an English bittering hop used in some English ales and has an Alpha acid % of 13.5 - 16[101]. From the list I have it is at the higher range of alpha acid percentages but at this farm they also produce other hops which grow more

---

[101] www.//en.wikipedia.org/List_of_hop_varieties visited 08/09/2009

profusely as well as aroma hops such as Fuggles. That's the technical bit over with. Again, to be honest, I don't really understand. But as Ron says, "as long as 'arvey's as got enough. I'm more than 'appy!"

The presses in action

As we walk by the side of the machine we can see that it is a system of belts, cams and pulleys all with the same purpose, which is to get, at the end of the machine, hops and get rid of anything that isn't a hop. The last part of the process is known as the 'water fall' which was the part of the machine that had broken down earlier. Dorothy explains that this machine was invented by a woman called Cherry Hines. The idea is that the remaining hops which still have leaf attached are raised above ground and cascade down a series of conveyor belts leaving only the hops to fall to the bottom and the leaf is removed completely. And it works. At the end of the machine are thousands of hops being poured into a large hessian sack. "As this type of hop isn't a profuse grower the person filling the sacks can relax a bit," explains Dorothy. "But if we get a really profuse growing hop this area can be very, very busy indeed."

Once filled with hops the sacks are manhandled into a drying room. "In each of our drying rooms, and we have two" says Dorothy, "We hold about 600 kilos of hops. Instead of fires under the hops to help dry them we now use gas and the hops will stay in this room for about 8 hours." Dorothy explains that Richard, from experience, knows when it is time to remove the hops from these rooms to be packaged. While we are watching Richard leans into the room, puts his hand in the hops, rubs them between his hands, smells the hops and runs a few in his fingers before he is ready to have the whole room of hops, again by manhandling, brought out into the area near the presses where they will sit for another two or three hours to rest.

I will stop now and ask if anyone has ever weighed a flower? Neither have I. But consider this, a hop is a flower. And in front of me are flowers that weigh 600 kilos. For those of us who were brought up with real weights and not this mamby pamby European rubbish 600 kilos is over ½ton or over 1,120 lbs[102]. Whichever way you look at it, it's a damn lot of flowers. While I'm looking at Ron he's got that silly smile, "What's funny?" I ask, "Nothin'," he replies, "but ain't that a bloody lov'ely smell?"

The beautiful hop

We are now standing on the first floor. Just in

---

[102] http://www.onlineconversion.com/weight_common.htm visited 16/09/09

front of the 600 kilos of hops are three round holes. "What we do," continues Dorothy, "is we place a pocket in the hole, secure it with a metal rim, and suspend it to the floor below. We then sweep the hops into the pocket and press them, by machine, into the pocket. Each pocket will hold about 90 kilos of hops." We watch as the hops are brushed towards the pockets and the presses are switched on. Large round metal discs descend down, into the pockets, pushing down the hops. This process continues until the pockets are full, when they are released from the holding metal rims and sewn together by hand before being stored ready for transportation to the breweries.

This has to be one of the most enjoyable learning experiences I've had for a very long time. I was disappointed not to be able to take photographs but, as they say, rules are rules. Richard tells us that the farm has been in existence since 1684 which, in anyone's language is a long, long time. "The fields here used to be named," says Richard, "We've got one called six acre field, which must be due to a little Sussex logic as its only 3 acres." Unfortunately the hop growing business isn't what it used to be and, like any other local industry they are finding things a little difficult in these 'modern' times. I can only hope that in years to come others will take the opportunity to find out about the humble hop and how it is grown to help produce some of the best beers in England.

As a final note, both Ron and I agreed that the little secret told to us by some of the people working at the farm, would not be revealed by us, but we couldn't finish today without thanking the person who made today possible. So thank you, Tiger!!

Sad Sod's Sunday Lunch Walk

Some time ago a new organisation was formed locally, known as The Sad Sod's Sunday Lunch Club. The only requirement to being a full member was that you had to live on your own. Ron was one of the founder members to this elite organisation which numbered, in its infancy, a total of 7 full members. Since the start of the organisation a number have fallen by the wayside and, if you include Ron, the membership now stands at, would you believe, just three. The three full members are Ron, of course, Marian and Lyn. They are sometimes joined by others but by invitation only. To become a full member all you have to do was live alone and be able, once a week on a Sunday, go out, with the other members, for a meal. It's that simple. Well that's not strictly all there is to it. What you also have to do is mark the eatery out of ten. Not just the meal but also the décor, the waiting staff as well as the meal itself. Things can cause the score to be reduced, such as the plate not being warmed; having to wait too long for the actual meal is a definite no, no and the meal must, of course, be edible and, reasonably priced. So, on the basis that the group have been visiting a number of eateries every week for the past year or so, they have a good idea as to where to go and where not to go for a meal. Which brings me to the reason for this particular walk when I asked the group where I might take my wife, Emelia, for a nice Sunday meal? "Why not come with us," suggests Ron. "You could 'ave a nice walk, which would give yer both an appetite and then 'ave a meal in the company ov some o'yer mates." And I couldn't say no, really, could I? All I have to do is persuade the wife. But before I did this I'm told that Alan has a wonderful walk already planned for us. "But he's not a full member of 'the club'" I say, "'e may not be a member but 'e can be a sad sod now an' again," answers Ron. So it looks like a number of invitations have been sent out and, for this particular Sunday, the club will swell to 8 members. And which eatery is going to be blessed with our presence? Framfield is the town and The Hare and Hounds is where we are to eat.

Little Becketts

As usual, before we 'visit' a place I like to get a feel for the town or village. Framfield is to be no different. The name Framfield is thought to come from the Anglo Saxon 'Freme feld' which, roughly translated, means 'profitable clearing in the forest'.[103] The current church at Framfield, The St. Thomas à Becket, is said to date from 1288. In 1509 a fire burned out all the

Framfield Church

---

[103] http://www.villagenet.co.uk/ashdownforest/villages/framfield.php visited 27/09/2009

Marian checks the time

wooden parts of the church, and the tower remained in ruins until 1891 (381 years later). It was then that the High Sheriff of Sussex, Robert Thornton, had the tower rebuilt to its current glory.[104] Just outside the churchyard is a house known as 'Little Beckets'. It is said that just before Thomas was killed at Canterbury Cathedral in the year 1170 he stayed in this house and his ghost is supposed to haunt the tower. As with most villages and towns in bygone years there was a Manor at Framfield. This was owned by The Levett family for hundreds of years until the reign of Queen Elizabeth I when it became the property of Thomas Sackville[105] the First Earl of Dorset (b.1536 d.19th April 1608 and a relation of Anne Boleyn).

Just a couple of hundred years, after the fire, a gentleman named Thomas Turner, started a diary which was published and is available to buy. The full title is 'The Diary of Thomas Turner 1754-1765'[106], and is a wonderful read about, not only East Hoathly, Thomas's final resting place[107], but also other Sussex towns and villages and is an insight into the way we lived during the 18th century. Thomas Turner was born on 9th June 1729 in Groombridge. His family moved to Framfield when he was only six years old and his home town is mentioned on a number of occasions in the book which is why I mention it now. The book introduces you to Thomas and his family and is reproduced as the diary in practically the manner in which Thomas wrote it after he moved to East Hoathly in 1753, about eighteen months after his fathers' death. With the Framfield connection, I have reproduced just a little snippet:

Thurs. 16 Jan 1755 This morning about 1 o'clock I had the misfortune to lose my little
        boy Peter, aged 21 weeks 3 days........
Fri. 17 Jan 1755 Went to Framfield concerning the burying of little Peter.........
Sat. 18 Jan 1755 After dinner went to Framfield and buried my little boy......[108]

Such a 'matter of fact way' of writing about such a sad event. Luckily the book isn't all 'doom and gloom' and there are some very funny times to be found within the pages of this very interesting Sussex book.

I'm going to digress here for a while. Does anyone remember a firm called Satellite Engineers? They used to be based in Hackhurst Lane, Lower Dicker until they moved, with a Government grant, to Wales. I'm talking about 40 years ago. The managers' name was Kendall and the workforce used to be picked up and taken home by a green double-decker bus driven by a guy called Ephram. The reason I'm telling you all this is because when I first left school I worked at this firm. I wanted to be a capstan lathe tool maker and I was promised an apprenticeship with Satellite. Unfortunately things didn't work out for me but I do remember some of the people's names I worked with and I have to say that apart from a guy called Colin many of the names that I

---

[104] Ibid
[105] http://en.wikipedia.org/wiki/Framfield visited 27/09/2009
[106] The Diary of Thomas Turner 1754-1765, edited by D. Vaisey, published by CTR Publishing
[107] 'Left or Right Ron?' published by LR Publishers Walk 21 Pages 89-93
[108] 'The Diary of Thomas Turner 1754-1765' pages 4-5

remember are female. Salomi, what ever happened to her? Hazel was a secret love of mine, Linda, who still lives locally as does Margaret who, although older than me and married, I had a real crush on. Then there was Ada and Sid a complete opposite of each other in physical size but a devoted married couple. Ada used to work with Carol, my sister, in the packing department with another girl called Sue. Here is the reason for relating part of my work history. Sue, who worked with Ada and Carol, is married to Alan who is our guide on this walk. Although I had seen Sue a few times I never put two and two together and I hadn't realised where I'd seen her before until recently. I can also remember the nickname that the girls at work gave me but, I'm afraid, that will have to remain a secret between Sue and me.

The Hare and Hounds

Just to continue with the walk, I mentioned earlier that Alan was going to show us round today, so this means I have no map or any instructions to follow. This also means that I have nothing to jog my memory when we get home and I try to write about this walk. So, what I have to do is take lots of notes and lots and lots of photographs. When I got home I found that I had eleven pages of notes and took over fifty photographs so I should have plenty to go on. So, just for this Sunday 'The Sad Sods Sunday Lunch Club' will total eight people, Alan and his wife Sue, me with my wife Emelia, Ron and Frances, Marian and Lyn. The idea being that we would complete the walk around the fields and paths of Framfield and end up at The Hare and Hounds for dinner, where I have booked a table for one fifteen.

So, on a reasonably warm October Sunday morning we set off, from The Kings Head, and make our way to Framfield. Anyone unsure of where Framfield is there are two ways of getting there by car. One is to head towards Uckfield, on the A22, and when you get to Halland turn right and go through a number of country lanes or you can head towards Horam and Cross-in-hand where you turn left and follow the road straight to

The Quince

Framfield. We go the Uckfield way and park the car in The Hare and Hounds Car Park, to be met by, we assume, the Landlord who instructs us that we cannot park there. We tell him that we are all booked into his pub for a meal, and then he changes completely and guides us to our parking spaces. We all get out of the cars and get ourselves ready for our 'little' walk. Alan instructs us to head out onto the road, cross to the other side of the pub and head for the church.

Now this is all pretty straight forward but I notice that Alan isn't consulting any type of paperwork or a book as he guides us round the church. I'm impressed. Alan explains about the church tower being re-built and points out the ugly gargoyles above each window and the Sussex slate on the church roof before directing us behind the church and out onto a path. Still he hasn't looked at any instructions. I'm even more impressed and think that, perhaps, I should prepare a little better for any of our future walks so that I, too, could walk without the need to look at a guide book.

We pass an old kissing gate on the right (you need to remember the gate!!) as we head down this narrow path with gravestones on our left and open fields to our right. We pass a small tree which Alan explains is a quince. Actually what he said was "tis a quince that is, also known as *Cydonia oblonga* and it's very dry when you eat it. My brother-in-law gave some to a 'orse once and the damn beast bit into the quince and ran off, so it did. Must'a tasted awful." Ron relates a story about when he first tasted a quince. He thought they were pears but soon realised his mistake. "Made yer 'ole mouth go dry," remembers Ron.

Alan checks the road map

At the right bend in the path we continue straight ahead. I can hear Alan muttering something to his wife but didn't catch what he said. But then he stops, turns to look at us all, and waits as we catch up. "He can't work out where we are," says Sue, "he's looking for a path that should be on our right- hand side, but he can't find it." "We'll keep going up this path," says Alan, "we'll find the route soon enough." But we didn't.

All those people who have walked with Ron and me will know that even with a map and instructions we can easily get lost. So you can all imagine what we said about Alan not having a map! But then he surprised us all by producing a book from under his jumper and he and Sue study the pages. Now I'm really worried, because he's produced, from his jumper, not an ordinance survey map or an instruction book on this particular walk but they are studying a road map. I'm not joking. How can you find footpaths across open countryside with just a road map? "We must'a passed the path," admits Alan, "let's 'ead back and see if we can find it, sorry about this lady's and gents." So we all turn round and head back towards the church only for Alan to say, "No, hang on, I think we were heading in the

Easily missed?

right direction first time." So we turn round, again and head back along the path. When we reach the end of this path we emerge onto a road. By this road are three people dressed in day-glow yellow jackets and one person appears to be holding a speed camera in his hand. "No," moans Alan, "this ain't right, we'll 'ave to 'ead back to the church and start again," and he and Sue head back up the path. Meanwhile the three in day-glow ask us where we're heading and, of course, we have no idea. The only person who does know is now heading back up the path that we have just walked down. We found out that one of the three was, in fact, holding a speed camera and they check the speeds of

Spindle Berries

passing cars and take notes. It seems that it is used as a deterrent and not as a form of a formal warning should they witness anyone speeding.

We leave them and head back up the path and catch up with Alan and Sue. Do you remember the old kissing gate, just past the church? That was where we should have turned right. "We'll be alright now," says Alan, "we've found the right path so we can get on." We all get through the kissing gate and head through a small wood until we reach a stile. Here we turn left. Ron starts to hand out sweets and tells everyone that should we get really lost he's "got sweets an' water to keep us goin' fer days." Lyn lets us know that she's got her ciggies and checks with the other smokers to confirm that supplies of nicotine were plentiful. The path now drops quite steeply to a wooden bridge and another stile. Once over the stile we are now walking along an enclosed path which has an electric fence on the right surrounding a paddock holding horses. One of the horses had a hacking cough and let everyone know it. But what really got our attention was the electric fence.

Regular readers will be aware that Alan had a pee up against one of these fences and was lucky not to have done some real damage to himself, although he did say that his squeaky voice had calmed down since this event happened. Now, of course, we all reminded him of his unfortunate accident. We also found some dog poo neatly placed in a plastic bag and then tied to the electric fence rail. We thought this phenomenon was only found in West Sussex but it appears that the trend is on the move. Nevertheless it isn't a very nice habit. Something else we managed to find are spindle berries. Alan explains, "The spindle berry, is also known as *euonymus europaeus,* and the fruit is poisonous but because it is a pretty colour most of the casualties are children, yer know. In the extreme it can kill." Personally I've never heard of the spindle berry but I can understand the fascination for children. The

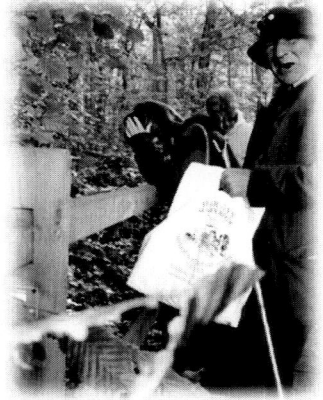
Ron makes a wish

bright pink colour of the berries is remarkable.   Apparently the Spindle gets its name from the wood, which is very hard and can be cut to a very sharp point and was used to make spindles for the spinning of wool. Alan is a hive of information. We leave the spindle berry and head further along the path to yet another stile and wooden bridge. Lyn and Frances get a little excited here because running water can be heard and any chance of playing Pooh sticks has to be taken. Both grab a small stick and encourage Ron to do the same. The rest of us look on as all three sticks are deposited in the water and they all run to the other side to see who won. Unfortunately the water wasn't running fast enough and we could have stayed there best part of the day and no sticks would have emerged on the other side. Ron made the most of the matter by dropping a coin over the edge and making his usual wish.

Once over the bridge we head uphill through the wood. Alan thinks this area is called Burough Shaw and it's really pretty. All the way up the slope are raised wooden steps. "That's because the area floods a bit," explains Alan, "there's a few ponds 'ere

Open fields, no signs

abouts where they used to dig fer iron. When it really rains, without these wooden walk ways, you'd never be able to pass through 'ere."

At the top of this slope is a really unkempt stile. Sue was the first over, and because the wood was rotten she fell quite heavily on her shoulder, but she insisted that she was ok because the ground was soft but, let's be honest, it could have been nasty. Perhaps we should report it but to be honest I have absolutely no idea where we are.

We now head across the middle of a field full of cowpats. If I didn't know better I would suggest that we were lost again because I haven't seen a sign for ages and we keep coming across electric fences which we have to get over, under or through. Thinking of cow pats did you know that they were used as a remedy for abscesses? Apparently it's an old gypsy remedy. What you have to do is get a fresh cow pat, extract the liquid from the pat, and put the liquid onto the abscess before breakfast and the abscess will break before dinner.[109] Go on, give it a try next time you have an abscess on a tooth!!

It's about now that our first aid skills are called into action. Frances has managed to cut herself. She can't explain how but blood is covering her fingers. "Don't you fret," assures Ron, "'cause in me carrier I 'ave a box ov' plasters." "And if it's any more serious than a plaster," says Lyn, "I'm a first aider." Ron is rummaging in his carrier bag, bringing out a hammer, a box of matches, some toilet paper, yes toilet paper "don't panic," says Ron, "'tis in 'ere somewhere." Now follows a newspaper, "ah, 'ere they are," and holds out a crumpled box of 'Boots' plasters. "They don't look very sterile," says Marian, "nothin' wrong with 'em," says Ron, "only been in me bag fer a year or so. Now let's 'ave a look at yer finger." Within seconds Frances had not one but two plasters on her right hand and the blood seemed to have stopped. Emergency sorted, we carried on.

Alan holds down an electric fence

But again we seem to be away from a public footpath and walking across open fields. "Are you sure you know where we are?" I ask Alan. "Not exactly," he replies, "but as long as we keeps 'eadin' in this direction we should arrive somewhere." Now I'm getting a little worried. "We do have to be back at The Hare and Hounds by 1:15," says Ron, "don't you worry," replies Alan, "as long as we keep walkin' we'll be there

---

[109] A Dictionary of Sussex Folk Medicine, by Andrew Allen, published by Countryside Books, Pages 41-42

We head for the gap

right on time. We've just got ter get to the next path, over there," he points his stick, "then we should pick up the footpath again. Trust me, come on."

We come to a track where we turn left and head for the gap between the hedges. Once through the gap we are on a concrete drive. Just a few yards onto the drive we come to yet another stile and a public footpath sign. "Told yer," says Alan, "we're back on the path an' now we cross this field and there'll be another stile. What time is it?" "It's coming up to twelve," says Lyn. "Better get a move on then or we'll be late fer dinner. We've still got some way to go yet." And off he goes. But we do find another stile where we bear left and walk diagonally across the field. Ron is getting excited and I'm not sure why until I see him bending down and picking something off the ground. At first I thought he may be trying out the cowpat theory but then I notice that what he's picking up is white. "Look at these luvely mushrooms," says Ron as he hastily picks up mushroom after mushroom and places them delicately in his carrier bag. We then pass through a small wood and bear right over, yes, another stile and we then turn left.

Coming to New Place Farm

This takes us into a field of Kale. I overheard Alan tell his wife what it was so I'm not being a know-it-all here. I'm not a great lover of the vegetable and what was really strange; as we were passing the crop, you could smell that horrible boiled cabbage smell which took me back to my days at school when Miss Kidd practically force-fed me the stuff. Perhaps that's

Red mushroom

why I'm not too keen on it now? We head along the path, passing the Kale on our right and the hedge on our left and it's very noticeable how warm it's starting to get. People, yes even Ron, has started to take bits of clothing off.

Our walk now comprises of a number of paths, fields, stiles and little yellow signs but at least we seem to be on public footpaths. This combination continues until we come to a five-bar gate leading us out onto a road, opposite the entrance to New Place Farm. Unfortunately that is all I can tell you about the place because I have absolutely no idea where we are. But as we walk up the drive, following the public footpath signs, the place is heaven. It is gorgeous. It has lakes, it has waterfalls, and it has grapes, yes grapes, growing over the top of the wall as we head along the drive. The place is just stunning. As we walk along I notice, what I first thought was a very large strawberry, lying on the ground near one of the biggest oak trees I've ever seen. But when we get closer I can see that it's not a strawberry at all but a very large mushroom. I wanted to ask Alan what it was called but he was getting a little concerned that we wouldn't be back in time for dinner and had gone ahead so I had no opportunity to find out until I got home. When I looked it up it seems as if it is called *amanita muscaria* and is poisonous[110]. Yet it looked so pretty.

A 'climb through' stile

Alan is now some way ahead so I'm being told to keep up. But I found New Place Farm a really interesting place to look round. Although it wasn't like your typical working farm it was obviously worth a few bob and it became a little difficult to realise that someone could actually own it all. As we are heading through the farm it is suggested that we wouldn't make it back to the pub on time. This got Ron a little worried because he was looking forward to a nice pint of Harvey's. In fact, with all the Latin names being spoken on this walk Ron decided that his favourite brew should be renamed 'Harveticus thirstus quensious' which in anyone's language is a bit of a mouthful.

A small repair is required

But we must press on; Alan is becoming a spot in the distance and we have to catch up. As the drive bears to the right we continue straight ahead. All you can hear all around us now are the sounds of pheasants and to our right is a sign which reads; WARNING – This is a shooting estate'. It's pretty obvious what it is they shoot and we did a pretty good job of keeping Ron off the subject.

As I'm writing this I am very conscious of how long this chapter is becoming, but please bear with me. I'm still only on page seven of my notes and we still have one or two things to see.

The track, away from the farm turns right but we go straight ahead, following the footpath signs until we reach a three-way sign. And yet another stile. Once over the stile we turn left and head across the field, aiming for the house in the distance. Suddenly, Emelia, whispers, very loudly (?) "A Deer!!" and points to it as if we couldn't see it. Sure enough a young deer shot across the field, in front of us, and disappeared over the hill. Emelia has never seen a deer in the wild before and was over the moon at the sight of this young animal. All she spoke about for some time was about the deer. Unfortunately he went past us so quickly I didn't have chance to get the camera ready. Better luck next time.

---

[110] http://en.wikipedia.org/wiki/Amanita_muscaria visited 19/10/2009

These are vines (not bines)

At the top of the hill we come to a gate which leads us out onto a road. Here we turn left and after a short distance, just before a lovely cottage called 'Pedlars' we turn right and yet again climb a stile as we continue to follow the footpath signs which tell us that we are now on the Weald Way. We emerge onto a road where we turn left and meet a large sign telling us that we are about to arrive at Blackboys. But before long, a matter of a few yards we cross the road and turn left down a public footpath. I'm not sure but I have the feeling we have been here before. As we walk along the path we come to a strange type of stile. This one you climb, as usual, but then at the top of the stile is a gate that you have to climb through. After some discussion we came to the conclusion that it must be to stop deer from getting into this part of the footpath, but, when you come to think of it I can't imagine a deer climbing over any stile? As we walk along the path there is a distinct smell.

My old mum always loved the smell of a bonfire and she would have loved this part of this walk because that bonfire smell was lovely and coming from somewhere to our left. Just passed the bonfire we come to another gate/stile and into a fenced path running alongside a vineyard. At the end of this path is yet another stile. I have no idea how many stiles we've been over because I've lost count but this one had a fair drop at the other side. Unfortunately Lyn managed to twist her knee so spent the remainder of the walk with a bit of a limp. Marian was also struggling to keep up with the pace that Alan was setting and the whole group now started to spread out. The path we now found ourselves on also dropped quite sharply under some electricity cables and at one point I couldn't see Alan and Sue in front of us and only assumed that they would wait at the bottom of the slope.

And it was at the bottom of the slope that we came to yet another type of stile known as a squeeze stile, simply because that is what you have to do to get through it. Once through this stile we turn left onto a gravel drive. Alan informs us that we are about to see Tickeridge Mill, which was once the home of Vivien Leigh. The name meant something to me but I couldn't remember where I'd heard it but both Ron and Alan explained that she was a very famous film star of the early 50's. (That's the 1950's) She starred in 'Gone with the Wind' when she played the part of Scarlett O'Hara for which she won an Oscar. She was born in India on the 5th November 1913 and died on July 8th 1967[111]. I read a trivia thing about her a long time ago that said she used to prop her bathroom door open with one of

A squeeze stile

---

[111] http://www.biography.com/articles/Vivien-Leigh-9378241 visited 21/10/09

The lake at Tickeridge Mill

her Oscars. Whether this is true or not I have no idea. But what I can confirm is that Tickeridge Mill is one of the most idyllic places I have ever seen. It is simply stunning. A very large metal gate, Alan tells me that the gate is cast in Sussex iron, ensures that you have no access to the house unless invited. For obvious reasons I am unable to photograph the actual house, although it is in plain view, but what I did take a picture of was through a hole in the hedge onto the lake which has a meandering path leading to it from the house.

Unfortunately, because of the beauty of the place, we stayed and admired it for far too long and Alan is ushering over the weir, with its fast running water, towards a metal gate.

I think I may have been the first to notice that on this gate was a little sign that stated 'Beware of the Dog'. Now you all know how I feel about animals. Since starting these walks with Ron I have endured all manner of furry, hairy, woolly and hoofed animals and to be honest I don't like any of them, and I'm sure that the feeling is mutual. So, as we pass through this gate my senses are on red alert. "You ok?" asks Ron as I creep up behind him, perhaps a little too closely. "Fine," I answer. "The bullocks won't 'urt yer," he continues, and I think bullocks? It said dog on the sign but as I peer over his shoulder there are a number of bullocks staring back at me. I will admit that they didn't look too big but, nevertheless I thought, they could do some serious damage, as my steps got a bit quicker. "Don't run," says Marian, and that's just about all I need, another person to tell me that 'they won't hurt yer' and 'don't show 'em yer scared' but, unfortunately I haven't perfected the art of looking carefree and relaxed when every nerve in my body is telling me to run like the wind! But we all manage to get through the field and over the next stile without any form of stampede, thanks mainly to Marian keeping the animals occupied.

Remains of the moat

Again things seem to go a little wrong now. All signs seem to have disappeared as we cross the middle of another field. This is where Tickeridge Castle used to be; all that is left is the remains of the moat. At the end of the path we come to a road. Alan was hoping to show us another mill known as Heavers Mill, but because time is against us and Marian is dropping further behind it is decided that we will continue but wait at different way points so that the ones behind could see where we turned off the path.

We don't seem to have time to stop anywhere now as it gets a bit closer to one o'clock. But we do manage, somehow, to find our way, by passing through a farmyard, around some barking dogs and a spooky path to eventually arrive at the playing fields at Framfield and back to The Hare and Hounds at twenty past one.

Greeting us at the door was the afore mentioned landlord who, I thought, was welcoming us back after what was a very hard and long walk. Emelia tells me that he wasn't welcoming us at all but checking to make sure our shoes we're clean! So we now come to the meal.

As I said earlier we have to mark everything out of ten. I thought that we had a good start when we had a table, with a reserved sign on it, for eight people. But…. the table was next to a blazing log fire!! We all decided to get our own drinks, the service was a little slow, mainly because the landlord had a few problems with the till and his dogs managed to escape into the bar and he had to usher them out. I noticed he didn't wash his hands after handling the dogs.

Reflections across the lake

The menu was a carvery and I have to say that the beef, carrots, cauliflower in cheese sauce, the roast and boiled potatoes and the cabbage were excellent. I was not impressed with the Yorkshire pudding which could have doubled as a muffin but I'm no expert. Due to the extreme heat from the fire Lyn decided to move to a different table. Ron and Frances, who sat close to the fire, stuck it out and I noticed that Alan didn't take his coat off? Emelia tells me that her chicken dinner was good and everyone seemed to enjoy their meal. When it comes to pudding I can take it or leave it. The fact that all the puddings on the board were £4.75 each made me decide to leave it. Marian and Alan managed to order the one pudding that they had run out of although the landlord didn't remove it from the board after telling us that the pudding was no more. The table was not cleared away after our meal and our puddings were placed to the side of our empty plates before they were removed.

All in all, at a cost of £6.50 for the carvery I thought was pretty good value. The full members of the Sad Sod Sunday Lunch Club awarded The Hare and Hounds at Framfield 7 out of 10. Which, I suppose, isn't a bad score. But on reflection I thought there were more minuses than pluses, yes the meal was good, the service was friendly but a little slow but you can't beat being in good company and all in all that's what made today, the company.

Smuggler's Walk

This particular walk caused me some problems. Firstly I needed to find the actual walk which would include a bit about Smuggling. Once I found a walk I then put it somewhere for safe keeping to use at a later date, like now. So where is it? I've looked everywhere and can't find it. As it is Friday today and the walk has already been arranged for the following Wednesday I had to do some very quick research and find another walk. But I couldn't find one. My wife kept on and on that if I'd seen a walk then it must still be on the shelf. So back I went and, thankfully after another few hours of searching, I found it. It was located in the book titled 'Walks into History'[112] and it is walk 15 in the book.

Hastings was at the heart of smuggling in the 18th century. During that time what had previously been small time evasion of duty turned into an industry of huge proportions. The reason for this is simple: throughout the previous 100 years incoming governments had levied higher and higher taxes to pay for foreign wars. Customs duty had also been collected over this period but a new duty, called 'excise' was introduced which, basically, was a tax on consumption. Wool, silks, tea and chocolate were subject to the new tax, as was tobacco and spirits. Legitimate merchants were more than happy to buy tax-free goods on the black market, fuelling a growth industry.

A typical Hastings picture

Profit margins could be huge. Spirits and tobacco would sell in England at four times its purchase price in France or Holland, tea would sell at eight times its purchase price, and as smuggling increased so did the attempts to clamp down. But smuggling gangs were large and very well armed, frequently outnumbering the revenue officers sent to intercept them, and they did not hesitate to use considerable violence to evade arrest. With whole communities helping the smugglers, getting any information about them was very difficult. Even when evidence was found the squire or the magistrates were frequently bought off by the gangs. Such was the powers of the rich backers of smuggling that effective legislation was impossible and organised crime flourished throughout the 18th century.

It must be obvious to you all that I am sitting here, in front of a computer screen, writing this after I have completed the walk. Let me just say that I am knackered! My legs ache all the way up and my feet are killing me. This had to be one of the hardest walks that we have done, so be warned. If you don't do hills, don't even attempt this one! The book[113] describes the walk as '..*involving some fairly strenuous ups and downs, but route finding throughout is easy.*' I can confirm that the 'strenuous ups' are b$**dy steep and the 'downs' are practically sheer drops. So, you have been warned. But after

---

[112] 'Walks into History Sussex' by John Wilks Published by Countryside Books ISBN 185306 7903
[113] Ibid, Walk 15 Page 97

The start of the climb

saying all this the walk was one of the more unusual walks that seemed to leave some questions unanswered and the feeling that we wanted to find out more about smuggling and the way that smugglers went about their illegal trade in Sussex.

So on a warm October Wednesday we head towards Hastings. The 'we' today are Ron, me and Alan, who has expressed a desire to learn a bit about smuggling. You will note that this walk was carried out on a Wednesday afternoon because, to quote Ron, "it don't rain in Sussex on a Wensdi afternoon". I'm not sure if the wet substance on the windscreen of the car, as we arrive at Hastings seafront, is rain or one of Ron's 'sea frets' but both Alan and I put on our 'hoodies' as we left the car and headed towards the start of the walk.

Traditionally, many of England's seamen had used their skills in navigation to sneak a few illicit items into the country, but by the mid-18th century this private enterprise had become organised crime. Wealthy merchants and financiers, well-connected socially and politically, would provide capital, which was used by the middlemen to buy goods on the continent. These middlemen would contract ship owners to get the illicit cargo into England, and the ship owners, in turn, would hire local seamen to run cargoes across the channel. Once on the English coast, the contraband would be discreetly landed on deserted beaches and coves, where whole communities would arrange for the transportation inland.

As we head towards the start of our walk we pass, on our left, the tall timber net houses which are unique in Britain. These houses were introduced in Tudor times to store nets and fishing tackle and were also used as a temporary hiding place for contraband. Their odd shape is due to the desire to occupy as little ground area as possible,

Net Houses

and thereby reduce the land tax that had to be paid. Fishing took place directly from the open beach, called the Stade, in front of these buildings.

View from the top

At the start I advised you about the 'strenuous ups' so, just to the left of a pub called 'The Dolphin' we start our first climb. These steps are called Tamarisk Steps and are just the start of a long, long climb up to the top of the East Cliff, where we find the now disused funicular railway station. Right now I would have paid anything to use that cliff-side railway which had been carrying passengers up and down this cliff since 1902. Little did I know how much higher we would need to climb before we finished this walk. The one thing, obviously, about being this high is the marvellous views. I know we all stopped to get our breath back after the climb but being able to look out over Hastings in this way really was outstanding. Unfortunately the sea mist was a bit of a hindrance so you couldn't see very far out to sea but at least we could see the town.

Gaps handy to jump over?

But in the 18th century Hastings was not as we see it today but much smaller. The old town was fronted by the Stade, the economic heart of the town. Smuggling was an essential part of the local economy and lots of contraband was landed directly on the beach below us. The town's population were fully aware of the smuggling trade and could see nothing wrong in avoiding customs duties, and they

Towards Ecclestone Glen

were only too happy to assist the smugglers. Revenue officers were totally outnumbered and would be bribed or intimidated into making themselves scarce when illicit cargoes were being landed. Sometimes they would seize part of a cargo, with agreement of the smugglers, in order to demonstrate that they were doing their job.

From the top of the steps, by the East cliff, we turn right and head uphill (even more steps!) following the sign for 'cliff walks'. I notice that we are reasonably close to the edge as we head along this part of the path and both Ron and Alan start discussing the rather morbid possibilities of going 'over the top'. "Tends ter draw yer to the edge," says Ron, as we stop to get our breath, "and once at the edge it's just another step to 'over you go'," continues Alan. And I must admit that along this particular part of the cliff edge there are a number of ominous gaps in the fencing which look as if someone, at some time, has headed 'over the top'. But let's get off the subject.

Our instructions now tell us to continue, uphill of course, for ½mile and we have to stop on a number of occasions to get our breath. This had to be one of the longest ½miles I've ever walked. It seemed to take ages and with Alan and Ron still talking about going 'over the top' this didn't help. Eventually we reach a kissing gate where we, at last, have to descend down some steps towards a place called Ecclestone Glen.

Ecclesbourne

Although small cargoes of contraband were blatantly brought into Hastings at the Stade, the really large cargoes were landed at the more secluded coves, such as Ecclesbourne and Fairlight, further along the coast. Most of these landings were under the darkness of night,

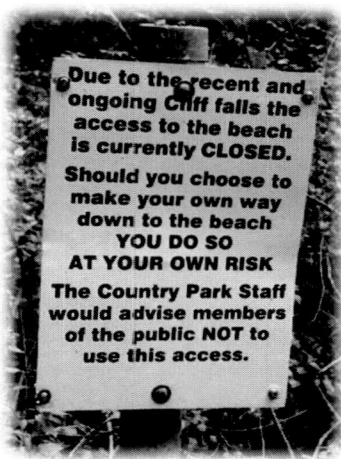

The 'Danger' sign

from large specially built black-painted vessels, rigged fore and aft to enable them to sail into any anchorage, whatever the wind. Lanterns and beacons on the cliff face would guide the ships into land and it was not unusual for 3,000 gallons of spirits to be brought in on a single trip.

Speed of unloading was the essence, and such was the organisation that the smugglers could muster hundreds of local labourers within hours, to be synchronised with landings. Anyone 'moonlighting' for the smugglers would be paid seven shillings for unloading (7 shillings in today's money is 35 pence). That same seven shillings would take a farm labourer a whole week to earn.

Discussions now take place between us about weight. "Can you imagine 'ow much 3,000 gallons of spirits looks like?" ask Ron, "sod what it looks like," continues Alan, "how much must it weigh?" "Well," says Ron, "I knows that a pint o' water weighs one and a quarter pounds." "How come you know the weight of a pint of water?" I ask, "Got asked in a pub quiz once," Replies Ron, "an' it's just one o'them things that yer remembers." "So, if a pint weighs 1¼lbs, and there are eight pints in one gallon, how much does a gallon weigh?" asks Alan, as quick as a flash Ron has the answer, "10 pound." "And if you had 3,000 gallons to shift you needed to be pretty fit," I offer, "an' all yer got paid fer shiftin it was seven bloody shillin's," comments Ron, as we move off and head for the next cove at Fairlight. To do this we have to go up even more steps and then walk along the cliff top for ¾ of a mile. Where we have a choice of paths we need to keep to the right so that we ensure we keep close to the cliffs. We then have to descend steps to Fairlight Glen, until, reaching the

Looking back at Fairlight

bottom we turn left along a broad path with the beach to our right, through the trees.

The discussion, as we walk along here, now gets a little political and heated. I'm not sure, exactly how to put it but you may or you may not know Ron's point of view with regards many things but let me just say that to some he comes over as not politacally correct in today's climate. Ron does not like scroungers and he made his point as we walk today. I'm not sure how the subject turned to criminals but Rons views are that should anyone be convicted of a crime where DNA has proven their guilt, they should be hung. "After all," rants Ron, "if the DNA 'as confirmed the person's guilt it's a 5 million ter one chance that the DNA's wrong so they must be guilty, 'ang em. That's what I say." And he does have a point. I'm all for having our legal system but you must have to ask questions when people who are found guilty 'beyond a shadow of a doubt' of some henous crime or crimes that involve children and are sentenced to 20 plus years in prison then have the cheek to claim that it's against their civil rights and appeal against the sentence. What makes it worse is a 95 year old judge sits on his pedestal in a court

More uphill!

room and agrees with the criminals. "There's no discipline," says Alan joining in with the conversation, "the local Police in Hailsham have stepped up patrols in the town during the evening to try and stop some of the hooligans congregating in the High Street at night. The hooligans just throw abuse at them, and what can the coppers do, nothing, because if they touch the little bastards they get reported. This country's gone soft." "That's why there's so many illegal immigrants," Ron is now in full swing, "we're too lenient with 'em. Other countries stone 'em ter death or cut their 'ands off, what do we do? Give 'em a warm room in a posh 'otel and £100 a week spendin' money."

It is now that we find that we can't get very close to Fairlight Cove due to cliff falls so now have to head away, climbing again and curving to the left. But it was the cove at Fairlight Glen that was the most popular destination for 18th century smugglers. The smuggling in Sussex was mostly controlled by large inland gangs operating out of Hawkhurst, Goudhurst or Mayfield. And it was the Mayfield gang, led by Gabriel Tompkins, that favoured Fairlight as the landing spot for his cargo. Gabriel was backed by many prominent citizens who gave him financial support. He could assemble up to 500 men for one night's work. Local labour would be recruited to carry goods up the steep path to teams of pack mules waiting on the cliffs above. Muscular thugs, known as 'Bat Men', armed with clubs would ensure that the operation was trouble free, but usually bribery combined with the threat of violence was enough to ensure that revenue officers stayed away. "How could you carry 3,000 gallons of spirits up this hill?" I ask, gasping for breath. "We never did decide 'ow much it weighed, did we?" asks Ron. We continue, uphill as the path curves left and then right again. We are told to ignore the steps on the right but continue, uphill, until the path flattens out. I'm shattered and both Ron and Alan look the same. I thought I heard Alan say that the smugglers must have sold the spirits on the Internet. I thought, 1700's – the Internet? When I started laughing he couldn't understand, but what he actually said was that "the smugglers must have sold the spirits to the Inns and that." But it was a simple mistake that I thought was hillarious.

This steep path was the route which the

We leave Fairlight Glen

Barley Lane

A gate to the right, but which one?

smugglers would bring up the goods from the beach to the team of pack mules waiting above. So organised was the trade that special packaging was designed for the contraband by Continental retailers. For instance, a standard hogshead of wine, holding 140 gallons, was impossible to conceal or carry up a cliff at the dead of night, so wine was decanted into manageable 4 gallon barrels before shipping. Additionally, barrels were made with flattened sides so that two could conveniently be worn in a harness and carried by one man. "'Ang on a minute," says Ron, "carryin' 4 gallons at a time could be a bit 'iffy but 'ow the 'ell do yer carry eight gallons?" We decide to stop and discuss the weight issue. "If one gallon weighs 10 pound then 4 gallons must weigh 40 pounds so double that and yer 8 gallons makes 80 pound," says Alan. "Then yer've got ter add the weight ov the container," chips in Ron, "and all for seven shillings," I add. "God," says Ron, "that's nearly a 'undredweight o'liquid sloppin about on yer back as yer try ter climb that bloody path in the dark." "They must have formed a chain gang and passed the barrels up the hill," says Alan, "I can't see 500 men all with barrels on their backs, 3000 gallons makes 750 4gallon barrels, it would have been chaos." It is decided that we should do a little more research and see if we can find out, exactly, how 3,000 gallons of spirits were transported up this path.

Just before our next uphill climb

Our instructions are a little confusing now. As we stand and watch one of the Hastings Country Park Rangers manoever his little tractor round us I read that we should ignore the kissing gate on our right, nor turn sharp left down into the glen. Instead we need to go half-left climbing slightly. Firstly the gate is in front of us and not to our right, secondly there is no sharp left turn but there is a sharp right turn but the correct way was to turn half-left and climb a bit more! We follow the path as it levels out and goes along the side of a field to a track. It is along this track that the contraband, now on the backs of mules, was moved inland to places such as Mayfield and Hawkhurst, where it was repackaged by legitimate merchants before being moved to its final retail markets in London and the Midlands. Vast convoys, with up to 150 men and 300 horses would move the goods, whilst the local population stayed indoors, asleep.

We pass through a metal barrier passing some cattle who seemed to show us no interest whatsoever (thankfully) and head along another track signed 'Barley Lane'. On reaching a tarmac lane we turn left and walk, on the level thankfully, for ¼ of a mile, passing some pretty cottages on our left. The Lane just seems to come to an end with a

Steps up to the church

footpath heading towards Ore in front of us and a very large gate with Fishponds Farmhouse stamped on it to our left. Our instructions are to ignore the path to Ore, but head towards the gate and bear right and then togo through a kissing gate on the right.

We now follow a clear path into a wood and I have to say that walking on the level was a treat. Unfortunately it wasn't going to last very long because out of the wood we follow the path along the side of a large lake before having to climb, yet again, towards a caravan park, where we turn left and follow the clear path as we return to nearly our starting point at the top of Ecclesbourne Glen. "Recognise, this," pants Ron at the top of the hill, "So you should," says Alan, "we were here over two hours ago. How long did you say this walk was, Graham?" he asks. "The book says 4½ miles," I answer. "'Tis more than that," says Ron as a matter of fact. "But we always think that it's longer than the book says," I tell them both, "the books can't always be wrong, can they?" But to be honest it did seem much longer but we did have to keep stopping because we were so tired. The next part of the walk was just as tiring because instead of walking back along the way we came we now bear right and climb even higher uphill untill we are able to see a sports pavillion in the distance. We eventually pass the pavillion on our right and head, now down a steep hill until we come to a road which we have to follow, with houses on our right. After a few yards we turn left and descend more steps and follow the tarmac path down to the road where we turn left and head for All Saints Church. I'm sorry, but when we got to the church I saw even more steps and I refused to climb any more. I was shattered! So we pass the church and head down the road passing The Stag Inn which was a favourite haunt of smugglers in the 18th century. Its cellars were once connected by tunnels to the cliffs above and contraband was hidden here. All Saints Street was one of the main thoroughfares in Old Hastings, and is still lined with many fascinating buildings. Once back on the seafront we turn left and head for a well earned pint in the Dolphin.

The Stag Inn

Returning to the subject of Gabriel Tompkins. He was eventually convicted for smuggling and murder but to escape sentence he turned in a number of his former colleagues and corrupt revenue officers and was rewarded by being appointed a bailiff for the Sheriff of Sussex. Unfortunately, Tompkins couldn't resist returning to his old ways and finally turned to highway robbery, for which he was hanged in 1750.

Smuggling flourished because it had the support of the local people. But popular support dissappeared in the 1760s when some local smugglers overstepped the mark. A gang known as Ruxley's Crew turned from running contraband to piracy. They would board ships, lock the crew below deck, steal the cargo and then scupper the ship with all hands. Ruxley was denounced from the pulpit at All Saints Church and the Mayor was attacked for not condemning the gang. The gang were eventually arrested by troops and despite the public revulsion of him no local jury dare convict Ruxley and he and his men were sent to London for trial.

So this is the end of our walk but not the end of our endeavours to establish some more information about smuggling. But please let me warn you just one more time. The walk is very, very difficult and not to be attempted by anyone with walking problems. A better idea is to head straight for The Dolphin, we received a very warm welcome and the beer is great. So my advice is simple, forget the walk, grab yourselves some cockles and sit on the beach or better still, head straight for The Dolphin.

Our next walk won't have any of these

Pub Walk (3)

Since our last walk a number of things have happened within the Pollard household. First of all Emelia and I have become grandparents again. Harry came into our world on November 4th 2009 at a very healthy 9lb + ounces and is an adorable brother to Chloe and Megan. Mum, Nicole, and baby Harry are both well and Nicole is, understandably, pleased that it is all over, although labour with Harry was reasonably short.

Another bit of good news is that Emelia has submitted two of her teddy bears into the 2009 British Bear Artist Awards and has found out that both have reached the finals, to be held at Hove on the 13th December 2009. The bear she entered last year came second in the 'newcomers' category but this year she is entered with the big names in the teddy bear design industry. I'll let you know how she gets on.

Readers may be aware of my interest in family history. The walk we carried out titled 'Smugglers Walk' has caused a bit of a stir. Not because of what was written, although we still have to follow up on one or two issues for Alan, but what I have discovered may involve my family. One of the books that I tried to locate prior to completing the walk was titled 'Smuggling & Smugglers in Sussex'. I thought that I

The Church of St Laurence, Catsfield

would learn something of the smugglers in the area but, unfortunately, I was unable to locate the book in time to carry out any research. However, since then, I have managed to download the whole book from the Internet and found out that one of the notorious smugglers from the Mayfield gang was Nathaniel Curtis and one of his aliases was, would you believe, Nathaniel Pollard. A bit of a coincidence perhaps until I tell you that I have a relation (an uncle) with the surname Curtis. This uncle of mine actually lives in East Grinstead, the very home town where Nathaniel Curtis lived

during the 1700's. I'll have to follow this up and, you never know, it's a bit of a long shot but I might have stumbled onto something.

Whilst on the subject of family history, have any readers, tucked away somewhere, some photographs of close family? If you do then these photographs should be cherished. It turns out that both Ron and I have a distinct lack of photographs of both our parents when they were young. In Ron's case his mother asked his dad to get rid of an old suitcase that was no longer needed and his dad threw out the wrong suitcase. The empty one remained and the case full of old family pictures was destroyed. In my case, my maternal grandfather, Tom, decided, for some reason, that no-one would ever see the pictures of his or my grandmother's children and, in a rage, destroyed everything. But today Ron has handed me this weeks copy of the Sussex Express and within these pages is a copy of a picture, taken in the 1940's of the children from the school in Rushlake Green. The very school that, I believe, was attended by my mum. As my mum, Joan, was born in 1926 she would, at the time the picture was taken, be 14 years old. She may have left school by then, I don't know. She might be in the picture, again I am unsure. I will get in touch with the newspaper and let you know how I get on.

But, in the mean time, I must get back to the matter in hand and I have found, what I hope will be, an enjoyable walk. It's got a pub, so I know Ron will be happy!!

The walk I have chosen is around a small village called Catsfield, which isn't a stone's throw away from where we completed our smugglers walk in the last chapter. I'm hoping that this walk will not be so strenuous although hills are mentioned in the instructions taken from the book 'Pub Strolls in East Sussex'[114] but the walk is only 4 miles long so how many hills can there be in 4 miles?? I'm also hoping that as the hill mentioned in the instructions is at the start of the walk we will be reasonably high up so as not to be too wet underfoot. The rainfall during the month of November (2009) has exceeded all others and is said to be the wettest since records began. Although I accept the stories that 'global warming' can cause us one or two problems in the future I still

The Lady Brassey epitaph

think that dredging our rivers and ditches to ensure that the flow of water is maintained should be carried out. When was the last time our local rivers were cleared? Today the River Cuckmere, once a navigable river, can be leapt across in some places because the rivers course has not been maintained. All that rainwater must go somewhere. But I'm straying from the subject and must get on with our stroll around Catsfield, with a visit to The White Hart.

Catsfield was the home of the 'Brassey' family. Thomas Brassey worked with George Stephenson (the builder of the first steam engine)[115]. Thomas and George spent many years pioneering rail travel all over the world, and Thomas retired to Catsfield in 1865. He brought a large area of land and built a French-style château which he called Normanhurst Court. Unfortunately he died before it was completed. His son, also called Thomas, was knighted in 1881, made a peer in 1886 and was created an Earl in 1911[116] He was known as 'Tab' to his friends and in the village. Thomas Brassey (the father) married Annie Allnutt, the daughter of a wealthy wine merchant and jockey. Although the home was Normanhurst Court they spent much of their time aboard their steam yacht 'Sunbeam'. Lady Brassey (Annie) contracted malaria whilst on a trip with her husband and died on September 14th 1887. She was buried at sea and her epitaph in Catsfield church reads:

SACRED TO THE MEMORY OF
ANNIE LADY BRASSEY
DIED AT SEA 14TH SEPTEMBER 1887
COMMITTED TO THE DEEP AT
SUNSET IN LAT. 15° 50' S, LONG 110° 35' E[117]

---

[114] ' Pub Strolls in East Sussex' by B Perkins, Published by Countryside Books ISBN 1853066702
[115] 'Hidden Sussex' by Swinfen & Arscott a BBC Radio Sussex publication Page 41
[116] 'People of Hidden Sussex' by Swinfen & Arscott, BBC Radio Sussex, Page 44
[117] 'Dead and Buried in Sussex' by David Arscott, SB Publications, Page 68

I can't wait to see Catsfield. So, on a damp Saturday morning, I collect Ron from The King's Head and we head, through Herstmonceux and Boreham Street and turn left at Ninfield. Has anyone driven through Boreham Street lately? The speed limit is 30 mph. The signs on the posts at the side of the road tell us that. But the writing on the road says 40mph. So who do you believe?

We arrive at Catsfield and park the car in the free, yes free, car park in Church Road, which is opposite The White Hart. We change into some warm walking gear and head out of the car park, turning left into Church Road. Our instructions tell us to pass the village school but before we get that far we come across what, from the outside, looks like a church but is, in fact, two private residences. The old Methodist church has been converted but, obviously, still looks like a very religious house. "I wonder if it's 'awnted?" says Ron, "can't say that I'd like ter live in a place like that. Most churches feel damp 'n cold. Must cost a fortune ter keep warm? Still, 'tis close ter the pub so it ain't all bad."

This is no longer a church

We find the school on the right-hand side of the road and need to walk another 60 yards where we find a gate. Here we need to turn right. "It would be nice to see Catsfield Church before we get our shoes muddy," I say to Ron, "and I think the church is a little further up the road." We both agree to walk a little further and we aren't disappointed. The church stands high on a bank and can be approached by two entrances. One, which we came to, leads you from the back of the church to the front and the more obvious entry, which is in desperate need of repair, is through the lychgate.

The lychgate, Catsfield

The earliest tombstone recorded in the churchyard is 1680 and there isn't a stone dated later than 1877. It is assumed that this is when the cemetery, across the road, first came into use.[118] The church is entered through a porch which gives access to the door set in a semi-circular arch. And inside is typical of all really nice churches. "'Tis cold an' smells just 'ow a church should," says Ron as I follow him inside. The church is well maintained and the pamphlet we purchased[119] tells us all about the history of this pretty church. I managed to find the epitaph to Lady Brassey which is magnificent with its candles and prominent position. We also discovered that

Stained windows in the Chancel

---

[118] 'The Church of Saint Laurence and Parish of Catsfield' pamphlet purchased at church 50p
[119] Ibid

Thomas Brassey (the father) died in 1918 and Thomas Brassey (the son) died the following year after being run over by a taxi near the Houses of Parliament. The little pamphlet is a hive of information and, should you visit this lovely church, is 50 pence well spent.

On leaving the church we retrace our steps back along Church Road, towards the White Hart, until we find the gate we need to go through to start our walk. As you all know some walks can change and you have to leave an open mind to the instructions you might read. The writer of this walk is Ben Perkins and we have used him many times and found that he is,

The diverted path

usually, pretty accurate. But we are unable to complete our first instruction because the path we need to take has, obviously, been diverted. Our instruction is to go straight up the fenced path but the gate is locked. We will need to take the path on the left and, hopefully, we'll end up at the same place. This is our first hill and I can't speak for Ron but I am wearing a large anorak, thick socks and a woolly jumper. At the top of the hill I'm beginning to sweat. Although the wind is a bit on the cold side the weather is surprisingly warm. I think I could regret the extra clothing before too long.

As we cannot follow our instructions it is a case of heading in the general direction and hope that something looks familiar in the book.

Parkland

We are given a little map to follow but it is pretty basic. Thankfully, though, we manage to find our next way point which is parkland with a waypost at the corner of a wood and a bungalow where we join the B2095. "That 'as ter be one o' the biggest bungalows I've ever seen," comments Ron as we approach a large white building with out-houses. "I always thought a bungalow was a single story building. This place has outbuildings bigger than my house and it's got windows in the roof," I continue. "You'd not get a lot o' change from 'alf a million fer a place like that," says Ron, "an' look at the views from the back windows, must look straight across all this parkland, lucky buggers." It is a pretty place and the location is great but we have to get on.

Once on the road we turn right and look out for some staggered railings. If you come on this walk be very careful here because there is no

Not so much staggered as broken railings

Thrown away?

FISHING
PRICES
£10 per person
per day
Two Rods
Visitors
£5 per day

ALL DOGS ON LEADS

Ron's confused

WYLAND ANGLING CENTRE
CHARGES JUNE 1999
ANGLING
£ (New Speci Lake £) per person per calendar day.
Each angler may use 2 rods but these cannot be shared
with another person. A night session is a 2 day ticket.
An accompanying spouse (not angling) is free.

VISITORS
Definition – anyone on site and not fishing
£ per adult per day. £1 per child per day.

BIVVIES
One bivvi per angler free. Extra Bivvis: £2 per night.

LARGE DOME TENTS
Some are so large they are no longer classed as bivvis and
subsequently will be charged £2 per night.

RUBBISH
Overnight stayers must purchase local authority green
bags from snackbar to leave their refuse on site.
Anyone found not complying will be told to leave.

INSURANCE
All these charges reflect our legal responsibility to
carry insurance against liability for all who visit here.

CHILDREN
Children not fishing must be kept away from the lakesides.
Roaming children spoil the anglers peace and quiet.

Ron now thinks it's free

path and the traffic hurtles along the road. One slip and the results could be really nasty. The book tells us that the railings are 100 yards from where we came onto the road. Sure enough we managed to find some railings; again this was something else that could do with some tender loving care. There was no sign here either, so it was a case of heading along the drive and, hopefully, we should come out at an Angling Centre.

Throughout our walks, over the years, we have seen all manner of things dumped in some strange places. People will, apparently, drive miles into the middle of nowhere just to dispose of some item or other. Some items are large, a fridge, a cooker or pieces of furniture but today we found the ultimate: a Fire Engine. Not just any Fire Engine but a child's pride and joy? It used to run on batteries and I'm sure it was a much loved toy but now it's dumped, up a lane, thrown away, never to be played with again. Why would anyone do this, and why not put it in a bin to save the trouble of walking all the way out to the middle of nowhere where it may do damage to wildlife????

At the end of this short drive we come to an Angling Centre which appears to be open to the public. The sign at the top of the drive tells us that one person can have two rods and the fee is £10 per day or a person can be classed as a visitor and the cost is £5 per day. "Cheaper ter be a visitor and 'ave a rod for a fiver," says Ron, "I don't think that's what it means, Ron," I offer. "Don't matter what it means," he continues, as only Ron can, "it says they're goin' ter charge me £5 fer bein' a visitor. There ain't no mention that I can't 'ave a rod with me. If yer ask me it's a bloody silly sign." Their cause isn't helped by the next sign we come to, a little further down the drive, which, according to Ron, means that this angling centre only charged people in June 1999. 'As it's December 2009 now it must mean that it's free," argues Ron. I'm not sure if he's winding me up but he seems pretty serious. Thankfully it isn't too long until we come to what I think is my favourite photographic opportunity, water. You will know that nothing gives me more of a thrill than reflections in water. Unfortunately today the water is not still so reflections are difficult to obtain but I did have a go but it wasn't until

We walk along a field edge

An odd squeeze stile

Ron's on a dream trip?

we got to the other side of the Angling Centre that I managed to get a really good reflection.

We followed our instructions around the various ponds or lakes, I counted five but there may have been more. The lakes seemed to be well-kept with various signs advising fishermen what should and should not be done. One sign advised them to 'dip your net' which, according to Ron, was to ensure that your keep net, if dipped in the receptacle provided, would not contaminate the water. Another sign insisted that barbless hooks were to be used at all times. "Gives fish a fightin' chance," explains Ron, "when you went fishin'," he continues looking at me like I should know better, "I bet you used 'ooks with barbs on." And he's right, I didn't know any different. "If you use barbed 'ooks," says Ron, "fish can't get off the 'ook an' it ain't very sportin'. But if you don't use 'ooks with barbs the fish, if you don't play it proper, it'll come off the 'ook, see, and escape fer another day. Not only that but the fish ain't 'armed if y er don't use barbs on the 'ook. It don't split the lip nor don't it get stuck in its innerds" Which all seems a bit of a long winded way of catching something, just to throw it back? I prefer sea fishing; at least you can eat most of what you catch. But I must admit that millions of people fish for a hobby so who am I to criticise?

We leave the Angling Centre and head along the field edge and cross a footbridge within a wood. The path here is a little difficult to follow because, simply, there isn't one. We need to squeeze between two tree trunks and follow our noses. Our map shows us that we should follow the edge of the wood and continue in a straight line but this was a little difficult with fallen trees and broken branches strewn on the ground. But we eventually managed to find the footbridge that is in our instructions but we seem to have ended up on the wrong side of a fence, because we should have arrived at a stile and, you've guessed it, we didn't find one.

But at least the mistake was obvious and we were soon back on track. Although the final large pond with an island was a little bit of a surprise I did notice that Ron had to stop a while and dream about things as he looked across the water. "Are you ok?" I ask, "Just lookin' across the water ter that island," he replies, "look at all them fishin' floats 'angin' from the trees where they've cast their line too far. Must be able ter make a few bob if only I could find a way over there!"

Nosey sheep

Once we were back on track it wasn't too long before we needed to turn left and head, uphill along a fenced track. Just in front of us was Miller's Farm where we forked right, over two stiles and skirt around the farm buildings.

Large padlock

Walking the plank

The instructions are a little vague here. We are told to keep close to the perimeter fencing and to join a concrete access drive which would lead us out onto a road. Firstly the field was full of sheep (not my best friends) and secondly, halfway along the perimeter fence was a gate on our left. Ron said we should go through the gate and head for the concrete access drive that would lead us out, onto the road. I disagreed and said we should continue along the perimeter fence until we came to the corner of the field. Ron, I'm sure, continued along the fence just to amuse me because, to quote my father-in-law, I'm not always right and I was wrong again! We headed back to the gate and found the concrete access drive that would lead us out, onto the road.

Here we cross the road and go through a gate, almost opposite. This is the path which would lead us through Powdermill Wood. But I notice that the gate has an extremely large padlock on it? "The sign says no entry," Ron says, "what shall we do?" "The book says go through the gate opposite," I reply, "this is the only gate opposite so it must be o.k. It looks as if people just walk round the post." So that's exactly what we do.

We find ourselves heading downhill, steeply and it is evident that water is running, and running very fast. Our instructions tell us that we are approaching the outflow from Farthing Pond and we need to get across an earth dam. Yes I did say an 'earth dam'. Now I've conjured up all sorts of pictures as to what an 'earth dam' must look like a long time before I actually got anywhere near it. The sound of fast running water didn't make the picture I had in my mind any nicer. But Ron is way ahead of me and looks as if he's actually standing on top of a waterfall. It isn't until I get down to his level that I realise that he's actually standing on a wooden walkway, over the water. But the feeling when I stood on the same plank was really strange. If you looked down it was hypnotic and tended to draw you towards the water. But I think it was the speed with which the water moved that was most surprising. I'm not sure how many gallons of water shot under our feet but it was certainly an impressive amount.

The grassy path

Again our instructions weren't quite correct here. There had been some recent work carried out around Farthing Pond and instead of forking right you need to just continue along the clearly defined path which climbs through the wood and a stile which leads us across another field and another stile.

After this stile we turned left and climbed through a coppice. It was getting a little warm now and both Ron and I regretted the extra clothing. At the top of the hill we turn right and walk along a grassy path which narrows to a path through a holly thicket. Once through the thicket we are in a plantation of Christmas trees and the smell is unbelievable. Wall-to-wall pine. And these trees had to be about 20 feet tall. We marvel at the trees but can't understand why they would have been left to grow to such a height. The tops were very spindly and wouldn't make good trees for decorating. Ron thought they may have been left to grow this height to protect the smaller trees on the inside of the plantation, but to be honest, they all looked the same size to me.

Christmas trees by the hundreds

We leave the wood over a stile and head along a field's edge to another stile. This leads us out onto a concrete drive and onto the main road. Again you take life in your own hands as we turn left here. The traffic is relentless and fast moving, although the speed limit is 40 miles per hour, cars feel as if they are going faster than that. But we are instructed to cross the road and after a couple of attempts we manage to get to the otherside, where another stile is climbed so that we can cross a field and come out, again, onto the fast main road. Just a short distance from the White Hart and the end of our walk.

Before we started this walk I had a look on the Internet[120] at what was said about this country pub. Sadly the comments weren't that encouraging and then I realised that

---

[120] http://www.beerintheevening.com/pubs/s/26/26524/White_Hart/Catsfield visited 30/11/09

the comments about poor food and grumpy landlord were old and I decided not to say anything to Ron and just see for ourselves. I must say that the pub was very well decorated for Christmas, the young lady behind the bar was very cheerful and the open fire was more than inviting. Both Ron and I decided to have a meal and, again, I must say that the food was not only delicious and well-cooked but the service was both pleasant and welcoming. All in all, a very nice day.

At the start I mentioned hills and 4 miles and although the walk is short the hills can be a problem. But at the end is a nice warm pub which will make you very welcome. I liked it and wouldn't hesitate to take my family there in the near future. What better recommendation can Ron and I give?

Ron rolls up his sleeves for the White Hart

Town Walk

Looking back over the walks that Ron and I have completed for this book we were a little surprised that we hadn't completed a town walk. So I thought it was about time to correct the situation and look for a town that would fit the bill and have chosen Bexhill-on-Sea or, as some others call it, God's Waiting Room. Bexhill got the nickname purely because of the numbers of pensioners who seem to flock to this seaside town. Some arrive on holiday to enjoy the comforts of the healthy resort whilst others decide, after a holiday here, to return and settle down. But whatever the reason Bexhill-on-Sea has become the place to be for many of our elderly. It is also the birth place of British motor racing when, in 1902 the first official motorcar race took place organised by the then 8th Earl De La Warr. More than 200 cars took part in the spectacle with straight sprint races taking place along the promenade at speeds of 50 miles per hour.

Fords first racing car

Image obtained from
http://www.speedace.info/speedace_images/ford_1902_arrow_race_car_henry.jpg

Which doesn't seem that fast today but back in 1902 the speed limit was just 12 miles per hour.[121]

John Logie Baird died in Bexhill on June 14th 1946. For those not familiar with the name John invented the television. He was born on January 19th 1925, in Hastings, and from his workshop in the town he successfully transmitted the first '*pictures by wireless*' – the hand of his assistant, Victor Mills, and a Maltese cross.[122] Since these events not a lot has happened within Bexhill-on-Sea until, that is, Ron and me turned up in December 2009.

Today's walk was obtained via the Internet and is described as '*...an edge of town walk of about 6 miles. It includes riverside fields and farmland, hedgerow remains of ancient woodland, reed beds, vegetated shingle and a wonderful mile of rock pools at low tide*'[123]. So, all I have to do is line up the walk with the low tide and we should end up with an enjoyable walk? Another play on the Internet and I now have a tide chart which lists, by day and by length, the incoming and outgoing tides at Bexhill and Hastings[124] and Wednesday the 23rd of December looks good, providing we leave a little earlier than usual, because low tide is at 09:15 in the morning. So a good start time would be about 8 o'clock. I hope that's not too early for Ron. One slight deviation from the planned route, and to ensure we are able to see the rock pools at low tide it will be necessary to start the walk on the beach and not, as our instructions say, finish on the

---

[121] http://www.discoverbexhill.com/bexhillmotorracing.php visited 12/12/09
[122] 'Hidden Sussex Day by Day' by Swinfen and Arscott - BBC Radio Sussex Publication Pages 20 & 79
[123] http://www.riverocean.org.uk/ocean/webwalks/Bexhill%20Circular.html visited 21/11/09
[124] http://www.hastings.gov.uk/tides/default.aspx visited 12/12/09

beach. I hope all will become clear when we arrive at Bridge Way, Bexhill-on-Sea which is instruction number eleven on our planned route.

We see the sun rise

For some reason this walk is worrying me. So much so that I have produced another map of our route which is larger than the one provided. This wasn't as easy as it seems because I couldn't find an appropriate sized map and had to produce one from the Internet[125] which turned out to be eight little street maps, joined by sellotape to produce one big map. I have also noticed that our instructions give pole directions i.e. turn north; veer north-east etc., so I will be taking a compass with us, just in case Ron can't find the sun!

So with new batteries in the camera we're all set for our last walk of 2009.

The weather forecast for today wasn't too good. In fact it was bloody cold. Snow fell a few days ago and, as always, we were nowhere near prepared for it even though we'd been told it was coming. But since then it has got very cold and the snow is fast turning to ice and becoming very dangerous. The forecast for today is that the temperature will drop to minus 7 and it's going to rain. Ron insists, yet again, that 'it don't rain in Sussex on a Wensd'y afternoon' but, as I head towards picking him up on a very cold Wednesday morning it is teaming it down. We also have Alan for company today so with the three of us kitted out for foul weather we head towards Bexhill-on-Sea.

We cross the railway line

Conversation in the car seems to involve our local pub. Alan can be seen helping out behind the bar some evenings and both Ron and I have noticed that a number of regulars have stopped coming in. 'Use ter 'ave a lot o'regular people in on a Friday night," says Ron, "all use ter sit round the big table in the public bar, chattin' an' discussin' all manner o'things, we did. Use ter be a big laugh, but 'ardly see some o'the locals now." I know Ron and quite a few of the older regulars have a bit of an issue with loud music and although others have spoken about it, it only seems to be Ron who complains. "Makes it sound like I'm the only

Ron's there somewhere!

---

[125] http://www.streetmap.co.uk/newdefaulte2.htm visited 22/12/09

Towards Galley Hill

one complainin', continues Ron, "but I ain't. We don't want that thump, thump music on when the average age o'the customers in the bar's over 60 an' all we won'ts ter do is 'ave a chat and play dominoes. I got nothin' against background music but over there, just lately, the music is the only feature o'the pub." I have to admit that I don't visit the pub as often as a used to but my problem is more financial. How many can remember saying that once beer got to a £1 a pint they'd 'pack it in'? I know I did, and here it is costing over £2.50. But I can remember closing the door between the bars at the King's Head once, because the music in the public bar was very loud and Ron and I needed to discuss one of our walks, and I received a very frosty comment from behind the bar. The discussion continues in this vain until we get to Bridge Way where I can't find anywhere to park so we end up in a free parking area just a few hundred yards up the road.

As I said at the start we would be joining our walk instructions nearly at the end of the 6 miles and this was just so that we could see the low tide. Our first instruction is to get back to Bridge Way and cross the railway line by way of the footbridge. Once over the line we find ourselves on the beach and turn right, heading towards Bexhill-on-Sea.

Surprisingly the photographs have turned out really good, even if I say so myself. It was still raining, it was very cold but the walk along the beach was very pleasant and the pictures, due to the low sun out at sea gave a silhouette appearance. All along this beach there are enormous granite boulders to protect the beach from erosion. "Yer wouldn't get many o'them ter the pound up at the garden centre," chuckles Ron. They are enormous but obviously doing their job. Without these granite rocks

Walking below the cliffs at Glynde Gap

protecting the cliffs the erosion would be very quick indeed. The latest addition to these enormous Scandinavian granite blocks took place during the summer of 2005. But one of my main reasons for being here at low tide was the opportunity to see the outline of the wreck of the Amsterdam, once owned by a Dutch East India Company. In January 1749 it was travelling from Rotterdam to Batavia (Java) with 330 crew, one of whom came aboard with yellow fever. By the time the ship had reached the Sussex coast 50 of the crew were already dead and 40 were sick. In a storm there were not enough crew to man the ship and its rudder was damaged. The ship was wrecked on the sands here but unfortunately, this morning, the tide wasn't long enough to see the outline.[126]

We continue along the beach, passing various beach huts, brightly coloured and now securely bolted against intrusion as well as the weather, as we now climb slightly

---

[126] http://www.riverocean.org.uk/ocean/webwalks/Bexhill%20Circular.html visited 21/11/09

towards Galley Hill. At the top of the hill used to be a Martello Tower, built in the early 1800's as part of the coastal defences against Napoleon. But it was from this point that, in 1828, a call was raised to assist in stopping the local smugglers, known as 'The Little Common Gang', from escaping with their contraband. The men from the Tower, known as Blockademen headed west along the beach to intercept the smugglers. As the Tubmen attempted to carry the illegal gains up the beach they were confronted by the Blockademen, who were armed. Some Tubmen dropped their cargo and ran into the night but others stood their ground. Suddenly the Blockade men were up against a large number of Batmen armed with nothing more than six foot lengths of wood. Whilst all this was going on the Tubmen continued the movement of contraband. Sources had told the Blockademen that the gang would be heading for Sidley Green which was about 2½ miles inland. Determined to out manoeuvre the gang the Blockademen dropped back, reformed and headed for Sidley Green via Galley Hill, where they gathered reinforcements. On the way to Sidley Green the Blockademen managed to catch up with some of the running smugglers and fights and skirmishes took place, but they caught up with the main body at Sidley Green where the smugglers, now armed, drew themselves up in a regular line and a fierce battle ensued. One of the leaders of the Blockademen was killed and, eventually the smugglers were forced to retreat to Cramps Farm but not before the Tubmen had managed to escape with the contraband into the Sussex night.

During the desperate fighting that took place several men fell wounded including an old smuggler who fell fatally wounded still clutching his bat which had been hacked almost to matchwood by the cutlasses of the Blockademen. No smuggler was taken alive that night and all the contraband bar a couple of tubs which had been dropped during the flight were safely carried away. In all, over six hundred gallons of spirit had been landed illegally. Two men lay dead and many had been wounded, some seriously.[127]

Ron inspects the graffiti/art/vandalism

We continue our walk up Galley Hill. On the right is a skateboard park, highly decorated with graffiti. On a plaque, in front of one of the ramps, tells us that '*The mural surrounding the skateboard ramp is the work of Blakstar and conveys the conflicting sides of graffiti: art and vandalism represented by heaven and hell.*' Due to publication laws I am not permitted to write what Ron called it but if you know Ron as well as I do then you are in no doubt as to what he said!

At the top of Galley Hill we now look down towards the town of Bexhill-on-Sea. It was here, as I said earlier, that the first motorcar race took place and we are now actually walking along the route taken by the racing cars. "Lilly the pink," says Ron, "Do what?" asks Alan, "Lilly the pink," repeats Ron and he points his thumbstick towards the blocks of flats to our right. "Lilly the pink," Ron says yet again, "I heard what you said," says Alan, "I just don't understand what your on about." "Over there," Ron says, pointing his thumbstick, "that block of flats 'as scaffolding round it. Lilly the Pink was sung by The Scaffold." You could hear the groan all the way to Hastings. "Back in 1968 it was, Lilly the Pink made it ter number one in the Christmas charts. One o'the members

[127] http://home.freeuk.com/whenham/prologue.html visited 21/11/09

was Paul McCartney's brother, I think 'is name was Peter. Strange that, just somethin' I picked up at a pub quiz somewhere. Stuck in the mind, it did." I have since checked what Ron said and he's right.[128]

As we head into Bexhill we need to look out for the War Memorial. "Why?" asks Alan, "Because opposite the Memorial is Sea Road and we need to head along Sea Road and walk past the Railway Station." I tell Ron and Alan. Looking ahead on our instructions I also see that I will have to produce my compass. It'll be interesting to hear what Ron has to say about it. By the way, it has stopped raining. It's started to hail now!

Walking along the 'race course'

We stop and admire the Memorial. "Now that's some monument to the fallen," says Ron, "Look at how many names are on it," comments Alan. Apart from the names being in alphabetical order they are also listed in Service. It is a very well kept monument in memory of both the men and women who fell during two World Wars and I can only hope that the wreaths are tied down due to the wind and not due to vandals?

The War Memorial

We now cross the road and head up Sea Road which, in the 1800's used to be called Sea Lane. The land, at that time, between Bexhill (the old town) and the coast was marshy and uninhabited. This lane was used to get to and from the beach by both fishermen and smugglers. During the first half of the 1700's smuggling in the area was run by the Hawkhurst Gang who, in November 1744, smashed up the house of the Bexhill Riding Officer and terrorised his family, apparently to keep him occupied and out of the way during a major landing taking place that night.

Just past the Railway Station is Buckhurst Road. At this junction we have to cross the road and continue uphill (no-one mentioned hills?) until we reach Manor Gardens. "Bit slippery up 'ere," says Ron and both he and Alan are now warning all the elderly people heading down the hill to watch their step. "Council 'ere are the same as 'ome," says Ron, "done sod all in the way o'saltin' the paths. 'Tis bloody treacherous on the paths, walk in the road you get 'it by a motor, walk on the path, you slip an' break yer ankle." Ron is now on his soap box. But just then, as we head uphill, I notice a sign on a wall that tells us that 'the last residing address of J. Logie Baird was, what is now,

---

[128] http://en.wikipedia.org/wiki/The_Scaffold visited 24/12/09

179 | P a g e

St Peter's Church

Baird Court. "CB Fry," says Ron. "He used to make chocolate, didn't he?" asks Alan. "No," says Ron, "'e was one ov' England's greatest athletes," Ron continues, "yet 'e never won an Olympic medal." "Why not?" I ask, "'cause 'e didn't know they were goin' on," chuckles Ron, "was captain o' cricket an' football as well as athletics fer Oxford University. Played rugby, he could box, swim, play tennis and even throw javelin. In 1901 'e scored centuries (100+ runs) in six games runnin' an' that record 'as never been beaten. I think 'e also 'ad a record fer the long jump." "How do you know all these things?" asks Alan. "Don't know," Ron replies, "just come inter me 'ead."

We are now at Manor Gardens where the Manor House was built in Medieval times to provide accommodation for bishops visiting from Chichester. In 1891 it became the property of the De La Warr family and for the next few years aristocratic visitors could play tennis and cricket or try the new sport, cycling. Unfortunately the house was demolished in 1968 as part of, would you believe, a road widening scheme? Just opposite Manor Gardens is Quakers Mill and it is here that we have to cross the road again and head towards the parish church of St Peter.

Sadly for us the church has a ceremony going on so we couldn't look inside. But from the outside it looks very large. Our instructions tell us about a window in the church, which is dated 1470, depicts various saints, one being Saint Zita who is the patron saint of domestic servants. Between 1804 and 1815 the area to the north and east of the church was occupied by King

The twitten between hedge and fence

George III's Hanoverian legion. These 2000 troops met with considerable suspicion from the local people (Bexhill's population was about 200 at that time) but it seems that the German soldiers won their locals' hearts by their singing and musicianship in their band and by the quality of care they gave their horses. "Not changed a lot, then," says Ron, "we're still a bloody soft touch fer a bleedin' 'eart story." To make sure that Ron gets off the subject of foreign immigrants I notice that our next instruction is to head for the north-east corner of the church and ask him for directions. "Our instructions say that we could have difficulty here," I continue, "we need to locate a twitten between a beech hedge and a wooden fence." "It's that direction," says Ron, pointing his thumbstick towards the back of the church. I had secretly got my compass out of my pocket and checked Ron's direction, and he was spot on. How does he do that? As we walk in a north-easterly direction Ron say's "Did yer know that the word 'twitten' is only used in

I missed Southlands Court

Sussex ter mean an alleyway or path?" "I come from Kent," says Alan, "and I'd never heard the word until I came to Sussex." "What do the call them in Kent?" I ask. "They're a path, so that's what we call it," answers Alan. "A 'twitten' in York is called a 'snickleway'," I add. "I've read about them in one of my Candace Robb books."

We continue along the twitten for about ¼ of a mile, chatting about things in general as we walk behind peoples gardens. It is quite noticeable how much litter is dropped along the path. Ron makes his usual comments. As the path (twitten) curves to the right we come out onto a dual carriageway road. We come to a footbridge on our left, which we cross over the road, and we now find ourselves on part of the '1066 Bexhill Walk' route. Everyone must know the connection to 1066 and this area of Sussex but for those unsure of the events I'll explain briefly. William's troops (the Normans) landed at Pevensey Bay and Bexhill and some made their way up Sea Lane wreaking havoc as they went. Basically that's it.

Somehow I missed our next instruction; I don't know how I managed it. But we needed to turn left at a place called 'Southlands Court'. We had gone some way passed the derelict building before I realised that things didn't look right. When I stopped and asked if anyone had noticed a place called Southlands Court Ron, immediately said, "we passed that ways back, don't say we're lost, 'cause I thought you we're doin' so well, with that compass, an' all." We head back

Our next 'twitten'

up the road and find the turning. How I missed the instruction I'm really not sure but both Ron and Alan are suggesting eye tests when we get back.

From this lane we find another '1066 sign' so know we are heading in the right direction. We are now in a modern housing estate and our instructions tell us to keep to the path until we come to a wooden seat between two hedges. We didn't find the seat but we did find yet another '1066' sign which pointed us towards yet another twitten between two hedges. Our instructions tell us to walk along this path until we come to a road. Once across the road we come to a stile which will give us access to open fields. Once through the squeeze stile (even Ron had a problem getting through) we find an open space, obviously used by youngsters for some recreational purposes. "Look at the litter 'ere," says Ron, as he pokes empty beer cans with his thumbstick. "It's not just the beer cans," continues Alan, "but at least the youngsters of Bexhill are practising 'safe sex'. By the numbers of empty condom packets laying on the ground, this must have

We keep the hedge on our right

We have to wade to the stile

The 'landmark pine'?

been some party!" All along this short path towards the fields rubbish is laying on the ground. Again Ron starts on about 'layabouts, on the dole, should be made ter come out 'ere and clean up the bloody mess and earn their dole money'. Again it is time to change the subject and move on.

We are now in open countryside with views across the valley. Our instructions tell us to walk along the field edge with the hedge on our right. "Are we into Wednesday afternoon yet?" I ask Ron, "Why d'yer ask?" "'Cause it's started to rain again and I want to prove you wrong about the Wednesday afternoon thing." Ron looks up at the sky and say's, "tis only eleven o'clock," and continues walking towards our next stile. I look at my watch and its five past eleven, so the sun must be five minutes slow. At our next stile we need to head in a north-easterly direction. Again I ask Ron, he points, I don't bother to check. We are now heading along field edges and over stiles the rain is making going a little treacherous. Large puddles are appearing everywhere and I've noticed that Alan is beginning to limp. Then it starts to hail. Big chunks. I look at the map and we are a fair way from the car. We have no shelter and we are getting very wet. All Ron say's is "it ain't cold though, is it?" It's freezing! As we arrive at the next stile the hail stops as suddenly as it started. "Told yer it was just a clearin' up shower," says Ron who, by this time is wearing wet weather leggings, coat and hat. We wade across to our next stile and head up the lane, past Boulder Cottage and bear right past Worsham Farm. Our map doesn't show these buildings but it does show Upper and Little Worsham Farm, which we didn't see? Alan is still limping. "Are you o.k.?" I ask, "I got a pebble in me shoe when we were walking on the beach," replies Alan. "But that were ages ago," says Ron, "you'd better get 'er out before she rubs yer sore." We find a post for Alan to lean on so that he can take his boot off and get rid of the pebble.

It is here that we now leave the '1066 walk' and head up a lane where we should find '…a landmark pine tree'. It's started to rain again. I look at Ron. "It ain't afternoon yet," is all he has to say.

The lane is very muddy, with puddles and ruts that need care when walking. The lane eventually turns into a track and the puddles and ruts get even deeper. To our right is a water treatment works and I can remember my late father-in-law, who used to work at one of these treatment works, telling me that they didn't smell. Well I and Alan can tell him that this one certainly did!

The edge of the landfill site

We eventually reach the end of the path and we are now walking to the side of a very large landfill site. This site was due to close in 2008 but the site is producing so much methane that the local authority is planning to use generators to produce electricity for local use. It has now stopped raining. I look at Ron. "Tis midday an' tis a Wensday. It won't rain no more ter day," he says with that smug grin. We follow the edge of this site, down into a valley until we reach a kissing gate. It is at this gate that I see a large dog. A very large dog. A very large brown dog and it appears to be on its own. "It looks like one o'them dogs owned by Royalty in the old days," says Ron. I think they were Irish Wolfhounds and were used for hunting. As we got to the gate this one stopped in front of us, and just stared. I'm not sure what the owner shouted but the dog immediately sat down. Around the corner came a man carrying, and I'm not joking, a bird of prey, a real 100% hooded, flying, killing machine. I have never been this close to a hunting bird before. Of course I'd seen them at shows but never this close up. "Just off to scare a few sea gulls from the landfill site," says the birds' owner, "trouble was she managed to catch one back there," blood is on the birds' claws and the owners' glove. And the man has gone as quickly as he arrived. It is at this point that you have so many questions to ask and kick yourselves for not asking them. And why didn't I ask if I could take a photo? It would have looked fantastic in the book, a man with his bird of prey on a gloved hand complete with Irish Wolfhound by his side. I'm gutted!!

Cross the Comb Haven

We turn right, after the kissing gate, and head towards Combe Haven. We cross the river by way of a wooden bridge, which is relatively new; the old metal parts can still be seen. But just before we cross Ron notices a boundary stone which was one of many that used to be used to signify the parish boundary. The tradition of beating the bounds went out of favour, in Bexhill, in the 1920's. The area we are now in is also known as the Filsham Reedbeds and, when the landfill site eventually

Boundary stone

closes, will become part of a new country park. There is also a proposed new road due to

Looking back along Combe Haven

be built around here which, we are told, will reduce the amount of traffic using the much used coast road. Unfortunately local opposition to the road had been voiced. The reedbeds are home to lots of plants and creatures and conservationists are trying to get the road re-routed so that the wildlife in the area can be preserved. We'll have to wait and see what happens.

We now walk along Combe Haven, with the Holiday Park just over the river to our left. Thankfully, Ron was right and the rain has stopped and we manage to arrive back at the car, somewhat wetter than we started. But the six mile walk was pleasant although a bit muddy in places. This would be a much better walk in the summer, when the weather wasn't so bad.

Our next stop, on the way home, was The Star at Pevensey Bay. We have eaten here before and, again, we are not disappointed. Christmas dinner and all for £4.95. As Ron say's, "a bloody bargain."

As I write this chapter December the 25th has come and the festivities are well in hand. Emelia has spent the last few days preparing for the number of parties we hold over Christmas and all our families are able to eat, drink and be merry so that a good time is had by all. It is also the time that we think of members of family that are no longer with us. It's only been a few years since I lost both of my parents and I still miss them terribly.

On a much happier note, if you remember, I told you all that Emelia had two bears in this year's British Bear Artist Awards and I'm both pleased and very proud, to let you know that one of her bears came second in the competition. Well done Mele XX

All that remains is for both Ron and me to wish you all a Merry Christmas and a very prosperous New Year.

**Say hello to Charlie, placed 2nd in
British Bear Artist Award 2009**

Short Walk

This is a walk that has been arranged for some time. But, due to weather conditions, we have had to put it off until now. The reason for a short walk is simply because we are to be accompanied by Derek. Everyone from our local knows Derek. He's one of the most popular regulars, and if we needed to work it out mathematically, he's probably the oldest regular to currently use The King's Head. Derek is one of those people that I have rarely seen in a 'dark' mood. Even whilst he nursed his much beloved wife through her illness he always seemed to be cheerful, although at times, it must have been very, very difficult for him. He is a gent; he can talk about anything, and everything, and is one of the nicest people I've met. He also makes a real mean home-made wine that has seen some hardened drinkers go weak at the knees. Derek has a couple of daughters, Sally who is featured in these pages[129], currently living in Canada with her husband, and Susan who lives in Worthing and visits dad on a regular basis.

Some news on the Pollard front is that I have decided to stop driving the school mini-bus. Not an easy decision to make but one that I hope will prove beneficial to one and all. Ron is over the moon! "Means we can go back ter walkin' on Wensd'ys," he says, "what with you not 'avin' ter go back ter the school at 'alf past four ter take them girls 'ome. Be like old times, so it will." Of course this is just one of the benefits (?) but I'm hoping that health matters will also improve and stress levels will be reduced. Only time will tell.

The real title of this walk!

Before I go on to write about the walk I will just mention that the photographs for this chapter will not be taken with my usual camera. For the technically minded all the photographs I have used in the other chapters are taken on my 5.1 mega pixel S5600 digital camera and then downloaded onto the computer for use in these pages. But today the pictures are to be taken on my old 35mm SLR (single lens reflex) camera purchased in the 1970's, processed in the normal C41 manner at JR News in Hailsham High Street and then scanned into the computer before they can be used in these pages. All I have to do prior to the walk is to read the camera instruction book again to make sure I can remember my f stop theory as well as the 'depth of field' preview technicality. And I bet you thought it was easy?? Should the next few pages be without pictures you can rest assured that the experiment didn't work. On the other hand if pictures are seen then I may do it again!

So, to the walk. As I said at the start of the chapter it is a short walk around Litlington. Short meaning that it's 3½ miles in length and described as 'A very enjoyable and peaceful, scenic walk at first across farm land, through woods on wide grass tracts, leading into Lullington Heath Nature Reserve before returning along a down land bridleway. Although hilly the walk is not too strenuous…'[130] I will say right now that Derek actually chose this walk for us to do. I'm sure that we have been to the fore

---

[129] 'Friends Walk' Page 22
[130] Pub Walks in East Sussex by Mike Power, Published by Power Publications, Dorset – Walk No. 23 Page 56

mentioned Lullington Heath Nature Reserve before and, if memory serves me correctly, it's a b^~~dy long way up! So it is worrying me. So much so that I decide to express my worries to Ron over a couple of pints, just a few evenings before we are due to carry out the walk. And little did I know that Ron was thinking the same thing. So, what to do? "We can't tell 'im we ain't doin' the walk 'e chose 'cause we don't think e's up t' it," says Ron. "And on the other hand," I continue, "we can't let him start the walk and then for him to tell us that he can't manage the hills." "Trouble is," says Ron, "'e probably wouldn't let on. 'E's the sort o'bloke that wouldn't say a thing." So we both decided to come clean and explain to Derek our worries and, thankfully, he accepted our thoughts and we have decided to do a different walk that is not too distant from Littlington. In fact

Alfriston Church

it is a walk we have completed before, and is written about in one of our other books[131]. I know it is one of Ron's personal favourites and I'm sure nothing has changed since we completed this walk in 2006 although I am hoping that I find something different to write about.

And then things didn't go to plan, again. As some will be aware I have had a couple of 'events'. Due to these I am constantly being seen by doctors for one reason or another. My medication has recently been changed and I have some discomfort. Because a doctor thought that I should not be taking a certain dosage of a tablet he halved the dosage, and, because of this, things are not working as they should. So the walk has to be postponed yet again. Luckily for us (?) on the day we were to carry out the walk it snowed hard, so I didn't feel too guilty about postponing our little walk.

Thankfully, after a few days I'm back on my usual medication, I'm feeling a little better, although more trips to the surgery are arranged, but more importantly the snow didn't last long and it has come to the time when we must brave the elements. For reasons that I'm unsure about we are unable to carry out the walk on our favoured Wednesday afternoon so it will be done on a Thursday afternoon instead. Which was a real shame because Wednesday was a gloriously sunny day and Thursday turned out to be the exact opposite. We set out from the King's Head at just after 1.30 in the afternoon. It's been raining

Market Cross

hard on and off all morning. I noticed that Derek was wearing casual shoes and I was going to mention the expected mud but, I don't know why, I didn't say anything.

---

[131] 'Left or Right Ron?' by Graham Pollard, Walk 5, Page 17, 1st March 2006

A sailor's tomb?

Unfortunately it turned out that I should have said something, because all was not well when we got halfway round our circular walk. But all will be revealed……..

The church at Alfriston, dating from the 14th century and dedicated to St. Andrew, can be found in The Tye, which is located behind the main road. Once you are in the village it is signposted at regular intervals but I have found that as you approach the village from the Drusillas Zoo roundabout there is a pay-and-display car park on the left which is an ideal starting point for this walk. There is a wonderful story about why the church is built where it is. Apparently the villagers tried to build the original church on open land very close to the houses in the village, but work was constantly interrupted because every morning they found the stones they had laid the previous day had been uprooted and thrown through the air onto the large mound on the Tye. The villagers didn't know if this was the work of the devil or a sign from Heaven, to be obeyed. The puzzle was eventually solved when four oxen were seen lying together on the Tye with their rumps touching forming an equal armed cross. The sacred symbol, created by innocent beasts, settled the problem, which is why the church is where it is, and has the shape that it has.[132]

As always, a trip inside the church is called for. As you will all be aware I have this phobia about church organs playing and the last time I came here I had to leave the church when the organist started giving it 'some wellie' but today all was peace and quiet. This is one of my favourite churches. It has so much atmosphere and, because it is built in the shape of a cross, it holds a little more interest. Derek hasn't set foot inside this church before and loved the serenity and peacefulness. Just outside is a tomb to William Thomas Harris Evans who used to be at sea? At least that is what is assumed, simply because of the style of the memorial. It has a rustic cross atop a large boulder with a ships anchor resting against the cross. A very touching memorial, especially if you read the inscription on all four faces. It is as we are leaving the church that Derek

Complex stained window

says, "Used to know a bloke, years ago. We always called him Captain. Never knew his real name but when I asked him if he was really a captain he said he was. Then I asked him what was he a captain of and he told me that he used to be on a steam powered submarine." Now I'm not sure if Derek is telling a yarn but he assures us that it was true, "When they submerged," he continues, "they used to have to lower the funnel and seal it off." It wasn't until I got home and looked it up did I appreciate that steam-powered submarines actually existed. Experiments as early as 1800 were taking place to perfect a

---

[132] 'The Lore of the Land' by Westwood and Simpson – Published by Penguin - Page 722

submersible fighting ship that could be driven by steam. One successful pioneer was an Englishman called George Garrett who, in 1879, designed a new type of boat. His boat, the Resurgam, steamed underwater for 4-5 hours at speeds of between 2-3 knots. Garrett's experiments were so successful that they attracted interest from all over the world. Further submersibles were tried and some of these early vessels were in operation during the First World War[133]. So, as unreal as it may seem, Derek's 'captain' was telling the truth.

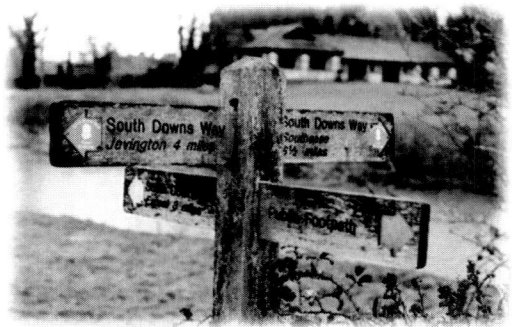

Clear signs

We leave the church and head towards the white bridge to our left. Those who have followed our walks will be aware that on our visits here the water level of the River Cuckmere, which flows under this bridge, was very shallow. I'm not sure whether it is

Over the wooden bridge

due to the amount of snow or the abundance of rain that we have experienced during this long winter but the water level now flowing under our feet was exceptional. Thankfully the rain is holding off as we stroll over the bridge and head along the clearly marked footpath, heading towards the road which will take us to Litlington. One of the reasons for taking this walk at this time of year was to see the abundance of snowdrops that seem to be everywhere in Alfriston. But our last visit here, if memory serves me correctly, was around March time and as now it's early February I feel we are a bit too early to see them at their best. Ron seems to think we may be a bit too late, as the weather, although very wet, temperatures have been slightly warmer than usual and he thinks the snowdrops may have flowered sooner. We'll just have to wait and see, because although some of the flowers were out at the church I have known it to be a blanket of white and today it wasn't such a spectacular picture.

At the end of the path, just before the road, we come to a small wooden bridge over a little stream. The water is crystal clear and we stop and admire the flowing water before heading towards the road and turning right. Just in front of us, just before we turn right, is a very old flint barn. The inscription reads, 'Built in 1698 – Restored in….?. "He's dead, you know," says Derek, "'oo is?" asks Ron, "the bloke that built that barn," is the reply as he continues to walk along the road.

In our previous walks in Alfriston we have turned off the road here and walked along the fields and paths but I'm very conscious of Derek's footwear and it is obvious that the field paths are going to be very muddy and slippery. We also need to climb uphill along this stretch of the walk so I decided to keep to the road. The views to our right take in the magnificence of Alfriston church standing high on the mound of the

---

[133] 'Steam-Driven Submarines' by Michael. L. Hadley – Published in 1988 – Pages 57-61

Tye. The discussion between the three of us now turns towards Derek's much loved wife, Elizabeth. "Her ashes are scattered over the Long Man, you know," says Derek, "and that's were I want to be when I'm gone." I ask Derek why Elizabeth's ashes were scattered at the Long Man. "We used to go there often," reminisces Derek, "she loved it there. You know it's been a year on Saturday, since she's been gone." Today is Thursday. "My daughter, Susan, is coming down from Worthing to be with me over the weekend," he continues, "probably to make sure her old dad's ok. It's going to be very difficult for us. We'll be heading for the Long Man on Saturday and probably have a meal at the Giants Rest. Do a nice meal there." Neither Ron nor I knew what to say. So we hoped our silence helped in some way.

The church in the distance

To break the melancholy feeling it was Derek who cracked a story about one of his colleagues being caught in the wrong place during his career with the Railways. This person, who, according to Derek was a bit of a rough diamond, was travelling in a first class carriage when he shouldn't have been. The guard confronted the man who, in very colourful language, told him what he thought of the guard. The result of the story had me and Ron in hysterics but, due to publishing rules I am unable to tell the story as it was told to us. But if you see Derek, ask him to re-tell the story. It is very funny!

Putting theory into practise

The road ahead is closed to traffic due to resurfacing work but we are told by one of the workmen that we could pass and get to the pub, The Plough and Harrow, which, the workman tells us is open all day. On our left is a large house with a very private drive. Padlocks on the gates, and a security system, gives us some idea that the occupants don't like visitors strolling up the drive. But they did have a fantastic show of snowdrops on the bank-side which begged to be photographed. So I tried to remember my theory with the 35mm SLR and hoped that the foreground and background were slightly out of focus but the centre was in focus. I think the picture is ok.

I mentioned a workman, but shortly we came across more than one workman. In fact there were another four. All standing across the road by a large lorry. All wearing the obligatory hard hat. All pointing at the road and, needless to say, all doing absolutely nothing but watching the one man who we had spoken to earlier. The only one working.

But shortly after this we come to Litlington church on our right. The notice on the gate informs us that the church is open to the public from 10.30 'or thereabouts' so

A touching reminder

we head for the door. We explain to Derek my phobia with church organs whilst I try the door. It's locked. It's now 3 o'clock in the afternoon so, according to the sign it should be open. We decide to just look around the grounds. Ron has spotted a war grave and heads towards it. The stone is in remembrance of a W. Stobbart from the 14th (Kings) Hussars who sadly lost his life on the 4th December 1918. He was a married man, 31 years of age and lived at Church Farm[134]; just next door to the church where he is buried. At the base of the stone has been left a wreath of poppies, presumably from the Remembrance Day service in November. Not an uncommon sight in our graveyards you must admit, but it is the first memorial I've, personally, seen in remembrance of a 'Shoeing Smith'.

It is just a short walk from the church to the Plough and Harrow. Again those familiar with our walks will remember my confusion when Ron and I first came to this little pub. I thought it was called the Plough and Arrow and said so in the book but I was confused by Ron's pronunciation. On our first trip we were also not able to try the ale in the pub because, at that time, it was closed. But not today. We are warmly greeted by the staff and Derek is first to the bar and ordered the drinks. "Blimey," says Ron, "that ain't bad look, fish an' chips fer a fiver." "Where did you see that?" I ask. "On that board, over at the end o'the bar," replies Ron. Now my eyes aren't that good but I couldn't see fish and chips, and tell Ron so. "Tis at the top o'the menu," says Ron a little agitated, "it says 'addock an' chips an' somethin' else I can't quite make out. But it's a fiver look." I now know where he's looking and have a little giggle. "What's up?" asks Ron, "That isn't haddock and chips, Ron," I explain, "it's haddock and potato soup with a baguette." "But that can't be right," says Ron, heading towards the blackboard for a closer inspection, "yer can't 'ave ter pay a fiver fer a bloody bowl o'soup." When he came back to his pint of Harvey's he was complaining about the cost of the food. I noticed that the cheapest meal on the board was over ten pound. "Still," says Derek, "the beer isn't bad. I've tasted worse." "P'rhaps yer right" agrees Ron, "but it ain't as good as it is at the 'ead."

Ron and Derek at the Plough & Harrow

We leave the pub after just one drink (honest!) and turn left, heading back in the direction we came until we come to a little public footpath on our left which will take us back to the River Cuckmere and our route back to Alfriston. It is here that we made an error of judgement. I really can't blame the

---

[134] http://www.roll-of-honour.com/Sussex/Litlington.html visited 21/02/2010

others; after all, they were following me. What we should have done was turn right as soon as we reached the river. If we had done that we would have been on the much dryer stretch of the river bank. But we didn't do that. At the end of the path we turned left and crossed the bridge to the other side of the river. This stretch of the bank, on the way back to Alfriston was very muddy, very wet and, above anything extremely slippery. And yes, it happened. I said earlier that Derek's shoes were not meant for walking in the countryside. And I was proved right. I decided that as the path was a little narrow I would lead. I was hoping to locate some less perilous stretches of dry ground but the first that I realised of the error of my ways was when I heard a "aarrghhhhhuck it!!!"

We're on the wrong side of the river now!

Nearly home!

Derek is flat on his face. His feet had slipped on the mud and down he went. "Went down like a sack o'potatoes," explained Ron, in-between giggles. "Help us up lads," says Derek, "it only takes me seconds to get down here but it'll take me ages to get up if you don't help me." To be honest both Ron and I panicked. If anyone could have seen us, slip sliding about as each one of us grabbed a shoulder and hoisted Derek back on his feet they would have thought it a comedy show. Thankfully Derek wasn't physically hurt but I think his pride took a bit of a bashing. His leather jacket was covered in mud as was his trousers and shoes. Luckily we could all see the funny side of it after it had happened but it could have been really nasty. Derek is a big bloke and it worried me that although he was ok now he could be covered in bruises by the morning. If only we had taken the other turning none of this would have happened. Derek was clearly shaken by the experience even though he put on a very brave face. For the remainder of the walk back to Alfriston he was very unsteady on his feet. Even with the help of Ron's thumbstick Derek took the remainder of the walk at a very steady pace.

We are greeted at The Post Office in Alfriston by Beverly and her staff like we are long-lost relations. Derek is a little embarrassed about his appearance but they all invite him in and offer to clean him up a bit. But Derek will hear nothing of it and heads back outside and waits for both Ron and me. Every time we come to Alfriston we always stop and buy some of their delicious pies. It's become a bit of a pilgrimage for us but Emelia, my wife, loves the steak and stilton pie and the cheddar and bacon tarts are to die for. As Ron says, a little pricey but delicious.

So another eventful walk comes to an end. As we have done this walk a few times I'm hoping that Ron will resist the temptation of the 'pie shop' and we can now put this one to bed. We've seen Derek since the walk and he's fine. Nothing broken and, thankfully, no bruises. It did take him some time to clean his clothes but he is ok. As he said he should have looked where he was going. But I will take the blame. Next time, I'll think before I act.

A muddy Derek

So, what do we think of the pictures. Personally I'm not too happy. Although I ended up with 36 photographs from the film they cost me £6.50 to process. If I had used the digital camera I could have taken over 200 pictures with no outlay. Scanning the filmed images with a flat bed scanner and then saving them onto the computer was very time consuming. Downloading from the digital camera is much, much faster. I'm also not too happy with the colours on the filmed images. The colours seem too harsh. Perhaps it has something to do with the way I used the camera, I'm not sure. With the digital camera it is just a case of point and shoot, whereas the SLR had to be set up for every shot, focused and shutter speed checked. All in all it is so much easier to use the digital camera. So that is what I'll be using in the future. But at least I've found out that my old camera can still take half decent pictures.

I would like to thank Derek for his company on this walk. His humour and knowledge were appreciated by us both. We hope that his trip back to the Long Man with his daughter, Susan, gives him strength. Sadly I only met Elizabeth on a couple of occasions but her warmth and friendliness will stay with me.

Both Ron and I appreciate that Derek may not be as nimble as either of us. I didn't actually witness Derek 's little mishap when he fell flat on his face like '...a sack o'potatoes', but Ron, who was walking close by, has awarded Derek 9.6 for artistic impression and 9.8 for degree of difficulty. Not quite as good as my perfect 10 when I came a cropper on a walk around Waldron. On that occasion I cracked a rib! Which only proves that it can happen to any of us? So watch it. Next time it could be you.

Coastal Walk

Today is a bit of a downer. We have just learnt that one of our dear friends and followers, who has walked and drank with Ron and me, has lost his fight for life at the age of 71. Sadly Mally, who 'walked' with us in Chapter 3[135] of this book, has passed away in hospital after a long illness. Our thoughts and prayers go to his wife Sheila and his family. The King's Head will not be the same without his cheerful smile and witty comment. The story of him swapping his wheelchair for a helicopter in the chapter 'Wheelchair Walk' gave everyone a giggle. I'm told the photograph of him standing by the helicopter waving at the camera has pride of place on his wall at home. Mally's ability to make people laugh was a credit to him, even when people were taking the 'mickey'. One of the things that Mally would have loved to have done was walk along the cliff top at Beachy Head. Due to his illness, and being confined to a wheelchair if he needed to go any distance, this walk was not possible for him. So, living, as we do in Sussex, we have decided that we must include a walk that will incorporate the wonderful rolling South Downs and Beachy Head.

So this walk is for Mally, who will always be with us.

Beachy Head Lighthouse

I have decided not to use the 35mm SLR camera for the remainder of these pages. It is too time consuming and, to be honest, it's a bit long winded when all I need is a simple picture. With my digital camera it's just a case of 'point and shoot' so it couldn't be easier. So, on a cold March afternoon, but it is a Wednesday, we head towards the Beachy Head pub. I've never been to this pub but I'm sure Ron can tell me how to get there. "No idea," says Ron when I ask for directions, "only ever played darts there," he says. "So you must know how to get there then," I say. "Why must I?" asks Ron, "when we went in the dark an' I wasn't drivin'" "So you've no idea how to get to the Beachy Head pub?" I ask, "Not a clue," is the reply, "but there's no need ter worry 'cause we got all afternoon ter find it." The one thing that did surprise me was that the book we are using today[136] doesn't give any directions to our start point. Yes it gives a section of map but if you didn't know the area at all you could have problems finding the place. The book does, however give GPS waypoints???? This tells us that we need to get to TV 590 959. But seriously, if you don't know where Beachy Head is by now there must be something wrong. Obviously I am aware of the cliffs location and I can only assume that the pub must be pretty close. So I drive towards where I think the pub must be.

Just for the record I have done some checking on Beachy Head facts. Locals will be aware that people come from miles to throw themselves over the 535 foot-high cliffs. They drive over, fall over, some jump or, occasionally, you get someone being pushed. Eastbourne Parish Registers contain entries of deaths at Beachy Head dating from the

---

[135] Chapter 3, page 15
[136] Jarrold Short Walks, Sussex and South Downs ISBN 978-0-7117-2424-2

1600's. So, it's not a new idea to plummet to the bottom. By the middle of the 20th century there was an average of 6-7 deaths per year but at the end of the 1900's this had increased to 17 per year.[137] Could this be an indicator of the times we now live in? I don't know. But looking over at Ron, as we head up the road towards Beachy Head, he doesn't seem to have a care in the world.

Belle Toute in the distance

As I said we are using a book titled 'Jarrold Short Walks' and the walk we are to complete can be found on page 66.[138] The book describes the walk as a '...*exhilarating and highly scenic route across Beachy Head with magnificent views westwards along the coast.*' "That means plenty ov'ills," says Ron as we pull up in the pay-and-display car park beside the Beachy Head Countryside Centre. This centre is next to the Beachy Head pub but we are not permitted to use the pub car park unless we are going into the pub for a drink. Today I have no intention of having a drink. Ron is gutted but I'll explain my reasons later. Our walk is to be 5 miles in length and should, according to the book, take us 2½ hours to complete. What the book didn't tell us was how cold it was going to be. Perhaps I had the heating in the car too high but when we got out of the car the temperature dropped dramatically. It was freezing. Not only was it very cold but the wind seemed to make you feel colder. It went right through our clothing. Before we had left the car park and passed the ice cream seller (honest) I couldn't feel my fingers. "Don't fancy a lolly then?" asks Ron. "You must be joking. I can't see anybody wanting to buy an ice cream in this weather. Must be some sort of a moron to come out here in this temperature thinking anyone is stupid enough to want an ice cream." "The answers no, then," says Ron with that silly grin, "just thought I'd ask."

A long walk ahead

Our first instruction is to cross the road, turn right and head in the direction of the Belle Toute lighthouse. Our instructions tell us that we are now on what is called the South Downs Way, but we have no signs telling us this. The wind is very strong and if I need to communicate to Ron I have to shout or he will never hear me. I'm sure it's getting colder! Just in front of us is what looks like a brick wall. When we get closer we find that it is, in fact, the remains of an old watchtower which has been converted into a resting place, complete with bench seats. "Bet this place 'as seen more than a little action,"

---

[137] http://www.forensicmed.co.uk/beachy_head.htm - visited 04/03/2010
[138] Page 65 – Walk 18 titled 'Beachy Head'

shouts Ron, "an' I don't mean durin' the war," he giggles, "'andy little place ter bring the girlfriend, this is, all secluded an' in the middle o'nowhere." The watchtower, according to the plaque on the wall, was in use during the Second World War when the Royal Observer Corp kept a lookout across the English Channel for enemy aircraft. The plaque is also to commemorate the Dieppe Raid, in 1942, which was partly controlled by the Radar Station close to this point. As we now head towards Belle Toute, in the grass in front of us is a little stone pillar with the following words:

MIGHTIER THAN THE THUNDERS OF MANY WATERS,
MIGHTIER THAN THE WAVES OF THE SEA,
THE LORD ON HIGH IS MIGHTY

Psalm 93:4

God is always greater than all our troubles

It is signed MB. The significance of these words in the Psalm are obvious, with its connection to the sea and where we are standing, but the words '…God is always . ….etc.' I'm not too sure about. Ron thinks it has something to do with the before

The 'up's and downs'

mentioned deaths over the cliffs, which are only a short distance from where we are now standing, but I also wonder who MB is, and why place the stone here, in the grass, in the middle of nowhere. But we must get on, and the lighthouse doesn't appear to be getting any closer as we battle against the headwind. Because we are on the South Downs what goes up, must go down and it is very noticeable how much warmer it gets when we are in the down part, compared with the up bit. "It's like bein' in the Bahama's down 'ere," says Ron as we drop down into yet another dip in the walk. "'Ter think, I was only goin' ter wear a jacket fer this walk," he continues. As he puts on a woollen hat underneath his 'Harvey's' hat so that he can keep his ears warm. "They won't believe us, at the King's 'ead, 'ow perishin' cold it is out 'ere. T'was lovely an' warm back in 'ailsham when I was waitin' ter be picked up."

Before we arrive at the base of Belle Toute I venture towards the cliff edge to get a photograph of the lighthouse that has been present since the early 1900's. The picture can be seen at the start of this chapter and is one picture that I've always wanted to take but, for some reason, didn't get round to. It was noticeable how far away from the cliff edge Ron stood whilst I took this picture. But this particular lighthouse wasn't the original. It is thought that as early as 1670 a light has shone from the top of these cliffs and it was in 1828 that James Walker erected Belle Toute Lighthouse on the headland. This remained in operation until 1899 when it was abandoned due to being frequently shrouded in mist and threatened with collapse because of recurrent falls of chalk from the cliff. In 1902 the current lighthouse was brought into service. 3,660 tons of Cornish granite was used in the construction of the tower. Beachy Head Lighthouse is 43 metres high and is sited 165 metres seawards from the base of the cliffs. The station gives out a

Belle Toute Lighthouse

The long driveway to Cornish Farm

Birling Gap, in the distance

white group flash of light with the intensity of 880,000 candelas, twice every 20 seconds which can be seen 25 sea miles away. This lighthouse was manned until June1983 but is now monitored 24 hours a day from the Trinity House Operations Control Centre at Harwich in Essex. On January 12th 1999 a huge part of the cliffs, immediately behind the lighthouse fell into the sea. Thousands of tons of chalk rubble, loosened by a winter of wet weather and storms (sounds familiar) collapsed to form a new spit of land reaching almost to the base of the tower. At the time, this cliff fall was said to be the biggest collapse of the cliffs in living memory. The cliff fall came as a big shock to the inhabitants of the privately-owned Belle Toute lighthouse that stands just feet away from the edge of the cliffs[139]. Their plans to move their home back from the edge of the cliffs were accelerated. I seem to remember that the Trinity Lighthouse was up for sale and was due to be de-commissioned. So another piece of history is likely to disappear.

We've walked all this way, from the Beachy Head pub to Belle Toute, and haven't seen a sign informing us that we are on the South Downs Way. I suppose having the lighthouse to aim for we didn't need signs but, according to our instructions we have now reached point 'A' of our walk. This is at the base of the lighthouse. Just as an aside, have you any idea where the name Belle Toute comes from? I thought it was French; Belle meaning 'Beautiful' and Toute meaning 'All'. But, apparently the origin is Saxon, derived from 'Bel', the name of an early Pagan deity and 'Toot' for 'Lookout'.[140]

The temperature is still falling as we cross the road, at the base of Belle Toute, and head up the concrete drive towards Cornish Farm, where, would you believe we meet our first sign. "That's 'cause we're near the road," says Ron, "shan't see another sign till we 'ead back on another road. You see if we don't. Always the same in East Sussex," he moans, "too lazy ter get off their ar?@s an' put signs out in the middle o'nowhere, ok if it's near a

[139] http://www.solarnavigator.net/history/beachy_head_lighthouse.htm - visited 04/03/2010
[140] http://www.belletoute.org.uk/belletoute.html - visited 04/03/2010

road. Get ter the middle o'the walk the signs'll disappear. You'll see."

And, of course, he was right. "See that, down there," Ron points to our left. "Birling Gap that is. When I used ter work fer the Council we 'ad ter clean the beach down there. Cleaned the beach of oil, we did. 'Ad ter fill buckets o'the stuff and walk up the steps ter empty the bucket 'cause we couldn't get any machines on the beach. At the top o'them steps there was a café. An' I'm goin' back a few years, but even then beans on toast was over a quid, and that tight ol' ba%^ard never even offered us

Not a sign in sight!

a cup o' tea. All the time we were there. Cor 'e was tight. Never forget 'im." The temperature is still dropping but I think Ron is warming to the walk.

Before we actually get to the farm we need to turn right, through a wooden gate and continue along an enclosed grassy track. As Ron said, not a sign to be seen. But I knew where to turn simply because I'd walked this part of the walk before. From this point it is a long stretch, nearly 2 miles, before we come to another instruction. All we need to do is follow the fence, in a straight line, for 2 miles. The views along this part are outstanding, if you like views of fields and rolling countryside. Personally I find it pretty but…. it's still very, very cold and the wind is now in our faces which makes the going even more difficult and it feels even colder. It's about now that I'm wishing I hadn't had that cup of coffee just before I picked Ron up. I'm not sure if it's just me, or does this happen to anyone else, but when I get cold, I mean really cold, nature seems to call at the worst time. The fact that we are now struggling up and down hills, with the wind blowing hard in our faces, it is very difficult to talk with each other. This seems to make matters worse because you start to think. And I think natures call has to be answered but we are in the middle of nowhere, only the cattle to keep us company and not a tree in sight. (I wonder why men always look for a tree.) Not only that, but memories of Alan peeing on an electric fence came flooding back to me, I thought I'll 'hang on'. But nature was having none of it! In the distance I can see a clump of trees. Now I'm not sure if Ron noticed but I quickened the pace a little. I was discrete but I really needed to get to a tree very soon. I can't tell you how cold it was but perhaps, just between us, I can. Have you ever heard of a Ninja? Basically he is a killing machine. A man who can enter a

Only trees in the distance

building, kill his opponent and leave without anyone knowing he was there. It was the Scottish comedian, Billy Connolly, who told a story about how a Ninja, when about to go into a fight, has the ability to withdraw all his genitalia into his body. This protects his vital bits should a kick be directed between his legs during the fight. Well, as we all know, this happens to us men, but naturally, when we get very, very cold. It was that cold by the time I got to that tree, and tried to have a wee, that I thought I must be a Ninja. Thankfully, after making sure which way the wind was blowing, nature was eventually relieved and all was well.

From the seclusion of the trees we make our way along the 2 mile path still with the fence guiding us in a straight(ish) line. In the distance a lady is walking her dog. Ron thinks it's probably a Labrador, and they are heading towards us. Ron has seen her and her dog long before I do. "She's got a bright red coat on," shouts Ron against the noise of the wind. I didn't see her until, in the distance I managed to see what looked like a red blob. Over the many walks that we have completed I've noticed that Ron's eyesight is far better than mine, and I wear glasses. Due to my diabetes I have to have my eyes checked every year. I'd just had mine checked and paid £180 for a new glasses, (thought I'd got a bargain - buy one pair get another pair free. The pair I brought had a price ticket of £70 so how come I end up paying £180?? – but that's another story) But like I say, Ron's eyesight is much better than mine and I don't know why. He thinks it's his chaste lifestyle and sensible eating habits but I'm not sure. Ron can see things so much quicker than me. He points to a bird flying high and I can't even see a speck, he shows me things in the distance that I have no idea what I'm looking at, simply because I can't see it. "That's odd," shouts Ron, "she's turned round and is walking back the way she came." All I can say is, "Is she?" because, all of a sudden, the red blobs gone. Perhaps I should get my eyes tested at a different optician??

We now come to a flint wall. This flint wall went all the way round a very large field. It is a masterpiece of skill that must have taken a long time to build. But it's in the middle of nowhere. There are a few barns in the distance which, we assume, from the little map supplied in our instruction book, is part of BullockDown Farm. But the wall looks out of place. It is, obviously a very strong wall, although Ron did point out some frost damage. "Can you imagine what it must be like up 'ere in the winter?" asks Ron. I'm not sure if he's noticed the temperature or if he's now immune to the freezing cold wind that is howling around us as he asked that question. I don't think it needed an answer so I just looked at him. "Stupid question," says Ron as we continue, past the wall and head for the road, where, would you believe, we found another signpost.

Part of the flint wall

Heading towards Beachy Head Road

Our instructions are to cross the road and head towards Beachy Head Road by following the way marked bridleway. At last, we started to head downhill and, hopefully, a bit of warmer weather. The path was easily found and, in the distance we could see Eastbourne spreading out before us. At a little woodland we turn right and, I must admit that the shelter offered by the trees was very welcome, the temperature started to rise and the walk was more comfortable but it was short-lived. Because it wasn't long before we were out in the open again and heading back to the car park where we had left the car only 2 hours ago. But before we got to the car, on our left, was a young couple out for a stroll. The wind was now at our face and the chill factor must have been well below zero. But the couple must have been in love. They were walking hand, in hand. Looking at each others eyes, smiling, and laughing, without a care in the world. She was wearing a summer frock and a hoodie. She had on large dark glasses and summer shoes. She must have been frozen! Yet it didn't show on her or her boyfriend. "If you were a gentleman, you'd offer that girl your coat," I said to Ron. "If I were'nt so bloody cold she could 'ave me 'at, coat and anything else I could offer ter keep 'er warm," replies Ron. "But what about the boyfriend?" I ask, "'e can 'ave your bloody coat." says Ron, "I'll stick with the young lady!"

Not a bad walk, this. Bitterly, bitterly cold but I think it was worth it for the views which would have been even better if we had carried it out later in the year. Mally would have enjoyed it. Although there were no stiles, only gates, the ground underfoot was a bit uneven and it would not be possible to complete this walk with a wheelchair. As there were no churches, or a visit to a public house, on this walk I'll probably have to make up for it on the next one. Hopefully my diabetes will have improved enough for me to attempt some alcohol?

I wonder how far you could see on a clear day.

Village Walk (East Sussex)

This walk was a last minute thing. Over the past few days a number of people have been asking about our next book, this one. And it came to me that it had been taking too long to get this particular book completed. So I've decided that it is time to get my act together and finish our last walks. Originally I had set out to complete 50 walks, and this is number 28 so we've got a fair way to go. Also I wanted a theme for each walk. That is why each walk is titled the way it is. But as time has progressed it has become increasingly difficult to find titles for the walks that I, personally, have wanted to do with Ron. So a little license has been taken with titles, I hope you don't mind.

Of course I have been reminded, on more than one occasion that I should be taking it easy and not traipsing around the countryside with someone whose no spring chicken (sorry Ron, not my words, honest) but whilst I appreciate everyone's concerns, and I include my wife and family in this, I just love to be out in the fresh air. But unfortunately my health has had some effects on what I can and can't do. More recently, as some will know, my doctor has had to change my medication which means that I am not permitted alcohol. "Yer mean, none at all?" asks Ron with a real worried look. And that's exactly what I mean. "But when we goes fer a walk," continues Ron, "does it mean that we can't stop fer a drink," And of course it doesn't, but I have to resist the temptation to have a pint and the easiest way of doing that is to keep out of pubs for a few days or weeks until I get used to it. As I've been visiting the King's Head for more years than I dare to remember it may not be so easy, but I must try really hard. So our first walk, after letting Ron know about my alcohol ban, is a short walk that doesn't include a pub. I'm sure Ron will understand.

The Church of St Alban, Frant

We have completed a village walk in West Sussex[141] so to balance things up we need a walk in East Sussex. And I think I've found just the walk. A few days ago Ron went to a birthday party. The party was for a lady who was born in 1910. 100 years ago. In anyone's language that is a great age to be. The lady was born in Frant. I have passed through Frant on many occasions but never stopped. Why should I? There's nothing there. Just a village green, a few houses and that's it. But do yourselves a favour. Next time you arrive at Frant village green, on the way to or from Tunbridge Wells don't keep going, but turn off, into the village and visit the magnificent church. I promise, if you like churches, you will not be disappointed.

---

[141] Page 58

So it was on a warm Wednesday afternoon that I pick Ron up and head for Frant. Of all the things we could talk about on the drive we end up by discussing badgers. Not alive, pretty black and white creatures which turn out to be one of Ron's favourite animals, but the amount of dead ones we see on the side of the roads. "Never used ter see it," grumbles Ron, "council always used ter come an' pick 'em up," he continues, "take 'em away and test 'em fer that t'berculosis, yer know, that TB disease. But what 'appens now is they leaves 'em ter

High Street, Frant

rot by the side of the road. It ain't right." But what is strange, and why we got onto the subject of badgers, is the numbers of dead ones. It seems nearly every road you drive down you see a dead badger. "That's 'cause they use the same route ter get about," Ron tries to explain, "they've been usin' the same routes fer centuries." But I'm still not sure why so many are getting killed.

But back to our walk. We arrive at Frant and park in what is called the High Street. The fact that a small village has a street called a High Street must be unusual in itself. Probably because I'm used to seeing shops on a High Street and Frant High Street certainly isn't what I imagine as a shopping mall. In fact it has one shop and, I'm afraid to point out, a pub called The George, right next to the church. Perhaps Ron didn't notice it? But what I must do, before we get started is to let you know something about today's

The church interior

walk, which can be found in a book titled 'Village Walks in East Sussex'[142]. The walk is described as being 3 miles in length and is '… *short and easy, almost entirely through woods and open parkland.*' But we don't take any notice of that now, do we??

I'll give Ron credit, as we headed towards the church we had to pass The George, and he didn't even look at the building, let alone make a comment about 'having a jar when we get back'. But we both headed straight for the lych-gate of this beautiful church. As I said earlier this church is a real gem. Surprisingly large for such a small village but it certainly has appeal. The church is relatively modern, by church standards, being built a few years before Queen Victoria came to the throne (1837). The original church was constantly in need of repairs, being somewhat ramshackle and it was during these repairs that a boy was killed by falling stonework.

---

[142] 'Village Walks in East Sussex' by Ben Perkins, Published by Countryside Books – Walk 12

The result was that in 1819 the church, apart from the tower, was demolished, and construction of the new church was completed by 1821[143]

But it wasn't just the interior of the church that was so appealing. Leaving the church and heading down the right-hand side of the building you find yourselves in one of the most peaceful churchyards that we have seen with some interesting memorials, one of which I will detail here. It is the grave of John Harvey who, *"...was killed by a stone which stands at the foot of his grave falling on him from the top of the old tower of this church on 19th November 1818, aged 19 years'*.

The kissing gate, at the start of the walk

The view towards Tunbridge Wells

As we head towards the far corner of the churchyard, looking for the starting point of our walk we notice, sitting on one of the benches, a very old couple gazing across the churchyard. They answer our greeting but seem very intent at looking elsewhere. Perhaps they were checking out the best place to be laid to rest, who knows, but you couldn't find a nicer place. I have many books on Sussex but one describes this church as *'...rebuilt in 1821, and is unworthy of so charming a place...'*[144] but don't you believe it!!!

We find the kissing gate in the bottom of a perilous slope in the far corner of the churchyard. This is the start of the walk. There wasn't much of the kissing gate left but our directions now take us along a field edge with extensive views towards Tunbridge Wells. "Used ter play football 'ere," says Ron, "when I played fer Upper Dicker it was. Beat Frant 6 nil we did. 'Ad ter chase the sheep off the field before we could start playin'. Not only that but after we got changed we 'ad ter walk through the 'lotments ter get to the field an' then walk back through the 'lotments before we could get changed back again. The pitch still 'as a slope on it."

The 'level grassy path'?

[143] 'A Short Guide to Frant Church & Churchyard' purchased at the church – 50p
[144] 'Sussex' by F G Brabant, M.A. The Little Guide – First published in 1900 by Methuen & Co

After a few yards of casual walking we come to what is described as a '...*pleasant level grassy path which contours along a gentle slope.*' We need to turn right here. But our 'grassy path', over the years, has turned into a gravel drive. The views along here take you into Kent. As soon as I mention our neighbouring county I had a feeling that Ron would have to say something. I wasn't disappointed. For the next few minutes I heard about the cricket teams, and how Kent beat Sussex. "But it's only a game, Ron," I offer but that only made matters worse. Apparently it's more than a game, it's cricket. But as we discuss the finer points of leg before and silly mid off (whatever they are??) I notice a lady out exercising her dog approaching from our right. You will all be aware of my love of things on four legs (?) and this one was to be no exception. Whilst the lady was cheerfully telling us about the virtues of the village of Frant and the fact that a new school was going to be built and that cricket was still played on the green and, yes, football was played on the slope on most Saturday afternoons, the dog, which I believe was a cross between a jack russell and a crocodile, rolled its lips and growled at me every time I looked at it. I wasn't sorry to wish the lady a cheery goodbye, "what a lovely lady," gushes Ron, "shame about the dog!"

It isn't the first time that our instructions do not go with what we have in front of us, because we should now come to a stile. But there isn't one. We should turn right, onto a drive, and walk towards Garden Cottage. In front of us is a pretty impressive driveway, complete with a mini round-a-bout and some very imposing metal gates. But we find Garden Cottage, just to our right. So that's ok. We then have to turn left and walk for another 30 yards before we turn left again and pass through a gate. But the gates padlocked with a sign that says 'No Public Right of Way'. So we walk back to the Cottage. It's then that a kind gentleman comes out from the back garden of Garden Cottage. He is pretending to put something in his wheelie bin but I'm positive that he was a little worried about two characters wandering outside his property and decided to investigate. He advises us that the gate is now padlocked by the new owners and we need to head for the gates and a new stile for the footpath can be found just to the right of these gates. We thank him for his help and head for the new stile. But little did we know that things were to get a little worse. Because just over the stile we

Looking towards Kent

The stile is just to the right of the gates

That!! sign

The last resting place of pets

Climbing hedgehog

find another sign that makes both Ron and me believe that 'someone's' out to get us. Of course it's that sign that tells you that the path 'has been diverted' but it doesn't tell you how, why or to where or by how much! All it says is 'official path diversion', which is about as useless as a chocolate teapot because our instructions now tell us that we are 600 yards from a road where we need to turn right. Because of this diversion that road was over a mile away! Whilst this part of the walk was pleasant, you do start to wonder if you're heading in the right direction, because all of a sudden, as is typical with most of our walks when in the middle of nowhere, all signs seem to disappear. "We must be 'eadin' fer a road," says Ron trying to encourage me. "What makes you say that?" I ask, "'Cause I can 'ear a motor," is the reply. Not a lot of comfort when your not sure if it's the correct road he can 'ear a motor' being driven along. But like I said the walk, through scrubland, was enjoyable and we did find a couple of unusual things on the way. Like the animal graveyard which nestled in the woods to our right, complete with headstones. Two stones for loved dogs and one for a much loved horse. And, of course, I must mention again the climbing hedgehog which I still find a fascinating growth on trees. The diverted path we are now on is a bit slippery and it's quiet steep in places. It doesn't look as if the path is used much so some of the brambles can get caught round your legs. I nearly went flying a couple of times, much to Ron's amusement. But be warned it can be a bit tricky if you're not careful. Thankfully we eventually arrive at the road. As I said our instructions say it is 600 yards from the previous stile and I'm hoping that we've come out at about the right place, because, according to our next instructions we should now turn right and walk along the road for about 150 yards when we should see a house called Brookfield. Again a word of warning. There is no path here and you take your life into your own hands. As we are walking along the road a 4 by 4 roared up behind us and took the left-hand bend so fast that the tyres squealed. "Bloody idiot," shouts Ron shaking his stick at nothing because the car had gone. "Did you see 'ow fast that idiot was goin'?" Ron asks, "Yes Ron," I reply. "Bloody showin' off 'e was. 'e'll be wrapped round a tree one day, you see if 'e aint!" "Yes Ron," is all I say

Uphill through Stubby Grove Wood

because, really, that's all you can say.

The house we are looking for, Brookfield, is thankfully just a few yards along this road and here we need to turn right and walk through 'Stubby Grove Wood'. Unfortunately I can't find anything about this wood in any of the books I have or on the Internet. But with such a lovely name it must mean something to somebody. What it meant to Ron and me was steep. That's steep with a capital st. "I didn't realise that we went downhill when we were in that scrubland earlier," I tell Ron as I stop, again, to get my breath. "This path is really steep," I continue, "And it's a damn long way up, too," offers Ron as he rests by some of the trees. Part of the path is also very slippery and it's obvious that the track is used by horse riders because there are a number of 'jumps' scattered about. What is surprising is that our instructions don't mention the Sewage Works we have to go pass nor the stables with its well turned out stable girl. I'm not sure if Ron saw her, because he didn't say anything, and that's not like Ron? Thankfully we manage to clamber up the hill, after a few stops for air and emerge, from the wood into a field with views towards Kent again. This time I didn't mention it to Ron!

Here we head along the field's edge until we reach a concrete drive. The owner of the land is having what looks like a new barn erected. A monster of a building with workmen clambering all over it as well as ground workers, preparing for concrete to arrive, around the edges of the construction. But what was interesting, if that's the right word, was just past the site was, what looked like, an aerial mast. And perched on every inch of the wire were pigeons. "Why do you think all those pigeons are sitting on that wire?" I ask Ron and straight away I knew that was a mistake. "Its 'cause they're females," replies Ron, "not only does the wire keep there little feet warm but they also likes the vibration," he chuckles. Personally I don't know what he means. Do you??

Our next instruction is to follow a concrete drive until we reach a redundant tarmac drive which is reverting to grass. As we head along this path I noticed, on a gatepost, three old horse shoes, pinned to the post. The bottom two I had seen before but the top one was different, in that it was an all round shoe. Ron thinks it may have been for a Shire horse but we'll have to ask an expert when we get back.

Birds on the wire?

The top shoe?

Just a short way up this drive it becomes private property with all the signs that encourage you not to go any further. Here we turn left, over a stile, and into an enclosed path which takes us out onto the road. We turn right here, again being careful because there is no path.

We now need to turn left at what is described in our instructions as '...*the imposing brick gateway to Manor Farm.*' But it isn't the brick that we found imposing but the gate is a real work of art. Why it is being left to rot on its hinges is a mystery. Because it must have taken a skilled craftsman a fair time to make this wooden gate. But ours is not to reason why, but it is certainly a nice piece of woodwork.

A marvellous wooden gate, just left to rot?

At the end of the drive our instructions are a bit off again. We are told to walk along a gravel drive towards a stile but there is no stile along a gravel drive. There is a stile on the right, just before the gravel drive. Our next instruction is to walk along the fields' edge, but the footpath runs right through the middle of the field. We are told to climb over two stiles, but there were three before we got back onto the road which would lead us back to the High Street in Frant. One strange thing, when we were heading back towards the High Street was that we couldn't see the church tower. Normally it is one of the first things that come into view when you walk into a village. But not today.

When Ron asked me how long this walk was I told him that the book says that it is 3 miles. He couldn't stop laughing. "'tis more like 5 miles if not 6," he says but that may be because of the diversion, I'm not sure. What I can say is that apart from the steep hill at Stubby Grove Wood, this was an enjoyable walk but it certainly isn't one for the less able. But, as I said at the start of this chapter, take a look at the church, it's well worth it.

Spooky Walk

This walk could also be a 'Forest Walk' because that is where we are heading, "...but you've already comp'leted a Forest Walk in previous pages," I hear you say but, let's be honest, that one was a little disappointing. I'm hoping that this one will be a lot better. The reason it is called a 'Spooky Walk' is because some strange things are said to happen in St. Leonard's Forest that involve ghosts, serpents, dragons, mysterious disappearings and, last but not least, a race against the devil. But before we get into the less than 'normal' goings on let us discuss some things about St. Leonard's Forest. First it's nowhere near St Leonard's. I must admit that when I first heard the name my immediate reaction was that there isn't a forest at St. Leonards, near Hastings. Well there isn't, is there? That's because this St Leonards Forest is between Horsham and Mannings Heath, in the west of our county. In medieval times any area of open land in private ownership was called a 'chase', while tracts owned by the king were 'forests' – whether wooded or not. St Leonard's Forest used to be owned by Henry III, and on 23rd August 1234 he made a special gift of fifty oak trees from his forest to help in the building of Chichester Cathedral.[145]

The name St. Leonard's Forest is said to come from a former chapel to St Leonard, a saint popular in the medieval period, but legend maintains that he actually lived in the forest as a hermit and on one occasion confronted a dragon and, after a long and fierce battle, he slew the dragon. As a reward for his bravery God decreed that wild lilies of the valley would grow forever at every spot where blood was shed, and that no nightingales would ever sing in the Forest again, since Leonard had complained that they distracted him from prayer.[146]

A little more recently, in 1936, there was believed to be a very unpleasant ghost in the Forest; it was a headless spectre which lurked amongst the trees at dusk waiting for some horseman to ride past, whereupon it would leap up behind him, wind its skeletal arm around his neck, and cling on till they reached the far side of the Forest. The spectre is said to be that of Captain William Powlett who died in 1746. But that is not the entire strange goings on that I have discovered about St. Leonard's Forest[147]. So, it would seem to be just the right place for Ron and me to take a stroll??

Is this supposed to be the start?

And the stroll this week is taken from another of my Ben Perkins books published by SB Publications[148] and is described as being 6¼ miles, of '...*sandy paths and tracks, mostly well-drained but can be muddy in places after heavy rain.*' The book also says that there are no stops for refreshments, so I expect we'll have to find somewhere on the way home? What could be a problem for us is the weather. The forecast for Friday is not good. Unlike the name of the day we are completing this walk;

---

[145] 'Hidden Sussex Day by Day' by Swinfen & Arscott a Radio Sussex publication
[146] 'The Lore of the Land' by Westwood & Simpson – Published by Penguin
[147] Ibid
[148] 'Classic Walks in Sussex' by Ben Perkins, Walk 16, St Leonards Forest

Good Friday. The day before was really nice, the sun was shining and the air was warm. But Friday the weather was due to change. The temperature was due to drop, the rain was due to drop, and we weren't disappointed, on both counts....

Due to the strange goings on around this walk we are to be joined by Marian and Lyn who are hoping to perhaps experience just a little of the strange phenomena that is St. Leonard's Forest. So it is on a little chilly Good Friday morning that we head towards Mannings Heath and Horsham.

As we circle the roundabout at The Boship and head towards Uckfield, on the A22, Marian, from the back seat, sits upright and says, in some panic "Where are we going? This isn't the way to St. Leonards." It's obvious that her taxi driving training has kicked in and alarm bells have started to ring.

W. Sussex hedge decoration

"We ain't goin' ter that St. Leonards," chuckles Ron, sitting next to Marian in the back of the car "we be goin' t'other St. Leonards." "Where the hells the other St. Leonards?" asks Marian, clutching the door handle by her seat. "I knew you weren't listening," interrupts Lyn, "we're going to St Leonard's Forest, near Horsham." Marian mumbles something about '…not being told anything and anyone can make a mistake…' as she settles back to enjoy the ride.

It isn't long before the discussion comes round to strange things. But we do not discuss the strange things that happen in the Forest. One of Marian's friends has a friendly ghost. "They call him 'Arthur'," explains Marian. "They've brought a very old house in Market Street and started to knock down walls and discovered all sorts of strange things. Apparently there's a grave in the back garden. They did a bit of research and they think the grave is of somebody called 'Elizabeth'." How we got onto the subject I'm not sure but does anyone from Hailsham remember a lady who used to wander around the town, wearing a face mask? She used to live in a house in Market Street somewhere and when I was working for Royal Mail she always complained about her delivery of mail. Not when it used to arrive but she insisted that the person who delivered her mail wasn't a postman and that 'that type of person was not welcome at her letter box'.

The path drops down

Apparently Ron had seen her at the cemetery and when she got to a certain grave she would say, out loud, 'there, I've made the effort again, and again, you're not here' before walking out of the cemetery. Lyn used to 'meet' her and hear her life story on a regular basis and can practically tell you her story word for word. I haven't seen her for a while now and it's thought that she now resides in a Nursing Home somewhere in Hailsham.

Whilst on the way to the Forest we pass a road, on our left, called Slugwash Lane. I think we were near Haywards Heath. The conversation now turns silly as we try to work out how the lane got its name. All sorts of theories were spoken about, most involving the 'things' that would be needed to wash slugs (that's the black slimy creatures) Marian suggested that every conversation from now on must include the word slug. That was until Ron, who had been unusually quiet in the back of the car, suggested that perhaps the word 'slug' referred to a bullet and not the black slimy creature after all.

Our book tells us to park in 'Roosthole Forestry Commission' car park. Thankfully I had studied a couple of maps of the area so had a rough idea on where to find the place. Parking was no problem, plenty of spaces, but we had a problem trying to find the start of the walk. I should have realised that we might have a problem when I read the first line of the instructions: *'From the right hand corner, just inside the entrance to the circular parking area follow the path which starts between staggered railings.'* How can you have a corner in a *'circular parking area'*? We found staggered railings but they were halfway round the car park and nowhere near any corner. I noticed that our next instruction was that the path '...*drops down through woodland...'* and this path certainly dropped so we decide to go for it.

The slippery slope to the bridge

I'm a little worried about the weather and I share my worries with Ron, "Don't you worry 'bout that," he assures us all. "It ain't gonna rain, might get a bit o'forest mist that's all. Trust me." But the forecast is for torrential rain from the middle of the day, it is now 11.30 and clouds are gathering in the distance. But we set off, wearing just short coats. This turned out to be another mistake. The ground underfoot was treacherous. Very muddy, very wet and very, very slippery. We didn't walk down to the wooden bridge that was at the

The steady climb

bottom of the steep slope, we slid most of the way. What was worrying was that what goes down must also go up and it's not long before we are trying to get back up the other side of the dip and into the Forest proper. But our instructions tell us to continue in a straight line. But there isn't a path that heads in a straight line; they all head off at different angles. The question has to be asked, are we on the right path in the first place, because I really am not sure. As yet we haven't found a single sign to let us know that we are actually on a public footpath? To quote Marian; we decided to carry on - 'sluggishly' (sorry!) I am now totally confused as to where we are and in which direction we need to head. Looking at our next instructions gives me no ideas. We should be at the top of a slope but we aren't. We should soon be dropping down again, but we are still

Can you see us in front of the tree?

heading uphill. We should cross Sheepwash Gill, whatever that is, but who knows? Not one sign on the path to let us know where we are, just path after path of mud!

We continue to climb up the slope, simply because there is little else to do. I can't find anything that remotely resembles what the book is telling us. Apparently we need to turn right at a 'T' junction – we didn't find one. We need to go across an earth dam at the head of a small pond, nothing came into sight. We've only been walking for an hour and we are lost! Did I feel a spatter of rain?

"Perhaps this is the tree that people disappear from," says Marian as we head towards a very large and old specimen. "If it is," says Lyn, "you lot can stand near it and I'll take the photographs, just in case you lot disappear," and she takes the camera from my neck. I still haven't managed to find anything about the strange disappearances but Ron insists that somebody told him about a tree which has some spooky effects. "Go on," says Lyn, "you three stand in front of the tree and I'll take a picture." We oblige with Ron and me at the front and Marian peering from behind the tree. When the picture was developed, which turned out to be the 13th picture, I, with a little computer technology, managed to obliterate all three of us. I tried to kid Lyn that the tree stories must be true, but Lyn didn't fall for it. The actual picture Lyn took is at the end of the chapter. By the way, it has started to rain! Also, I still have no idea where we are!

A clearing, but where are we?

We continue to walk around the forest hoping, or expecting, to see something that is described in the book. But I could find nothing and I'm starting to get worried. The rain is getting harder. We come to a clearing, is this Sheepwash Gill, it looks like a long path, is it Mick Mills Chase where, according to legend, Mick Mill, a local smuggler, raced with the Devil along this wide track on which no tree has been able to grow since. Or are we standing on the long distance path across the High Weald of Sussex and Kent which meanders for over 90 miles and finishes in Rye. For no other reason other than to keep walking we head for a small path in front of us. After a short distance we see who I hope is going to be our saviour. A lady is out walking her dog. She doesn't know how pleased I was to see her and, for once, her dog. After some pleasantries and a quick look at our map she tells us that we need to continue along the path we are on, turn right and once we come to the 'T' junction we need to turn right and that is Mick Mills Chase, go straight across and that would lead us to the road, which was position 4 on our map. I could have kissed her. What a very helpful lady and I'm

Is this Mick Mills Race?

sure she was totally unaware of the hope she gave me. So we head off towards Mick Mills Race and the rain is getting really heavy now. I speak to Ron. "'Tis only a forest mist," he assures me, "t'wont last long." But, by God, it did.

We find the logs, "We have to turn left here," says Marian sitting on one of the logs, "No, we have to turn right, and then we turn left. This is Mick Mills Chase, so we have to walk down the chase for a few yards and then turn left." I reply. "That lady said we have to turn left," insists Marian, "but we have to turn right at the logs, first," says Lyn. "But we've already turned right to get to the logs," says Marian. I'm getting confused again. If we are standing at Mick Mills Chase, and we have no idea really that that is where we are, then we need to turn right now, walk a few yards and then, according to our map, if we are standing on Mick Mills Chase, turn left, where the path should drop sharply deeper into the forest. An executive decision is made. We turn right. It is now throwing it down and we are getting soaked.

Thankfully something else goes right, just a few yards along this clear path is another path to our left, just as the map said. And, once we turned left, it was pretty obvious that the path dropped considerably, deeper into the forest. For the first time since starting this walk I think I have some idea where we were. But the rain was getting harder. It had already gone through my coat. The camera was also getting wet and my trousers were starting to stick to my legs. It was also getting very cold. My walking partners didn't look any better than me. In fact they looked worse.

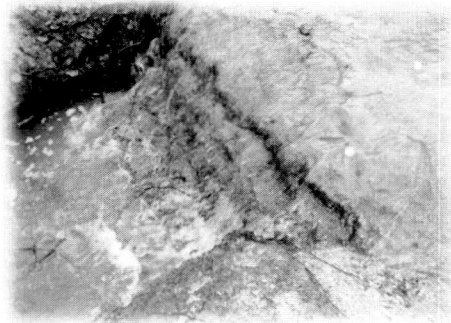

Water running down the path

Before we got to the drop in the path I decided to stop and ask what the others wanted to do. "If we carry on down this slope and the rain doesn't ease up, we've got to climb a long hill on the other side of the forest," I advise them, "what we can do is call it a day and, if we can assume that the path back there is Mick Mills Chase, we can head back along the Chase and we should, eventually arrive back at the car park." So, for the first time in four years we are beaten by the rain. It would be silly to continue. We are all soaked to the skin already. We are all getting very cold and as the rain continued to fall the paths were becoming streams. The most sensible thing to do was to turn back. All I had to do was find our way back to the car park.

Simple thing to do, just get us back to the car park. But I really had problems finding the right way to go. I kept consulting the map that came with our instructions and although I had little confidence in what I was looking at I had to assume that the map should resemble where we had to go. And I reasoned that when we reached what we

Ron is soaked.

A wooden bridge, but not the one!

hoped was Mick Mills Chase we had to turn left and walk along the chase for some time but at some point we would need to turn right. But where that point was I had no idea. And still it rained.

Thankfully the rain didn't dampen anyone's enthusiasm. Marian was still trying to suggest sentences with the word slug included. Lyn slipped a couple of times and was heard to mutter 'oh! Slug it!!" under her breath and Ron kept singing 'Teddy Bears Picnic' at the top of his voice as we headed down Mick Mills Chase, which Marian insists is an old Roman Road and that's the reason for no trees growing and it has nothing to do with the devil!

After about ¼ mile I spot a turning on the right. Our instructions tell us that should we have followed the complete route we should have come out of the forest at this lower section of Mick Mills Chase where we would have to turn left and then pick up the path on our right. I get everyone to stop and I retrace our steps back up the chase and I find another path which I will assume is the path that we should have arrived on. I go back to the group and, with a little more confidence, tell them that we are on the right path for the car park. What I didn't realise was how far it was.

If we were at where I thought we were it doesn't seem very far because the instructions read '…*turn right along a wide forest track which takes you back to the car park…*' Unfortunately, and I didn't let on to the others, but we were not on a wide forest track but a tiny public footpath. But I was sure that this path would get us back to the car, somehow. But we seemed to walk for ages. Now I was beginning to think that we had a real problem. To our left was a steep drop towards running water. All the time we were walking along this path I assumed that this running water was where we crossed over the wooden bridge at the start of the walk, all we needed was to find a way down to the bottom and, hopefully a path which would take us up to a road, or even luckier to the car park. The more we walked the more I worried until, in the distance I could see what I thought was a wooden rail leading down the slope on the left. This must be it, please let this be the right path. Very carefully we managed to get to the bottom of the slope where we found a wooden bridge. But it wasn't the same bridge we crossed over 3 hours ago, when it wasn't raining and we were looking forward to this walk. It didn't matter that it wasn't the right bridge, what did matter was getting over it because just at the other end of the bridge the water had overlapped the end of the bridge and we needed to jump across, onto some round concrete pipes. I was first across and held my hand out to help Lyn across. She didn't have too much of a problem but when I offered to help Marian she couldn't stop giggling and it took a couple of attempts before she could get across. To make sure there was room for Ron to get over, I started to go up the hill and the inevitable happened. I slipped and landed front forward. Luckily no damage was done but I could hear the laughter behind me as both Ron and Lyn doubled up. Marian didn't know what had happened and could only say, "What are you laughing at," which seemed to make the other two laugh louder. But I had the last laugh because as we approach the top of this climb I can see my car at the top of the rise. But we are all soaked to the skin and I couldn't feel my fingers.

This is not a walk for the feint-hearted, especially in the rain. I was also very disappointed with the instructions. There are no signs to guide you around the walk, nor are there any signs let you know where you are. The number of paths is confusing. The instructions from Ben Perkins are misleading from the start. For once, perhaps, compass bearings may have helped but at a couple of points I was beginning to think we would never get back to the car. The rain did do us one favour, the book of instructions that I kept having to consult during the walk is ruined, so we probably won't be using it again.

At the end of the day we decided to meet up at The Grenadier in Hailsham for a drink and a chat. Thankfully my walking partners didn't hold a grudge and the evening was a pleasant one. I'm hoping our next walk will be a little easier and much more pleasant. And, hopefully, in the dry!

Not really a disappearing tree

More a Stroll than a Walk

This walk/stroll was a last minute arrangement. We had been asked by a couple who were aware of our exploits if they could accompany Ron and me on one of our walks. What could we say? The request was made a few weeks ago, yes Ron and me are getting really popular now and people are booking us up weeks in advance! "Do I know Annette and Neal?" I ask Ron, "You will when yer meets 'em," says Ron. "But I'll introduce yer on Wensd'y," he continues, "you'll see. You'll recognise 'em, sure yer will. Somethin' ter do with camera." "What," I ask, "they take lots of pictures?" "Not that sort o'camera," chuckles Ron, "they wander round pubs, tryin' out the beer." "You mean CAMRA," I say as the penny drops, "It's the CAMpaign for Real Ale." "That's what I said," he says, "camera." For anyone unsure of what any of this means I'll try to explain. CAMRA is '...*an independent, voluntary organisation with over 100,000 members and have been described as the most successful consumer group in Europe. CAMRA promotes good-quality real ale and pubs, as well as acting as the consumer's champion in relation to the UK and European beer and drinks industry.*'[149] And let's be honest it's not a bad way to spend your spare time, is it?

But at the last minute Neal, the husband of Annette, advises us that he can't get time off work but could meet us at a start point at about 1:30 in the afternoon. Neal is a Postie based at Uckfield and, trying to be an accommodating sort of person, I thought I'd look for another walk, a little closer to Uckfield, so Neal wouldn't have to travel too far. So, on Tuesday, the day before the walk, I was frantically looking for somewhere that fitted the bill. Thankfully I found this 'stroll' in a book[150] on my shelf that would be ideal. So it was arranged that I would collect Annette and Ron at the pub, I would drive to the start of the walk where we would meet Neal, Annette's husband. Now that sounded like a plan. So I was somewhat surprised, when I pulled up at The King's Head car park to find Neal waiting for me with his wife and Ron. But the surprises didn't stop there. As I mentioned Neal is a Postie at Uckfield and the walk we were about to complete was at a village called Fairwarp. And where does Neal deliver his letters? You've guessed it, Fairwarp. So we spent the next half an hour heading back towards the place that Neal had spent all morning rushing around to get back to Hailsham in time for the walk. "Now that's what yer call a coincidence," giggles Ron who always seems to find the funny side to most things. But there is nothing for it, Neal is more than happy to walk around Fairwarp, Annette is happy and Ron is, well Ron is just Ron. So to Fairwarp we go. But what is really niggling me is that I've seen Annette somewhere before, not at the King's Head but somewhere and, for the life of me, I can't think where. But all the time we are heading towards Fairwarp I keep trying to work out where it was that I'd met Annette.

So what I can I tell you about the village of Fairwarp? Not a lot really. The place wasn't mentioned in the Domesday Book but the first written record is in the year 1519

Village sign at Fairwarp

---

[149] http://www.camra.org.uk/ - visited 21/04/2010
[150] 'Pub Strolls in east Sussex' by Ben Perkins – Published by countryside Books – Walk 6 Page 22

when it was known as Fayre Wharp and the main occupation in the area was charcoal burning which provided the heat to melt the iron produced at nearby Oldlands Farm. Just at the other side of the village, towards Nutley cannons were finished off with the centres being bored at Boringwheel Mill Farm. During the late 1700's regiments from the army were stationed at nearby Duddleswell, during the build up to the Napoleonic Wars.[151] So, apart from the charcoal burning, nothing much happened at Fairwarp but lots happened 'nearby'. "But I bet it 'as a pub," says Ron and of course in every village that has a church you will, normally, find a public house and Fairwarp has The Foresters Arms. The pub was, originally, a private house and became licensed premises in 1898. The longest reigning landlords were the Osborne's who had the Foresters for over sixty years[152].

The Foresters Arms, Fairwarp

So let's get on with the walk, or should I call it a stroll. Perhaps it could be a stride because Annette certainly took off in a rush. But first we had to overcome what I knew would be a bitter disappointment, especially to Ron... the pub closes at 2.30 and it is now 2 o'clock. "We could always 'ave a swift drink before we set off," suggests Ron. But I'd noticed the coach waiting outside the door and as we passed the windows, every table was taken up by customers sitting with meals. I needed to go in to the bar (just for politeness honest) to ask if it was o.k. to leave my car in the car park while we carried out the walk. It took some time for me to get permission simply because the people behind the bar were so busy serving a pub full of customers. (And our landlord thinks his dwindling customers is due to the recession?? There was no sign of that happening here).

Christ Church, Fairwarp

But once permission was granted it was off down the road, towards the village green where we should find a path, on the right-hand side which should lead us to Christ's Church, Fairwarp. I say should because right from the start we have a number of paths we could take and it took a little while to work out which was the correct path to take and it was thanks to Annette for steering us in the right direction but it was becoming more annoying because I knew her from somewhere. What I haven't mentioned, and think now might be a good time to bring it up, is that Neal hasn't stopped talking since we left Hailsham. "Can yer imagine," chuckles Ron, "what it'd be like ter 'ave Neal, Noel and Alan in the same car together? Yer wouldn't get a word in." And he's right Neal just didn't stop. As we approach the church I find myself with Annette. As I said Annette does stride it out and we were a little ahead of Ron and Neal, who were chatting away like long lost friends. With all the walks we have been on I have known the people we are walking with but

[151] http://www.villagenet.co.uk/ashdownforest/villages/fairwarp.php visited 22/04/2010
[152] http://www.forestersarmsfairwarp.co.uk/AboutthePub.aspx visited 23/04/2010

today it was different. Although I'm positive I've seen Annette before I am aware that I don't know either Neal or his wife. So I'm a bit worried that I might say or do something that I might regret. As we approach the door of the church I ask Annette if she was a religious person, "Yes," is the reply, "I'm Catholic and so are my children, but Neal isn't." So cracking jokes about the church is a definite no, no.

Sadly the church is locked so we are unable to get inside. The church is not that old, being consecrated in 1881, but I must admit that the churchyard is a place where you could sit awhile. Very peaceful. Very tranquil. And I find myself wandering around the church on my own. And I notice, to one side of the church very regular small humps in the ground. If you look in the pictures on the left you can just make out the humps to the left of the hedge. Are they unmarked graves? If they are, they are all very small. Could they be the graves of children? Just on the other side of the hedge are a number of larger humps. Are these the graves of the parents of the children? Again they are unmarked. I counted over twenty small mounds. What could have happened in a small village like Fairwarp to cause the deaths of so many? If, of course, that is what we are looking at. Ron thinks it could have been the plague but most 'plague pits' are located at a discrete distance away from the church and are,

Regular humps

normally, mass graves. These graves (?) are right next to the path leading round the church. Unfortunately we are unable to find out anything about them but perhaps a reader could help us out.

Our next instruction is to leave the churchyard as we came in and then turn left. We are now on the Maresfield Millennium footpath which takes us through woodland. I'm not sure if we are on the correct path because paths are leading off to the left and right and I haven't seen any marker posts. There's no point in asking Ron and Neal because they are still in deep conversation about the churchyard and Annette is striding it out in front of me. Where have I seen her before? We suddenly come upon a signpost. On checking the instructions we should now turn left here and head for the road. I read on a little and see that when we arrive at the road we should be opposite a drive leading us to Spring Garden Farm. Ron and Neal catch us up and due to my association with Royal Mail and Neal's occupation as a Postman it isn't long before we are talking about deliveries of mail, throwing off, OMV's[153], the rotation of duties and other such Royal Mail jargon. I think Annette has heard it all before. But to be honest when I was

Ron & Neal chatting away

---

[153] Royal Mail 'speak' for a van or Official Motor Vehicle (OMV)

We came out at the right place

working for 'the post' it was an enjoyable occupation. We had social gatherings, parties and, when I was manager at Hailsham I was not adverse to making all the postmen and women bacon sarnies to say 'thank you'. We always had a Christmas Raffle at Hailsham which I started to organise in August! But from what Neal was saying, and what I'd heard from some of my old colleagues, the fun has been taken out of postal deliveries. I miss the hustle and bustle of Royal Mail but I'm not sorry to be out of it really. As we come to the road we can see the entrance to Spring Garden Farm, opposite. So we did come out at the right place.

From here we cross the road and enter the drive. Just a few yards into the drive is a cattle grid. We cross the grid and bear right, heading slightly uphill walking along a forest track. We follow this broad track, ignoring all the little side tracks. Our instructions tell us that we should be heading, generally, westwards. Both Neal and Ron confirm this fact. Annette and I just keep walking. I've got to try and find out where I've seen Annette before.

Where the track splits into three we are advised to continue along the middle track which soon begins to drop down towards two footbridges. Neal and I, again, begin to discuss some of the things that we found funny at Royal Mail. Neal's story involves him tearing his trousers during his delivery and his wife, Annette, telephoning his manager to complain about a postman 'flashing' his red underwear. Neal was called into his boss's office and was informed that the complaint had been passed to a higher authority. It wasn't until

Uphill, along the forest track

he realised that the date was 1st April (All fools day) that he twigged as to what was going on.

As a manager you have to expect the unexpected. But I didn't expect one of my female members of staff to knock on my door asking to speak to me about a personal problem. When I suggested that we should have another member of staff present, which is Royal Mail policy, she refused. I then suggested that we should, at least, have her Union Representative present, she again refused. So I tentatively asked what the problem involved and she said it was about sexual harassment. Just the mention of those two words to any manager will bring you out in a cold sweat. Here I was, with a very attractive lady, alone with me, in my office, and she had a problem with sexual harassment. I chose my words with great care, "I will try to be of assistance

One of the footbridges

Ron gets close to the memorial

about this but I really need to know what sort of a problem you are having with sexual harassment." "I'm not getting any," she says with a broad grin, "and I want to know what's wrong with me." Again it was the 1st of April. I could have killed her.

We cross the first footbridge, Ron makes his customary wish and drops a coin of the realm into the water, muttering "costs me a fortune, so it does, every time I 'ave ter put money over the side an' make a wish. If me wishes all came true I wouldn't 'ave ter worry about money at all!" We now bear half-right and head uphill again towards 'The Airman's Grave'. This is a small, bricked enclosure containing a simple cross commemorating the crew of an aeroplane which crashed near here in 1941. The plane was a Wellington Mk 2 Bomber from 142 Squadron.

On the night of the 31st of July 1941 the aircraft was returning from a raid on Cologne. The weather was bad and the 'plane was flying on only one of its Rolls Royce Merlin engines, the left-hand one had stopped, and it was imperative for the pilot to reach an airfield as close to the English Coast as possible. The weather conditions were such that the aircraft mistakenly came too far, and picked up the beacon lights at Kingstanding that were intended for the guidance of returning night fighters.

Sadly, the aircraft could no longer keep going in order to reach the safety of a suitable landing place and crashed, nose down, on the southern slopes of the Forest.

All six crew members were killed on this their 13th. Wellington Mission[154]. The names and ranks on this inscription read:

First Pilot Harry Vidler 27 Hessle Hull
Second Pilot Vic Sutton 24 Sidcup, Kent
Observer Wilf Brooks 25 Ramsgate, Kent
Wireless Op/ Ernest Cave 21 Wallesey Liverpool
Air Gunner Stan Hathaway 23 Eaglescliffe, Stockton
Rear Gunner Len Saunders 21 Whitstable, Kent

In the centre of the memorial is a simple cross with the words:

To the glorious memory of
Sgt PVR Sutton aged 24 years
142 Bom. Sqdn RAF
also his five comrades
who lost their lives here
through enemy action
31-7-41

It is simply signed, 'Mother'

---

[154] http://www.ashdownforest.co.uk/Places/nutley.htm - visited 26/04/2010

Annette & reflection

We leave the memorial in silence and head further uphill, heading for an area known as 'Hollies'. But before we reach this car parking area we just have to stop, look and marvel at the views. To be honest I was getting a bit breathless and needed a little breather so that I could fill my lungs again. So looking at the views was a bit of an excuse. But you can literally see for miles. Ron starts pointing out landmarks that only Ron can see, insisting that you '…must be able ter see that," when I really, really can't. I really, really strain my eyes to see the church spires but I can't make them out and I'm not sure if Annette and Neal were saying that they could see things just to humour Ron or, in fact I am going blind?

We come to a pool on our left, just off the track. Everyone knows my love of photographing reflections so now was an opportunity to 'click away'. Even now Neal starts to relate a story about snakes and wanting to go for a call of nature which then turns into a story about volcanoes and all the time all I want to know is where I've seen his wife before. I keep looking at Annette and I'm sure she is aware of my staring and then Neal lets slip that Annette has seen some ghoulish scenes in her line of work when the subject he is talking about changes from volcanic eruptions to drinking and driving? That's it! Annette works at the local hospital. She is now a sister at the hospital. That is where I must have seen her before. She looked after me when I was in hospital some 20 years ago. Now I'm happy!

It is just a few paces from the water 'hole' to 'Hollies' which is really just a car park. Just before the car park we turn right and head along what is described as a '…wide forest ride.' We are advised that panoramic views of the South Downs will come into view and sure enough, to our right, are some fantastic views that you've got to see to believe. Now something isn't right. Our instructions tell us to keep the road to our left, I can see and hear the road. All is well. We are then told '…*where the ride divides, keep right (almost straight on)*' but we have a path that goes right and a path that goes straight on. Which one do we take? I make the decision to go to the path that

Tearooms, definitely closed

'goes right'. There aren't many times that I'm right and I'm wrong again. As Annette pointed out we should be heading towards Duddleswell Tearooms, which must be on the roadway. If we turn right, we will be heading away from the road. Why are women always so logical? So we head back.

As we approach the road Neal lets us all know that this is part of his delivery and isn't too sure if the tearooms are open on a Wednesday. They must have heard we were on the way because they were closed. Annette still wasn't convinced, even though it clearly said 'Closed' on the door she had to go and check it out.

We cross back over the road, find our path and head back along 'the ride' until we come to a point at the start of the walk. It is simply a case of retracing our steps back to the drive at Spring Garden Farm, pass the church and back to Fairwarp Village and the Forresters Arms which is, as expected closed.

"Never mind," says Neal, comforting a dissapointed Ron, "I know a little pub, not far from here that will still be open. It's called the Pig and Butcher." Sure enough, just a couple of miles down the road is a little pub who, according to both Ron and Neal serve a descent pint. I, of course stuck to orange juice. Apart from the noise of a very spoilt child who, let's be honest, really didn't want to be stuck in a pub on a glorious afternoon, at 4.30, but would rather be outside playing, we spent a pleasant half hour chatting and discussing the walk and Neal and Annettes involvement with CAMRA.

Well another walk is completed. The weather was warm and it was a bit difficult to know what to wear. At times a coat was needed yet at others you could easily walk around in a T-shirt. It was a shame that we couldn't get into the church but as Neal delivers the post around the village he has promised to find out some more information about Christs Church and its mysterious humps in the ground. As for Annette, when she got out of the car, back in Hailsham, I said that I was pleased that I, eventually, found out where I had seen her before, because it had been on my mind most of the afternoon. "If I can ask," she said, "why were you in hospital?" "I'd had a heart attack," I advised her. "Oh, I've never worked in Coronary Care," she says, smiling, "all my work has been carried out in surgical wards."

Neal needs help stripping off

A Day at the Cricket

It must be obvious from the title of this chapter that this isn't about a walk. What I thought might be a nice idea is for Ron and me to have a bit of our time. Well, to be honest, it's a bit of Ron time. I'm not a great lover of the game of cricket; Ron is a fanatic about the game. If you get to chat about cricket with Ron he will let you know that he had the chance to train and possibly, if he was good enough and Ron thinks he was, he could have ended up playing for Sussex. This was when he was still at school in Hailsham and, to quote Ron, "oo knows what I could 'ave achieved, but me ol' dad couldn't afford ter let me go ter trainin'. Money was a bit short in them days." So Ron remained doing what Ron did but found plenty of time to play his favourite game, along with others, in local teams around the area. "When was the last time you went to see a professional game of cricket at Hove?" I asked one evening over a pint of non alcoholic beer (I'm still not allowed to drink the hard stuff). "Must be over 50 years ago I last saw Sussex play at 'ove cricket ground. But these days they play that silly 20/20 over game, that ain't cricket. You can't play descent shots off the bat when the only idea ov' the game is ter smack the ball as 'ard as yer can ter get as many runs as yer can. Give me a four day match any day," he moans, "that's what yer call a real game o'cricket." (I will assume that the reader is familiar with how the game of cricket is played without me giving a tedious explanation.) This got me to thinking. Why don't I take Ron to watch a game of cricket? My treat, as a thank you for all the walks we had done together. But I can't afford to take four days off to watch a County game. To be honest I, personally, couldn't sit and watch one game of cricket that lasts a whole four days! But Ron doesn't like 20/20 cricket. Would you believe it, there is another type of game. This one is called 40/40 cricket, and you've guessed it – the game is twice as long as 20/20. So, as the game is a little longer to play I will assume that Ron would be happy and I will only have to take one day off. A quick look on the Sussex County Cricket website[155] gave me the programme of games. I chose a game against Lancashire, I don't know why but it seemed to fit what I was looking for. The game was being played on a Sunday, so I wouldn't have to take time off after all. I managed to order two tickets. Play starts at 13.45 and the gates open at 11.45. Now that's what I call a result.

But, apparently we aren't going to see Sussex play Lancashire. Ron tries to explain; "Sussex ain't Sussex when they plays 20/20 or 40/40 games. Same as Lancashire ain't Lancashire either." "So who are we going to watch?" I ask. "We be goin' ter see The Sharks play The Lightning," says Ron. "But I bought tickets for Sussex versus Lancashire," says I. "That's right," continues Ron. "But you just said that we're watching some fishy name playing thunder," I was getting confused. "When it ain't a county game Sussex is known as the Sussex Sharks and Lancashire is known as

County Cricket badges

the Lancashire Lightning," says Ron. Is it becoming clear to you because it certainly doesn't make any sense to me? "So you're saying that the Sussex County Cricket team change their name to the Sussex Sharks when they aren't playing a Sussex game and then change their name back to the Sussex County Cricket team when they are?" "Yes," says Ron, "all the county teams do the same thing." "Seems to me to be a bit of a rip off, I suppose they sell merchandise under the different names so people have to buy two of everything. And you say money hasn't affected the game of cricket." But I will admit that the cost of our tickets to watch the game on Sunday 9th May were very reasonable.

Not County cricket badges

But first I had to do some homework. Would you believe that the ground does not have parking facilities unless you're disabled or a club member? Can you believe that? Do they want people to turn up or don't they? I thought we might catch a train, I'm told the cricket ground is a five minute walk from the station. But we would have to change trains at Lewes and once we got to Brighton we'd have to catch a bus to get to Hove. So I've decided to take the car, after

Sign outside station

all, I can't drink alcohol anyway so the car is going to be our mode of transport. All I'll have to do is find somewhere to park. I'm hoping that it won't be too difficult, although I have been informed that, on match days, parking is a little bit difficult. So far I've only encountered things that are encouraging me not to go. Let's hope it's all going to be worth it. I've printed off a street map of the area and I'm hoping to be able to park in Hove Station Car Park and walk from there.

I've also checked the information on the game from the Sussex County Cricket Clubs website[156] and I'm told that Sussex have named an unchanged 'squad'. (Unchanged from what I have no idea??) Can anyone tell me the difference between a squad and a team? The only reason I ask is that, if memory serves me correctly, there are twelve men in a cricket team. Eleven that actually play and a twelfth man who does whatever a twelfth man has to do. The website lists the 'unchanged' Sussex squad for this game as follows: JS Gatting, MW Goodwin, AJ Hodd, CB Keegan, RJ Kirtley, RSC Martin-Jenkins, CD Nash, R Naved-ul-Hasan, MS Panesar, MJ Prior, OP Rayner, MA Thornely. You have to admit that we have a few well-known Sussex names in this squad. Now if you add up the number of names it comes to twelve which, to me, is a cricket team yet they call it a squad? On the same page as this information I'm informed that Lancashire have named a 13 man squad which will be captained by Glen Chapple – does that mean that Lancashire, with a bigger squad than Sussex, will have an unfair advantage? Will the

---

[156] http://www.sussexcricket.co.uk visited 08/05/2010

game get called off if one of the Sussex unchanged <u>squad</u> doesn't manage to get to the ground on time because they will not have enough men to make up a <u>team</u>? Perhaps it will become clearer on the day. And in a strange way, although I really don't like the game, I'm looking forward to it. But I will take a book with me, just in case.

First, just a few facts about Sussex County Cricket Club. Founded in 1839 Sussex is the oldest County Cricket Club in England. But it wasn't until the year 2003 that they won their first ever official County Championship. (Although they did win the unofficial County Championship in 1845, 1848, 1852(shared) and 1855) They repeated their success in 2006 and 2007. In 2006 Sussex beat Lancashire CCC to win the C&G Trophy, before trouncing Nottingham by an innings and 245 runs in the County Championship, thereby achieving the 'double'. Sussex first won the 40/40 title in 1982 and then again in the years 2008 and 2009[157]. Sussex are the current 40/40 title holders and have, this season played 2 and won 2. Today, therefore, is game number 3.

Lots of 'For Sale' signs

Spot the parking space

So, on a cool and cloudy Sunday morning we set off for Hove. "Do you know where the County Ground is, in Hove? " I ask Ron as he settles himself in the car. "No idea," is the reply, "It's been years since I saw a game, surely yer don't expect me ter remember where the ground is." I must admit I was hoping but, just in case, I've got a street map of the area. I've decided to head straight for Hove Railway Station and use the car park there. When I was working for Royal Mail I always used this car park because Hove Sorting Office is next door to the station and, from the map, it doesn't look like too much of a walk to the ground. I'm hoping that I'm going to learn something from today. As I said I'm not a great lover of the game of cricket. I've watched village cricket and a little of some games held on the recreation ground at Hailsham but it always seems a slow game. "Tis different when yer watch a professional game," advises Ron as we head along the A27, "you'll see a difference in the speed of the game and the accuracy of the players, trust me, it'll be good." I'm not so sure, and I check the back seat just to make sure I've brought the current book I'm reading. But let's go with an open mind and be positive. After all what is the worst thing that could happen? And, you never know I might even enjoy the day!

We arrive at Hove in record time. I was expecting a little more traffic on the road but we hardly saw another car. The car park is practically deserted. I used to remember when you could park at a railway car park free at the weekends. But no more. The cost is

---

[157] http://en.wikipedia.org/wiki/Sussex_County_Cricket_Club - visited 09/05/2010

223 | P a g e

What espresso coffee looks like

£4.90 for the day. So, with sticker on the windscreen we head out towards the County Ground. I'm not sure if the area is a little unsavoury but we both noticed a large number of 'For Sale' signs along the streets in Hove. Yet the houses look rather grand although everywhere, along the road, there are parking meters. When we get closer to the ground there are quite a few parking spaces that we could have taken, and parking on the street is 40 pence cheaper that at the railway station.

Because we got to Hove so quickly, we are now much too early to get into the ground. It's only 10.30 and the ground doesn't open until 11.45. "Fancy a cuppa?" I ask Ron, "Don't mind if I do," is the reply as we head off towards the sea-front. It's strange but when you're in a place your unsure of you notice different things. Like in Hove, on a Sunday morning at just turned 10.30 in the morning we noticed how many shops are open. And I have to admit, most of them are not run by English, but are mainly foreign shopkeepers. As we walk along a street there are restaurants for Indian, Chinese and Polish food. Italian restaurants are preparing to greet customers. The coffee shop we stopped at wasn't English but Italian. "What do you fancy," I as Ron, "I'll have a cup o'tea," answers Ron. "No I won't, make mine an espresso." "Are you sure?" I ask, "because I'm not too sure what an espresso coffee is."

"Neither am I," says Ron, "but it smells of coffee in 'ere an' it's changed me mind." So I order an espresso for Ron and a cappuccino for me. At least I know what to expect with mine. When I handed Ron his espresso I'm not sure what his expression said but it was obvious that he had never had this type of coffee before. Come to that neither had I. What he got was a very small cup, he couldn't get his finger in the handle and inside the cup was what looked like stale engine oil. "What the 'ell am I supposed ter do with that?" Ron asks, pointing at the little cup on the table. Rather than look as if he didn't know what to do with his coffee, when in fact neither of us had any idea, Ron picks up the cup, takes one swallow and puts down the empty cup. "Christ," exclaims Ron, "that must'a been neat caffeine, I'll probably be awake fer days now." I couldn't drink mine for laughing. But this little coffee shop with its tables inside as well as a few outside on the pavement was packed. I have to keep reminding myself that it is a Sunday morning. It's not long

The gate to The County Ground, Hove

before we are making our way back to the cricket ground. Just outside the gates is a pub appropriately named 'The Cricketer'. It's closed and I'm not sure if Ron is disappointed or not when he simply says, "Must be run by the English. If it were foreign it'd be open by now."

At precisely 11.45 the gates are swung open and we are permitted to enter the 'sacred' ground of Sussex Cricket. We hadn't gone far into the ground before Ron recognises someone, and is shaking hands with a steward. I don't believe it, but Ron is now chatting away to steward who he called 'Stimmy' Smith. When he eventually comes away he says, "'aven't seen Stimmy fer years." Apparently he used to play cricket against Ron years back and also played goalie for Ringmer when Ron played football. We've yet to go somewhere in Sussex where Ron isn't recognised by someone. It's amazing but there was more to come.

The game hasn't started yet!

As this was the first time I had visited the County Ground I wasn't too sure on where I could or couldn't go. It was obvious that there were certain areas that we were not permitted to go. These were marked with 'Members Only' and stewards were standing guard. All I knew was that I had tickets for area A, seats 117 and 118. When I asked for directions I was told by a steward to head away from the area we were now in, which apparently was a member's area, and head for the other side of the ground where all the deck chairs were placed. "Don't worry about the seat numbers, just grab yourselves whatever seat you want," we are told. "Looks good ter me," says Ron, "It looks like there's a bar as well as food over there. Let's go."

Like I've said this is a real first for me. And my first impressions are good. The ground is not as big as I expected but it is immaculately kept. The grass is perfectly green and at regulation height, although I noticed a groundsman with one of the biggest lawnmowers in existence wandering up and down the pitch. Is it called a pitch? It isn't

Warm up exercises

long before the players are out warming up by exercising and throwing cricket balls in all directions. In the distance a net has been erected and sets of cricket stumps put up. The idea is that one player rolls, or throws, a ball to another player and that player has to hurtle the ball at the stumps. And I do mean hurtle. It goes that fast I can't see it. Yet time after time the ball does hit the stumps. The speed and the accuracy is amazing.

After a brief walk round we head towards the club shop to make the obligatory purchases. A 'programme' complete with your very own score card is purchased for just a pound and the numbers that you are supposed to wave around when a batsman scores a four or a six are given away. There's even a weird bingo game inside the programme which involves cricket terminology which is free for everyone to enter with first prize being four free tickets to the 40/40 final at Lords Cricket Ground.

As the time approaches for the toss of the coin we head back to the seating area and relax in our deck chairs. We've only been sitting there a few minutes when one of

Ollie, the BIG no. 22

the Sussex players comes over to say hello to Ron! Can you believe that! The young man's name is Ollie and he has to be over six feet tall. He is enormous, with hands like shovels. It's obvious that Ron and Ollie have met at The King's Head and chat away together. Apparently he's a nephew of someone who used to visit the pub, but is, unfortunately, another of the lost regulars.

"If Sussex win the toss," explains Ron to me, "they'll put Lancashire in ter bat first." "Why?" I ask. "Cause it's a type o'wicket that'll get batsmen out," Ron tries to explain to me. Give Ron credit he did try. "I don't understand," I say, and I really didn't. "It's the atmosphere," Ron tries again, "its damp and its cold. The ball will swerve in the air. It's a grand wicket for bowlers. You see, if Sussex wins the toss, they'll put Lancashire in ter bat." At that precise moment the announcer informs us that Sussex had won the toss and will bat first. Lancashire will field first. I look at Ron. "That's why I ain't captain o' Sussex!" is all he said with that silly smile.

If you've never seen 20/20 or 40/40 cricket, and I'm sure that there can't be that many people who haven't, you will have noticed some things that are not the same with test cricket or championship cricket, apart from the length of time that a game takes. I will let you know of some of the differences that I have noticed for today's game. One, the cricket stumps, which are normally wood coloured, and bales are black. Yes I mean black. The sight screen, which is placed behind each of the wickets and again normally of a

The game gets underway - note lack of spectators

white colour, is also black. The ball that is to be used, which is normally red, is white. And all the players come out to play in bright coloured outfits and not the usual white ones. The umpires, that's the men in charge, normally sedate elderly gentlemen wearing all white outfits, look like overdressed traffic wardens. As the term implies 40/40 actually means that each team can play for 40 overs each, although there is also a time limit. Within the boundary of the pitch(?) are a number of coloured discs placed on the ground, in a circle. Only a certain number of players are permitted to be within this circle of coloured discs at anyone time. Within these 40 overs for each team (six balls are bowled in each over) there are, what are called, two power plays. One power play of 4 overs is called by the team that are bowling and the next power play of 4 overs is called by the team that are batting. So you end up with a total of 16 overs out of a possible 80 overs which are power plays. Simple, isn't it? Come on, keep up at the back! Ron did try to explain to me the principles of a four over power play but, to be honest, I hadn't a clue what he was talking about. I am, however, a little disappointed by the number of spectators. Perhaps it is the weather, which has turned really cloudy and very cold, has put a lot of people off. But the game goes on.

My scorecard and tickets for the game (match?)

I will not bore you with a blow by blow account of the game. (Isn't that good of me?) But I did learn something. And that is how to score at cricket. I don't mean hit the ball and run but I mean on paper, because we had purchased a score card each, and Ron explained the scoring system. If a run isn't made then you place a dot in the box which represents the over being played, if a run is made then an entry in the box corresponding to the number of runs is also entered in the box which represents the over. As six balls are played in each over there should be six numbers or dots in each of the 40 boxes. Everything was working well until we reached the 30th over of Sussex when Ron, looks over my shoulder and tells me that we were actually in the 31st over?? I have no idea how that happened! But I managed to loose six balls?? Never mind, at the end of the allotted 40 overs Sussex had scored 245 runs with 7 players being out. Or, for the technically minded, the Sussex innings was 245 for 7. It is now tea time. The players have left the pitch(?) and nearly all the spectators invade the area to play cricket with each other and everyone else. "Time fer a drink," says Ron and heads off to the bar. I'm left in my deck chair trying to fathom out how I managed to loose a complete over. When I look up there are cricket stumps everywhere, dads are bowling balls at little boys, and even little girls are having a go. There are balls flying about everywhere.

Ron comes back with his plastic pint 'glass' of Speckled Hen. As he sits down on his deck chair he is placing his full, foaming pint 'glass', on the ground. He couldn't have let go of his pint for a second before a ball came flying over the barrier and dropped straight onto his pint of beer spilling most of his precious Speckled Hen into the ground. I watched these events unfold before my eyes but couldn't do anything to prevent Ron's loss. All I heard was him mutter "b£$&*rd" under his breath as he handed the little boy his ball back. "At least he said 'sorry'," I offer but I'm not sure it helped. Ron turns on his heels and heads back to the bar. But when he returns I'm surprised to see that he has a very large hot-dog and not another foaming pint. "Can't afford ter loose beer like that too many times," says Ron, "better off with some food inside yer." I couldn't agree more and head off for the food bar as well. I thought it might be a good idea if I brought a cup of tea for Ron while I was getting my hot-dog. But be warned. One hot-dog, one small cup of tea and a small cup of coffee cost £7.00.

But, back to the game. Ron informs me that for Lancashire to win the game they had to score more than 7 runs in each over. "Is that possible?" I ask. "Certainly is if Sussex doesn't play it right," Ron answers. "It all depends on the delivery," continues Ron. "Which means what?" I ask, sure that my ignorance is showing. "Ow they bowl the ball, makin' sure it ain't short. Bowling a decent length. All them things 'ave ter be right," he explains, "just watch an' I'll try ter explain as we goes on." The game continues and Lancashire has scored 30 runs in 3 overs. "That means there on 10 runs an over," explains Ron, "which also means they are on the way ter winnin' the game unless Sussex can stop 'em from runnin'," "And they can do that how?" I ask. "By puttin' on a spin bowler and not bowling short." I must admit that as I continued to watch the game, rather than look at my score card, I could see what Ron meant. Sometimes the ball bounced a long way in front of the batsman (bowled short) and the batsman managed to hit it and get runs. But when the spin bowler was bowling the ball it inevitably bounced just in front of the batsman's feet and he couldn't get any momentum to take a swing at it. The captain obviously decided to bring on spin bowlers who then came into their own and managed to slow up the batsmen from Lancashire to only 3 or 4 runs an over. Ron was right after all. "An' that," says Ron, " is why I **could** be captain o'Sussex."

At the end of the game, Sussex were triumphant. With Lancashire only managing 206 for 9 with one of their players retiring hurt. Which made Sussex's record 3 wins from 3 games. And to be honest I really enjoyed it. At the end I was cheering and chanting with the other supporters as things swung in Sussex's favour. Ollie, Ron's friend, didn't have to bat but came into bowl and ended up by bowling 8 overs with 33 runs scored against him and managed to get 2 players from Lancashire out. He was happy, the crowd were over the moon with another victory. But I have to say that it was a long and very cold day and I'm not too sure that I'll be doing it again too soon. But Ron had a great day, and that was the main idea. But let's get back to walking!

Kiddies Walk

Those who have been with Ron and me since the start of our walks will be aware of the total lack of equipment we use. We do not, for example, take a compass with us, although, on the odd occasion I've slipped one in my pocket, but never used it; we rarely have an ordinance survey map. Ron has been known to produce a bottle of water and the odd bun from his Harvey's carrier bag on a few occasions but other than that we are pretty well equipment free. We have been known to walk with just a book and a thumbstick. But one thing is always sure. We always get home. But, having admitted to this we also used to sit in the King's Head and discuss where we were heading next. I have to admit that we no longer do that either! Not than Ron doesn't have his say on the next walk, we do discuss where we are heading but Ron normally lets me decide on where we are going and I arrange to pick him up. Lately we have had company and, we hope, that our company have enjoyed themselves with us and, I hope, should you ask any of them, they will agree that we didn't get lost too many times because we are getting better. We try to vary the walks so that we can make it as interesting as possible and we do not visit a walk over and over again. But one walk that we have completed before is a 'Kiddies Walk'. Now this walk does require a lot of organisation and setting up before we set off. I've been saving this particular walk[158] for some time. I've had it on the back burner for weeks. I had filed it away in my drawer waiting for the weather to brighten up. It is a good walk, suggested to me as being ideal for children. But, I had my doubts because of the title: The Beachyhead Walk. But I did some checking with the aid of my plentiful supply of walking books and have discovered that Len Markham has also written this walk[159] and has described it as suitable for children so I'm not as unsure as I was at first. Just to make sure that we have no problems on the walk, and more

Village Green, East Dean

importantly we are not going to get lost, I like to check out things with the help of my daughter, Michelle, who spends her whole working day with children, so is an ideal person to decide whether the walk is suitable for all age groups. Michelle also checks out the 'things to look out for' and ensures that any Health and Safety issues are addressed before we start. There can't be anything worse than taking a lot of people for a walk, especially children, and then end up getting lost because you've not done your homework. I will also point out that Ron takes no part in the following proceedings until the actual walk, with real children. When we completed our last Kiddies Walk we all ended up back at the King's Head where the children were presented with 'We've walked with Ron and Graham' certificates and photographs were taken. We had a lot of feedback, not only from the children but also from some of the parents. But we've decided to ignore that and do another one anyway, because Ron and I had a lot of fun.

---

[158] http://www.beachyhead.org.uk/assets/files/beachy_walk.pdf - visited 04/05/2010
[159] 'Kiddie Walks in East Sussex'

The idea for this walk is not only to get youngsters out in the fresh air but to also teach them a little something of our countryside. To this end, Michelle and I have set a little questionnaire for the children to complete whilst on the walk. There are no prizes for getting the right answers it is purely done for fun. Hopefully, a good day is had by all. The walk this year is to be carried out during the schools half term in May and, as luck would have it, there is a Bank Holiday Monday during this Spring break so most parents will not be at work so there is no excuse.

East Dean War Memorial

Ok, but first we must trial the walk, to establish if the walk can be completed by all age groups with or without buggies. There is a little difference between Len's walk and the walk from the Internet. Len estimates the time to carry out this walk is 4 hours and the Internet walk says it will take 1½ hours, for the same walk? Now that worries me. Len also describes the walk as not so good for youngsters; this also gives me doubts of the suitability. The Internet instructions do not give the same warning, but Michelle is up for it so, on a warm Sunday morning, we head for the starting point – East Dean.

From Hailsham East Dean isn't too far. This is a plus point straight away. There is little point in having to drive young children for miles before making them get out of the car and start walking. We park in the car park situated in Gilbert Road which is just a short walk away from the village green at East Dean. The pub, facing the green, is The Tiger. On our last visit here Ron wasn't too happy with the quality of his beer. But having a pub at the end of the walk is also a plus. Refreshments after the walk are very welcome so Michelle and I decide to stop off on the way back to the car to see if they will lay on something for the end of the walk. As I said the instructions come from the Internet and, unfortunately, they are a little old. We are told, from these instructions that a coffee shop will be opening in March 2006. It's now 2010 and the coffee shop has been built and is now open for business.

Has Michelle grown, or has the building sunk to its rafters?

As you approach the green it will be very difficult not to see the War Memorial. This has the appearance of an ancient village cross, and was erected in front of The Tiger after the 1914-18 War, the railings being hand-made by the last village blacksmith. One of the firebacks in the public bar of The Tiger is inscribed 1622 but it is in the 1800's that records tell of a disused Malthouse in East Dean which could be referring to The Tiger but as this was during Cromwell's reign it's true identity may have been suppressed. As with most Inns around the coastal areas of Sussex The Tiger was known to have been the base for smugglers and by far more sinister 'wreckers' who showed bogus lights on shore at night to lure storm-driven

Allotments with 'Zebedee'

vessels to destruction. It was customary for these wreckers to throw back into the sea any crew who escaped the destruction of the ship. The cottages adjoining The Tiger were used as barracks during the Napoleonic wars. Perhaps we could have a question about Napoleon?

Our next instruction is to '…*walk up the side of a large barn and cross the road at the top, outside the Village Shop and Post Office'*. Sadly neither of these exists but evidence is still visible. We now need to turn left into Went Way which, we are told, is the oldest road in the district. The old School House is on our right, built in 1850 by the daughter of Mrs Mary Davis-Gilbert who started an agricultural school, teaching digging, milking and stalling, along with the three 'Rs'. (Question: what are the three Rs?) The school eventually closed in 1964 due to the declining village population. A little further along Went Way is the Old Bake House, now a private residence, which once served the whole village and still retains the bricked up ovens. This used to be the home of the priest-in-charge of East Dean Church.

To our left are some allotments guarded by a fearsome looking scarecrow which has a placard round its neck telling us his name is 'Zebedee' and wishing us a nice day. (Question: What is the name of the scarecrow?) So far everything seems to be ok for the walk. Both Michelle and I have found a couple of questions for the children and it's looking promising. Until……

'…*Continue along the road until you reach a five-barred gate. Enter the gate and you are immediately on the first of the Seven Sisters known as Went Hill. Take the upward winding pathway and climb through a steep wooded area…*' This was not so good. It was steep. It was long. Obviously we are heading towards the top of the South Downs. Could we expect children to manage this hill? I didn't think so. But Michelle thought that as it was the start of the walk we may be able to encourage the children to reach the top. "But what if we have mums and dads with buggies?" I ask. It may be possible to pull the buggy up the hill

Steep, long climb

but we had strong doubts that this walk was good for children. And it's just because of this hill that we now sit and try to decide if we should continue with the rest of the walk or go home and look for something else. But what also made me think of turning back was the big heap of dog pooh that I managed to tread in as we started the climb! But after much deliberation we decide to continue. Should this be the worst part of the walk then Michelle thinks that we may be able to include some children but I do think that we will have to explain to parents before we set off that there is a steep hill at the start of the walk which may be difficult for the younger children and be even more difficult with a buggy. To be honest I'm not convinced that this is the walk we will be doing. But let's continue.

Once on the top of the Downs we need to pass the red roofed barn to our left (Question: what colour is the roof of the barn?) and head towards Birling Gap. Our instructions advise us to be alert during this part of the walk as there are many species of birds known to fly and nest in this area. We are also warned about sheep that graze freely on this part of the Downs, although all we manage to see are cattle. Due to the possibility of the presence of sheep we must remember to tell everyone that dogs must be kept on a lead during this part of the walk. It wasn't until now that I find my fear of animals has rubbed off onto my daughter. She really does feel unsafe as we walk fairly close to some big cattle and I can hear myself quoting Ron when I say, "don't let them know your scared," and, "whatever you do, don't run." But Michelle was only too pleased to arrive at the gate leading down to Birling Gap, even though she had some trouble working out how to open it!

We now head down a gravel road and arrive at Birling Gap which is the only access to the sea between Eastbourne and the Cuckmere Haven. There used to be eight coastguard cottages here, but due to erosion of the cliff face a number have fallen into the sea and the others have been demolished. Smuggling used to be a profitable trade during the 17 and 1800's when mainly wines and spirits were hauled onto the beach or up the cliff face. In 1828 a run of smuggled goods took place when 37 tubs were landed. The smugglers managed to get 25 tubs away but the alarm was raised by the firing of blockade sentries, so the smugglers had to let 12 tubs fall to the bottom of the cliff. And from Birling Gap, if you walk towards the sea you will get a magnificent view of the Seven Sisters. But.......... why does

A large animal

The troublesome gate

The Seven Sisters

Another steep climb

The saved lighthouse

Michelle makes the rapid descent

there have to be a but? We are looking at bringing children with us on this walk. We will have to check the time of the high tide on the day we are to carry out this walk. If we arrive during high tide we will not be able to get access to the beach. (Question: how many Sisters are there?)

The saying 'what comes down, must go up' comes to mind right now because our next instruction tells us to '...*climb the hill to the Coastguard Lookout at the top of the cliff.*' And again this is a steep and long climb with a sheer drop, over the cliffs if you wander to far to the right of the path. I think both Michelle and I came to the same conclusion as we got to the top of the cliff. This is not a walk for young children. It wouldn't be too bad should each and every child have one parent to keep hold of their youngsters but you'd need eyes in the back of your head if you let some children loose up here. The wind is very gusty and Michelle is fascinated by cliff top edges and insists on getting as close as she can to the edge. She terrifies me so much that I actually grab hold of her and pull her away from the edge. And Michelle is old enough to know better. No, I definitely don't like the idea of bringing young children on this walk. And the decision is made. We will not be doing the Beachyhead Walk as a Kiddies Walk. So it's back to the drawing board. We will have to look for something else. All we have to do now is get back to the car. But first we have to get some photographs of the lighthouse. Fortunately, due to popular demand, the lighthouse, built in 1902, has been saved so will continue to be on our shores for a few more years, at least. But I don't mind admitting, getting the photo was a little difficult. It was a bit windy and I was standing a little too close to the edge. Michelle loved it!!

The easiest way back to the car is to continue with our instructions which will get us back to East Dean. From our current position we have to make our way towards the Belle Tout lighthouse. I have written about this in another chapter so I don't intend to repeat all that information again. But once at Belle Tout our instructions read '...*now turn left, away from the sea and make a rapid descent towards the road.*' And rapid isn't the word. It is an awful descent along a dirt path and would be impossible for a parent holding on to children. With everything else considered there is no way that we could even think about completing this walk with kiddies, and both Michelle and I, once we slipped and slid to the bottom, are really pleased at the decision we've made.

Michelle didn't like the moo-cow

The entrance to the church

From here we follow the route taken in our previous chapter, Coastal Walk, where we head up the drive of Cornish Farm.[160] On that chapter we had to turn right and walk along the open fields but on this occasion we continue in a straight line, along the public footpath until we come out at the Seven Sisters Sheep Centre, which would have been a nice place to stop for some refreshments, if only they were open. But on the way to the Sheep Centre we needed to pass some rather big cows first. They were really big cows, with horns. I knew Michelle wouldn't be happy. But I didn't realise how unhappy until I decided to stop and take a photograph of the biggest cow. As I pointed the camera at the cow, it turned, menacingly, and looked straight at us. "I think I've wet meself," whispers Michelle as she tries to get herself as close to me as possible. "It's the sound of the camera being turned on that they don't like," she continues as she is now holding my arm with a vice-like grip. "Please, dad, let's go now!" She has started to raise her voice and she looks petrified as we quickly head for the last gate.

It is just a short walk along the road until we come to East Dean Church, which is set back off the road on our left. Access is via a brick archway and if you continue along the outside of the church, to the left, you eventually come out at the Tapsell Gate. But, as you know, I tend to wander around graveyards. It's not that I'm morbid, honest, but some tombstones tend to stand out. And today was going to be no exception. If your new to gravestone spotting you will not be aware that Military graves really stand out. They are made from a stone that remains clean and the inscription stays clear. What I first noticed about this particular gravestone was that the deceased, apart from being military was that he was so young. I was looking at the headstone of W.E. Kingley RNPS, who at the age of just 19 years, perished aboard H.M.S. Ocean Sunlight on 13th June 1940. I've done a little research when I got home and found that this ship was sunk just 800 yards from Newhaven Harbour. She is described as a 131 ton Drifter. Michelle had noticed a different gravestone, that of the Rev. Jonothan Darby who died 26th October 1726. This is the grave of Parson Darby who saved many sailors from shipwreck by the light from the cave he made in the cliff near Beachy Head.

After leaving the church, via the Tapsell Gate, a swing gate that is peculiar to Sussex, we head back to the village green and the car.

So, should we be doing this walk with kiddies, we would now head back home, compose the questionairre and invite as many children as we can to join Ron and me. But that is not the case with this walk. What I'll be doing is looking for somewhere else to go and then Michelle and I wil have do it all over again.

Church Walk

What I have tried to do with this walk is to find as many churches as I can within one, manageable walk. The maximum that I can find is three within eight miles. I think that eight miles should be achievable for Ron and me, as long as there aren't three churches with three pubs close by. Obviously if we are visiting three churches we must also visit three villages and the three we are to see today are Fittleworth, Egdean and Stopham all in the west of Sussex. The walk is taken from a book titled West Sussex Church Walks[161] and the terrain is described as '…*gently undulating.*' We've never walked with this book before and, if anything, I'm a little worried about the lack of directions given. But we will have to wait and see how it goes.

I can vaguely remember visiting Stopham before in our walks where, if memory serves me correctly, there is a bridge made famous, for some reason that escapes me at the moment. But the other two villages will be new to both Ron and me. Fittleworth was once made famous by the artist John Constable RA (1736- 1837) when he painted Fittleworth Mill in 1835, just 2 years before his death[162]. It is said that he lodged at The Swan Inn where, in 1924 the Ancient Order of Froth Blowers was founded. The order, whose motto was 'lubrication by moderation', was created '*to foster the Noble art and gentle and healthy Pastime of froth blowing amongst Gentlemen of leisure and ex soldiers.*' Between the 1930's and 40's the order had ½million members. But lager beer was ineligible. The Swan Inn rule book states *"it is unseemly and should be avoided always excepting by Naval Officers visiting German Colonies."*[163]

So it's lucky for Ron who, as you all know, favors real ale, and not so lucky for me, being a lager drinker.

The village of Egdean is tiny and, during the early centuries, always held a horse fair. It was at one of these horse fairs that, shortly before his death in 1837 at Petworth House, the 3rd Earl of Egremont was last seen out in public when he gave a £20 prize for the best three year old colt or filly at the fair[164]. And, since I started to look at doing this walk, I have found out just a few more facts about the villages we are to visit today which I will disclose as we go round.

The Swan Inn, Fittleworth

I have taken a few days off work supposedly for a well earned rest but my wife had other ideas. The hall, stairs and landing were in desperate need of decorating and we've had problems with the plumbing in the kitchen for a few months now. These had to be sorted out before I could even think about the walk and I was really pleased that I managed to get everything completed with just one day of my holiday (?) left. And it was a Wednesday, and the sun was shining. As the walk was a little on the long-side it was decided to make a day of it. So I picked Ron up at 10 o'clock on a bright, warm Wednesday morning and headed towards Petworth, where I'm hoping to see a signpost

---

[161] West Sussex Church Walks, by Diana Pé, Published by Sigma Leisure, Walk 25 Page 103

[162] http://www.information-britain.co.uk/county4/townguideFittleworth/ visited 01/06/2010

[163] http://www.jonedgar.co.uk/fittleworth.htm - visited 01/06/2010

[164] http://en.wikipedia.org/wiki/George_Wyndham,_3rd_Earl_of_Egremont – visited 01/06/2010

The Church of St. Mary

for Fittleworth. But just as Ron's bum hits the seat in the car he asks, "ave yer seen the squad we're takin' ter the world cup? My God! What ave we done ter deserve a shamble like that?" I had to admit that I hadn't taken a lot of notice to the England team. We played Japan, in a friendly, a few days ago and although England won 2 – 1 England didn't score a goal. Honest, Japan scored for themselves first and then scored two home goals. Ron was evil about the whole thing. "Emile, bloody, Heskey, for God's sake," Ron rants, "he's played over 50 games fer England an only scored 7 goals, an' e's one ov' our bloody strikers." There's no stopping Ron. We discussed Rooney, Terry, Lampard, Ferdinand. You name them and Ron criticised each and every one of them, "Can't even sing the bloody National Anthem at the start o'the game 'cause they don't know the words. Just stand there like melons, spittin' on the ground. Where are all the youngsters, them that wants ter put an English shirt on an' be proud ter play fer their country? We're bloody useless, can't even find a bloody English manager." I sit back and let him go on. Sooner or later he will slow down and, hopefully, calm down. For now I will assume that Ron will not be watching any of the World Cup 2010.

Fittleworth was really easy to find. I drove from Hailsham along the A27, over the Brighton by-pass and then onto the A283, passed Steyning and then stayed on the A283 to Fittleworth. It was straight forward and by the time we reached our starting point, Ron had calmed down and said he was looking forward to the walk.

Our start point was, in fact, Fittleworth church, the church of St. Mary which is a very pleasant little church built around the 13th century. As you must be aware I try to find as much out about the places we visit and then relate the interesting bits. Would you believe that when I went onto the churches website[165], yes even God has access to the World Wide Web, all it said about the church was 'St *Mary's is an ancient church with a growing friendly congregation.*' So, I've passed on the interesting bit. I didn't realise that the lack of information would have affected Ron in the way that it did. "I've brought a load o'change with me, weighin' me down, it is" says Ron, "I thought, as we were ter visit so many churches I'd be able ter buy leaflets an' postcards but all I can do 'ere is sign the visitors book." Ron always, buys the leaflets and cards at every church we visit and he's not too keen on walking away without something. And it's the walking away that caused us our first problem.....

It's a track, but the wrong one

---

[165] http://www.achurchnearyou.com/fittleworth-st-mary/ - visited 02/06/2010

At the start of the chapter I said I was worried about the lack of instruction. This proved founded right from the start when I read '...*From Fittleworth Church, cross the road to the track, heading south-west...*' We found a gate to and from the church. This was where I parked the car. Opposite the gate, that we entered was a track and with the help of my concealed compass (Ron would not be happy that I had a compass) by crossing this road and walking to the track, we were heading south-west. But it was from this track that none of the other instructions made a lot of sense. We should now be heading over Hesworth Common. But we came face to face with a scout hut? "That's got ter be a first," says Ron, "I don't think that we ever got lost on the first instruction before." Nothing, and I mean nothing, looked anything like it was

Ron is not impressed!!

described in our instructions. But at no time did I think that we must have made a mistake, after all we had followed everything that we were told in the book, hadn't we? Ron suggested that the writer of the book couldn't have walked it for the scenery to be so very wrong. But we battled on. We should come to a path, we didn't. We should soon reach a sandy mound, we didn't. We did find a wooden seat that Ron made the most of as I tried to work out why things were not as they should be. But we continued. Down slopes, along paths, around trees and all the time I'm trying to discover something, anything that looks as it should

We follow another path

from our instructions. And there it was, across the road was a sign that said 'Hesworth Common'. I was elated. "We've only been walkin' an hour," chuckles Ron "and we must now be 500 yards from the place we started." "Yes," I agree, "but at least we can now follow the instructions." "I thought we were already doin' that," says Ron.

Thankfully, as we walked through Hesworth Common, signs started to look good. Landmarks were beginning to look as they were described in the instructions. But we still never managed to find the steps which should lead us through well-spaced trees. We did, however, manage to find a lane. I just hoped that we would find '...*a small cluster of houses, including Hesworth Farm...*' when we turned left. Whilst walking down the lane Ron heard his first cuckoo in two years. The bird was some distance away from us but his distinctive call could be heard very clearly. At last, something has put a smile on Ron's face. We seemed to be walking along

Heading down the lane

The wall of Rew Cottage, where we turn right

this lane for some time before we came to some houses. "You'd think that they would put distances in the instructions," suggests Ron, "we could a' turned back ages ago if we thought we'd gone wrong again." But what annoys me even more is that our next instruction simply says '...*turn right here and go west...*' there's not a mention of the cottage called Rew Cottage, where the path hugs the wall. I wonder why.

We follow the wall until we come to a stile, this isn't mentioned in the instructions. In front of us, once over the stile are two fields, separated by a hedge, one field is to the right of the hedge, the other is to the left. All our instructions say is '....*go west across open fields.*' But which side of the hedge should we be? "Typical woman," mutters Ron, "I'm tellin' yer, she ain't walked this walk, probably just taken it from one o'them ordinance maps. She's got no idea." I must admit it's a bit of a puzzle and I wonder if I tend to look too deeply into the instructions given in some of the books.

For example, our instruction is to 'go west across open fields', this implies that there is to be more than one field. Because she has used the word 'fields', which is plural. So as we have a 50, 50 chance of getting it wrong (or right) I decide to walk along the left field, keeping the hedge to our right. And, would you believe, there is only one field. Admittedly, it's a big field and, I suppose, at some point it may have been two fields now made into one, but I must have got it right because we now find a gate which leads us to a lane. Which is exactly what we are told in our next instructions. We are also told that this is Woodruff Lane, but there is no sign along the lane telling us this, so why put this information in the instructions at all?

We decide to walk along the left-hand field

Opposite the gate is a converted barn with an absolutely fabulous garden. All Ron could say was "Blimey and ter think someone owns all that, bet 'e don't vote Labour. Can 'ere the election result now, Liberal; 110 Conservative; 49,853 Labour; 12." I took a couple of photographs of the garden with its little bridge over the water and the boat moored at the bank. It was an idyllic place and is obviously the pride and joy of the owners. But we must get on, we still have a couple of churches left to see and Ron is complaining that all the change in his pockets is beginning to get

Beautiful gardens

heavy. From the barn we turn right and head up the lane towards, we hope the main road. Funnily enough as we start walking up the lane Ron notices a public footpath sign, to our right that is pointing in the opposite direction to the way we are walking. Once again doubt is placed as to which direction we should now be heading. "The instructions definitely say turn right," I tell Ron, and show him the instructions. "Then why's the sign pointin' in the wrong direction?" he asks. And I have no idea, there is no mention of this sign in the instructions but there is another lane heading towards the sign, and opposite, so I can only assume that should we be coming towards the sign from another direction, and on another walk, we would need to turn right here. I think I've got Ron confused enough to carry on up the drive. He just grunts something and carries on walking. Thankfully the main road is found after walking about a mile up the lane.

Pointing the wrong way?

At this busy road junction we need to cross over and head up the lane opposite. If you complete this walk yourselves, be very careful here. The road is the main A283 and cars and lorries are doing a fair lick as they head towards Petworth or Pulborough. Our next instruction reads '...Cross to the lane opposite and Egdean Church is ahead, up the lane on the left...'.

The main road (A283)

So you'd expect the church to be up this lane on the left, wouldn't you? If you answered 'yes' you are wrong. Because the church is up the lane, take the next turning on the left and the church is at the end of the lane, on the left. At least the writer of the instructions got the left-hand side right. As instructions go we are a little disappointed, to say the least, but worse was yet to come, for Ron. The church is locked. We can't get in to take pictures and Ron can't spend any of his loose cash on postcards etc. so we are left to wander around the outside. The churchyard is well maintained and I noticed, just above the entrance to the church an inscription on the

brickwork with the numbers 1622, at first I assumed that this was the date when the church was erected? I have found out little about the church apart from it is dedicated to St. Bartholomew and was rebuilt of stone rubble and brick. I can find no mention as to why it needed to be rebuilt. We suspect that, like a many number of very early churches built in Sussex, this one was originally built of wood. I did manage to find a website[166] for the church which tells us that Egdean was once called Bleatham and the church has had many alterations since the 12th century when it was first

The path to Egdean Church

---

[166] http://www.sussexparishchurches.org/content/view/439/33/- visited 06/06/2010

Does this look like a Lane?

constructed so the date 1622 above the entrance must be there for another reason.

To continue our walk we head back towards the main road and find a path, now on our left which should take us in a northerly direction. Again the instructions aren't correct because they tell us that we are now on a lane, when in fact it is a bridleway? We seem to walk for ages along this bridleway which runs parallel to the busy A283. Because we are walking for so long doubt, again is being planted. Should we be on a lane? Are we heading in the right direction? Ron tells me that we are heading north and a sneaky look at my compass confirms this. But we should come to *'...a fingerpost at the top of the lane...'* Wherever this fingerpost is we need to *'...turn right through a gap in the woodland...'* Have we missed the gap? Has the signpost been removed? Have we missed the signpost? Should we turn back? And everyone we speak to can't understand why we get lost? After much discussion we decide to keep going. Sooner or later we must see a signpost and both Ron and me are beginning to get hungry and need to find somewhere to eat. It is now turned 1 o'clock and we've been walking since 11 which means we can only be about halfway round the 8 miles, although it certainly feels a lot longer.

Ron is still convinced that the writer of the instructions has not completed this walk and keeps on and on about it. And our next discovery does seem to bear out his theory. We do come to a signpost. But there is no gap in the woodland to our right. The signpost doesn't tell us to turn right but to continue straight ahead. "What now?" I ask

Ron. I must admit that I'm getting a little fed up. The instructions are really getting to me now and it's hot, I'm hungry and thirsty and I can feel temperatures rising even more. Ron, being Ron, is always calm and seems to take everything in his stride. He doesn't seem to worry when things don't go right. He starts poking about in the undergrowth with his thumb stick and tells me that he thinks he's found a path. Sure enough, a path is leading away from the fingerpost towards the road but it was very difficult to see. The path does lead us to the road and opposite is the gate we need to go through

We find the gate, at last

to continue with the walk. We now need to look out for a rickety gate, on our right, after about 200 metres. "'Ow long is 200 metres?" asks Ron. "It's as long as it is to the gate," is the only reply I can give. I've had enough and just want to get finished. I think Ron has realised my mood because he starts to talk a lot. He talks about anything and everything. Some makes sense and, typical of Ron, some things don't make sense at all. But it is all light-hearted banter and I start to loosen up. Even more so when something,

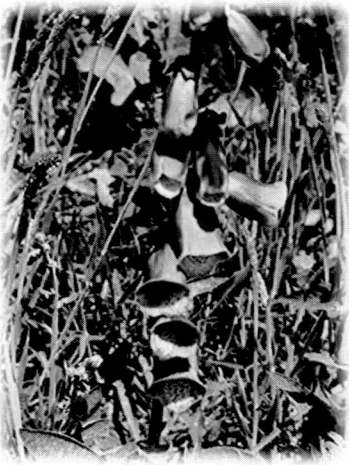

Foxgloves

at last, goes right and we find the 'rickety gate', although Ron did think it was further than 200 metres.

Once through the gate we tumble down and along a fenced path. Again our instructions are not strictly correct but I think I'm now just looking for mistakes and have to promise Ron that I'll stop complaining. To our left is woodland and to our right is open land which looks as if it goes on forever. The view is wonderful and, again, Ron makes the comment, 'some lucky bugger owns all o'that'. The path is reasonably steep as we head down into a valley. On our left are a number of foxgloves, growing wild in the hedgerow. "Although they're blue flowers you also get white ones," explains Ron, "but they always return to the original colour, a bit like lupins." Now I have a lot of lupins in my garden and they are all different colours. "You wait," continues Ron, "they'll all go back to their original colour." "Isn't the foxglove poisonous?" I ask. Ron explains that the foxglove is also known as digitalis which is used in the preparation of drugs but wasn't sure which drugs it was. "I think it 'as somethin' ter do with the heart, but I can't be sure. I don't think it's the flower that causes the problem," he continues, "tis the leaves that are poisonous."

We continue down into the valley remembering that what goes down must also go up, at sometime. "Farmer 'as done us walkers proud," says Ron. "In what way?" I ask. "Just look at the fence e's put up. Yer got no excuse if yer gets yelled at ter get off 'is land, 'cause yer knows exactly where yer can walk an' where yer can't." The fencing looks pretty new all along this path, or it has been well maintained. Our instructions are '…*to hug the woodland on our left and continue east to the houses of Little Bognor.*' But what our instructions didn't tell us was that we would have to cross a few fields before we got to the houses. I'm still not impressed with the instructions because the next couple of fields aren't even mentioned. And one of these fields is full of rape seed with just a wide strip left for walkers. "Just think 'ow busy them bees must be to pollinate this lot," chuckles Ron and as we walk through. That is all you can hear, the bees buzzing from one flower to the next. "I read somewhere that bee stings can be good for you," I advise Ron. "Can't see 'ow," says Ron. But in a little book

Down into the valley

A clear path

Yet more nice gardens

I've got at home[167] it explains how a man in Hailsham became so desperate for a means of relieving his rheumatism that he resorted to the painful but effective traditional remedy of applying enraged bees to his sore and swollen joints, apparently affecting a complete cure[168]. "I wonder how he made the bees angry." I ask.

We now arrive at, what we are told is the small hamlet of Little Bognor. Again this is another beautiful area with some very nice houses and even nicer gardens. We need to turn left here and our next footpath is on the right, after about 100 metres. This path takes us up and behind a garden with a small stream running through it. Ron starts to speak but I finish his sentence for him, "I know Ron, some lucky bugger owns all of this!" The path we are now on goes east with some great views across the Downs. Unfortunately, again, our instructions just tell us to continue until we come to a tarmac road. "Just because this bloke was a better thief than me dad, 'e gets ter own this lot and me ol' dad ended up as a rat catcher," says Ron, looking out across the vastness of the next farm. "Same as me, Ron," I reply, "my old dad ended up as a cleaner at the hospital." "Well, at least that makes me feel a bit better. But look at this view. 'ow about wakin' up an' looking out yer window an' seein' this every mornin'. You'd think yer'd gone ter 'eaven."

And now we just as well might have been. In heaven I mean, because the instructions in my hand are now meaningless. We managed to get to a lane, we turned right as if heading towards the farm, we then forked left along a slender

Ron admires the view

open lane. We did, as I could make out, everything that our instructions told us. We passed a cottage called Amen. Why, oh why then did it all go so wrong? We emerged at another road, which we crossed and then found ourselves in a field. We were to cross the field and enter the woodland but we couldn't find an entrance. We found plenty of stinging nettles that insisted on stinging both of us, even through our clothing. Eventually, once inside the woodland we are now completely off course, but luckily for Ron's astute 20/20 vision he could

We found the slender lane

[167] A Dictionary of Sussex Folk Medicine by Andrew Allen – ISBN 1853063665
[168] Ibid – page 86

see the next church tower, at Stopham, in the distance. Basically, we forgot about the instructions and just went straight towards the church. It is said that two local families who arrived with William the Conqueror settled in Stopham, the Barttelot family from the Manor and de Stopham family from Stopham House. Both families are commemorated within the church which is both beautiful and very well maintained. Thankfully the church is open and purchases were made which, at least, pleased Ron. Unfortunately the instructions now are a completely useless as we should now retrace our steps. Obviously we can't do that because

St Mary the Blessed Virgin, Stopham

we didn't arrive at the church as we should. So I consulted the map, looked at my compass and, basically stuck my finger in the air and said, "if we head down this road we should come to Sandy Lane. From there it's a straight walk to the Swan Inn." "That'll do me," says Ron, "I'm parched!" It has been a long walk. It is now just turned 2 o'clock and we still have a little way to go. When we come to the end of the road we find what

Sandy Lane??

we hope to be Sandy Lane. There are no signs to say that it was Sandy Lane but we went for it anyway. We should now be able to see '...*fine views south to water meadows and the River Rother...*' we didn't. We did see a few farm buildings but try as we might, not a sign of water. Thankfully we emerged at the end of the lane to find the sign telling us that we were, in fact, walking along Sandy Lane, so I did get something right. We headed straight for the Swan Inn, an imposing building on the corner of the High Street. We were greeted by a charming young lady behind the bar and Ron ordered himself a pint of Sharps Doom Bar, whatever that is and, now I'm being really honest, I just had to have a cold pint of lager, not the non-alcoholic stuff and, oh my god, did that taste fantastic. This was my first alcoholic drink in three months. Nectar.

Whilst Ron was ordering the drinks I managed to find the menu, after all we'd been walking since 10.30ish and it was now 2.45 in the afternoon. But when I looked at the prices I was a little taken aback. I only found the bar snack menu but the cost of sandwiches started, yes started, at £6.80. For a sandwich? We asked the young lady if the church was very far from the pub and all she would tell us was that it would be quicker to walk through the wood than go by road. While she was telling us we noticed another lady locking all the doors. Apparently the pub closes at 3 o'clock so we were out of luck anyway. And we didn't take the young ladies advice. I'd noticed a little shop along the road so we thought we'd pop in there for a pie. Would you believe it, they were closed as well.

All in all this was a very long walk. Pleasant in places not so good in others. It would have been nice to visit a few pubs on the way but all the churches were in the middle of nowhere. Perhaps we'll have more luck on the next walk?

Group Walk

As this chapter heading implies this was going to be a group walk, where a number of people join Ron and me for a little bit of fresh air and some exercise. I say should, because it didn't really happen in the way that I expected. We were let down by some people, not that it was the first time and probably will not be the last. But if you remember it used to be me that would make all sorts of rash decisions when the alcohol reached the spot. Now that I rarely drink alcohol I can see others doing the same as me. "Yes, I'd love to come for a walk," we are told, "I'll come on a walk with you but it must be on the level, I don't do hills," "You just say the day, Graham, and I'll be there," are all familiar phrases to Ron and me. But when it comes down to it some do not show. Not too surprisingly the people who let us down today are male, a few of the drinkers from the King's Head. The females were waiting for me with Ron when I went to collect them at 1.30pm on a warm Wednesday afternoon, as arranged. Both Helen and Pip were prepared for the walk and Helen had brought along Benson, a beautiful, high-spirited Alsatian puppy.

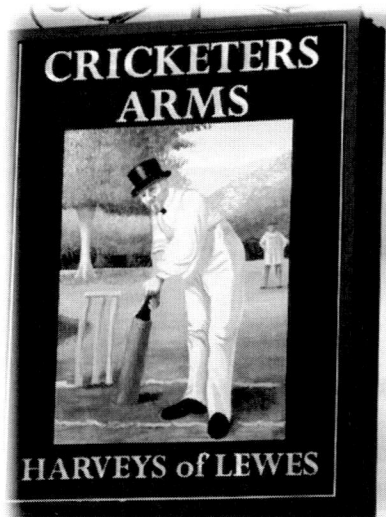

The sign outside the pub

The starting point for this walk is Berwick. Should anyone remember the last walk Ron and I carried out around this village it turned out to be one of my least popular walk although it did leave a lasting impression. The walk also has a connection with Ron's favourite sport, cricket, because we actually start the walk from a pub (surprise, surprise) called the Cricketers Arms. If you get the chance to visit this pub we thoroughly recommend it. Unfortunately it's a bit off the beaten track but it is well worth a visit. We didn't eat there but we sat and tried a tipple and what we saw coming from the kitchen looked very appetising. Perhaps I could encourage the 'Sad Sods' Sunday Lunch Club' to try out the food and let us all know what it's like?

Anyway, back to the walk. As we are only a small 'group' now, this walk could also be called a 'pub walk' but we've already done a few of those and both Ron and me are getting a little worried about our reputations. But I will have to be honest and tell you that the walk is, in fact, taken from a pub walking book[169], that is becoming a little dog-eared around the corners due to the amount of use it's getting. As this is a circular walk this will mean that we will start at the Cricketers Arms and then finish at the Cricketers Arms (isn't life unfair?) the obvious place to park the car is in the pub car park. And it was whilst we were walking from the car park to the bar, across a well-kept cottage type garden that I do believe Ron and I found fame. It may be a surprise to everyone that Ron and I were not first to the bar but got held back by a lady who attracted my attention with a wave of a gloved hand and a "cooie! Is your name Graham and is that Ron?" she asks as I approach the table and she points an accusing finger at Ron. "That's right," I answer; a

---

[169] 'Pub Walks in East Sussex' by Mike Power Published by Power Publications Walk 4 Page 12

Concrete farm road

little apprehensively I might add. "Are you doing a walk around here?" she gushes as she turns to her companion and says, "you know who this is, don't you?" It was obvious her companion had no idea what she was talking about. "It's Graham, from Ron and Graham, you know, the Graham that wrote that book about walks in Sussex." She turns to me and continues, "I loved the book, a laugh on every page, are you going to write another one or are you just doing another walk around here?" Ron has headed off to the bar with Helen and Pip as I explain that we are writing another book and to keep an eye on the local papers because we are hoping to release the title soon. "And what is the next book going to be called?" she asks. "It's going to be 'Thumbsticks, Boots and a Carrier Bag'." I am then given a lecture on what the book should be called and, of course, the lady has ideas about where we should walk etc. etc. etc. I thank her for her advice but have to leave to be with my friends and hastily make my way back to Ron. But it was really nice to be recognised like that, it's never happened to me before and made me feel pretty good.

But it is time to start the walk. Benson is on his lead and we're ready for the off. We leave the pub and turn right, heading towards the village which is Berwick but is not where you think Berwick to be. As I've said before I thought that Berwick was were the pub called 'The Berwick' and Berwick railway station is but of course that is not the true Berwick, or is it? Anyway we pass the mini-roundabout with its sign pointing to the church. Just on this roundabout is a minibus loading up with sightseers, obviously out for the afternoon and enjoying some good old Sussex hospitality. We keep to the right and walk up to the concrete farm road ahead. What is nice, so far, and I appreciate that it is early in the walk, there is no way that you can go wrong because the signs are very clear and easy to see.

Benson enjoys the freedom

Because the field we are in has no animals Helen lets Benson off the lead. No sooner is this done and he's off. Running around like a dog possesed. Our instructions tell us to walk across the centre of the field on a raised footpath. Again this is very easy to see and whilst we wander towards the distant hedge Helen asks if we know how far away the horizon is. I can remember I was once told that if you stand on a beach and look out to sea the horizon is 3 miles away. But, according to Helen, it all depends on how tall you are. "If you're of average height," explains Helen, "the horizon is 2½ miles away," "An' what is average height?" asks Ron, "Well, it must be about 6 feet," answers Helen, "I got that from the programme QI on the television," she continues, "just something I remembered." "That's why I didn't know the answer," says Ron, "cause I ain't got a telly." We continue the discussion by trying to work out that if you are smaller than six foot tall would that make the horizon further away or closer? Or does it really matter how tall you are??

For some reason Benson has decided to try and trip me up. He isn't bothered with anyone else but he insists on darting between my legs, he keeps running up behind me, pushing his way through and then going round for another try, but at least he's enjoyng himself. And once we get to the otherside of the field and turn left he gives up and leaves me alone. As you know I'm not that keen on animals but Benson, although small at the moment he is going to be a very big Alsation, he does have a very placid temperamant, but I'd be a little bit wary of him when he gets to be fully grown.

Unused path

Once we turn left and walk along the field edge we must pass any paths that lead off to the right. Luckily for us the only path that I saw was very overgrown and looked as if it hadn't been used for some time. Benson has now started to walk sensibly and I don't have to watch my every step. The views along here are remarkable. The Downs in front of us look very luschious and green in the distance. I'm surprised at how far you can see from here. Again we start to discuss the horizon and I notice that Ron has gone surprisingly quiet. At the end of this path we again turn left. Both Ron and Pip have noticed that the church spire can be seen over the trees. "Don't worry, Pip," says Ron, "as long as we can see that church spire, the pub won't be too far away." We are now on a bridleway which, again, is raised from the fields around us. Although it is obvious I didn't see any signs indicating that this was the way we should be heading. Pip is a horse rider and is unfamiliar with this bridleway but says that she would consider coming this way again, next time she is on horseback. It is very quiet and secluded and, as we approach another bridleway that crosses in front of us there must be a network of paths in this area. The church spire can still be seen over the trees to our left.

The distant Downs

Walking along towards the barn

Where the bridleways cross we need to continue in a straight line until we come to a dwelling. The temperature has started to rise now and it is getting a little warm. We are now walking towards a barn that has had considerable work carried out recently and is up for sale. My immediate reaction is to wonder why anyone would want to buy a

I can remember walking along the lane

large barn in the middle of knowhere but I'm sure there must be those that can afford to do that sort of thing.

And now I have a massive, massive problem! As I've said many times before, Ron and I, sometimes with others, complete the walk. I then download the pictures onto the computer and I then write about the walk. I've being doing it for over 4 years now. People who have walked with us have commented on my memory for detail because I very rarely write things down although on some occassions notes are very necessary. This walk wasn't one that needed notes. So why, oh why am I sitting in front of my computer screen and I can't think of what to write. All because I can't, for the life of me, remember any of the conversation between the four of us from this point in the walk until we got to the road. I can remember walking along the lane. I can vividly remember coming to a path where we turned left, and walked across a field, and I can even remember my wife phoning me to find out how the walk was going. But the rest is a complete blank. I've checked the pictures to see if anything jogs my memory. But no. I even went to the King's Head one evening to speak to Ron and even he can't remember what was spoken. "Benson kept 'eadin' fer the barbed wire," says Ron, "an' 'ellen kept callin' 'im back." "I can remember that and Benson was on a lead then. But what did we talk about?" "I can remember I were walkin' be'ind Pip," says Ron with a grin. I thought Ron would remember that, he

Just what did we talk about?

always does. "But what did we talk about?" I'm beginning to get desperate. "Pip asked 'ow many photo's we'd taken ov' er backside an' I said out o'79 phot'ers that you'd taken we'd only got 77 ov' er bum," chuckles Ron. I had to convince Pip that Ron was exagerating because, in fact, we'd only got the one photograph and Ron said he wanted that for a keepsake.

So, I'm afraid, whatever we spoke about has gone never to be repeated. Our instructions tell us that we should reach a road and we managed to get to that so all is not lost. At the road we turned left and headed towards Drusillas Zoo Park, a wonderful place to take young children for a day out, but it is a little expensive. Just before we reach the entrance to the Zoo Park we should find a bridleway on our left, but we didn't. Ron managed to find a public footpath which looked as if it was heading back towards the pub so we turned left here and made our way, slowly, through a couple of fields until we reached the church. As we have visited and described this church before[170] I will not

---

[170] 'Left or Right, Ron?' by Graham Pollard Chapter 4 Page 13

Just a glimpse of the murals

go on and on about it. But I would encourage anyone who is visiting the area to just spend a few minutes to have a look around this ancient building. Dedicated to St. Michael & All Angels the church is reputed to be of Saxon origin and is one of the most peaceful places you will ever find. There are few stained glass windows but what the church lacks in stained glass is certainly made up for by the 20th century murals that adorn the interior of the church. The work was carried out by Duncan Grant (1885 – 1978) and Quentin Bell (1910 – 1996) and was started in 1941, during the Second World War and completed in about 1996[171]. And I have to say they are stunning!

To get back to the Cricketers is just a short walk around the path to the road where we turn right and the pub is on your left-hand side. Obviuosly we couldn't leave without sampling just a little more of the hospitality of the establishment before we headed home so a quick drink was enjoyed by all in the garden. It was now that Ron decided to catch up with technology and wanted to take a picture, using my camera. After a quick guide on where to look and what button to press, Ron had a go. All he kept saying was, "I can only see me shirt!" as he clicked away, but I think the photo came out reasonably well, don't you?

A well earned rest

---

[171] 'A Guide to the Church and 20th Century Bloomsbury Murals' purchased at the church

The Last Walk

We have come to the final walk. Some readers will be pleased that at last we are stowing away our thumbsticks, putting our boots away and Ron can bin his carrier bag. My wife will be pleased that I'm about to turn off the computer, but it is a bit of a sad day for Ron and me. I honestly think that people could be getting tired of our ramblings and, although there are still many, many villages and paths we have not visited I am finding it increasingly difficult to find different things to write about. Currently we are going through World Cup 2010 so I suppose I could write a few words about England's performance so far but let's be honest, yet again, England just haven't performed at all. I have my views and anyone who knows Ron will be aware of his very strong views about English football and the players so I'll not write anything more other than to say to all those who doubted what I have said right from the start of the tournament – "I told you so!!"

But let us continue with the walk. Although I have titled this as 'The Last Walk' it could be called a 'Family Walk' or even 'A Kiddies Walk' because that, basically, is what it is. We are visiting Crowhurst, which is a little village resting in the folds of the hills of East Sussex. The walk is described as over '...*gentle field and woodland paths with slight gradients...*' and is only 2 miles long, taken from a book by Len Markham[172], so we will have a nice leisurely stroll in the countryside. As this is supposed to be a nice 'stroll' we have decided to invite some children with us for the afternoon, and those who have read the 'Kiddies Walk' in this book will know what that entails before we set out. All checks have been carried out, the questionnaire has been completed and a check on the route has been done just to ensure that it is safe and reasonably easy for the 'little ones'. Whilst on the subject of 'little ones' we will also be accompanied by a big 'little one'. When the walk was spoken about in our usual hostelry, and that we

We check out the walk with Peter

would be inviting kiddies Derek asked if he could bring his 'kiddie' with him. When I asked who he was bringing it turned out to be Susan, his daughter. Sue will be the oldest kiddie ever to walk with us. But she is still Derek's 'kiddie' so no rules have been broken.

As I said earlier, checks have to be made on the walk and normally these would be carried out by my daughter, Michelle, and me. Unfortunately my daughter is not available so I have resorted to taking Ron with me and we are accompanied by Peter who assures me that Ron used to be a 'kiddie' in a previous life so will be more than capable in checking things out. The walk that we are proposing has no real problems, apart from a little water that only I seem to worry about. But we will, if the weather remains as hot as it is at present, have to advise one and all to cover their heads, wear sun block, bring

---

[172] 'Kiddiwalks in East Sussex' by Len Markham published by Countryside Books

plenty of water and, because something crawled up the shorts of Peter and bit him in a personal place we may suggest some form of insect repellent. I say that we have no problem with the walk and we don't, but Ron did have a problem with the pub, it was closed. There is only one pub in Crowhurst, called The Plough. And it's closed when we finished checking the walk. So, to make really sure that **everything** on the walk has been checked out we've decided to go back to Crowhurst the following day, just to check out the pub. "After all," explains Ron, "we don't want the little kiddies ter be let down by not bein' able ter 'ave a drink after a long walk. Wouldn't be right, would it?" And I'm not going to argue.

Before we go to the walk I have found out a couple of things about Crowhurst that I would like to pass on. The very nice bar lady in The Plough advises us that Crowhurst is the most spread out village in the south of England. I have to say that, even before we start the walk, both Ron and I have visited the village twice and approached it from two different directions. When we drove home on the second visit we found direction number three and I'm sure that others will find their own way to the start of the walk. But in case you are unsure where Crowhurst is you can approach it from Battle, Ninfield, Hastings or Catsfield. The choice is all yours. We've now tried most of them and I think the Catsfield way is probably the quickest route.

In the Parish register for Crowhurst, dated 10th December 1680 the churchwarden has written *'A blazing starre appear. It did first shew itself 10th December which did gleam from the south right to the middle of the heavens, broader than a rainbow by farre and continued till latter end of February.'* It would seem that he was referring to what we now know to be Halley's Comet.[173]

Apart from odd snippets of information I can find very little about Crowhurst in any of the books that I have. I've also looked on the Internet without a lot of success so I'll get on with the walk. Originally we were just taking a couple of children with us but today both Ron and I

Crowhurst church

will be accompanied by Sophie, Rachel and Meghan, who are related to Ron and over on holiday from Canada with mum Lorraine, Jack, Susan and Will along with their respective parent, guardian or grandparent. Sadly my grandchildren are not able to make it as they are in quarantine and cannot mix with other children. My granddaughter, Megan, goes to a playschool which has a confirmed e-coli infection so all children at the school need to be tested for the condition. The tests have been carried out but the results have not been returned. Until they get the results the children are not permitted to mix with other children, purely as a precaution.

On our walk today each of the children will be armed with a little questionnaire (the questions and answers are included in the chapter) and a pencil to write the answers. We will also be taking them back to the King's Head for a bite to eat and to present each and every child with a certificate and a rosette. The last thing on this chapter will be a group photograph. So, we're all set, all we need now is some decent weather. Whilst on

---

[173] 'Hidden Sussex Day by Day' by Swinfen & Arscott – ISBN 0950951021 Page 149

the subject of weather I found out that on Monday 14th January 1987 Hastings had 16 inches of snow, the temperature was nearly -10C and at 5.30 in the morning a train left Hastings Railway Station. The same train was later reported to be snowbound, somewhere near Crowhurst.[174]

The first problem we have is making sure that everyone knows the way to Crowhurst. As I said there are so many ways to get to the village I thought it best that the other three cars followed me. That way we would all end up at the same place at the same time. This turned out to be a plan until I drove straight past the place where we had to park, so we all had to turn round and head for the little lane opposite the church which leads to the railway station. We didn't actually see the station so I can't say if there is an actual station or not. I think it was closed by Beeching but I'm sure someone will let me know, either way.

Once all the cars were parked I issued the questionnaires and pencils to the children, and Ron ensured that Susan, who after all was the elder of the children, was suitably supplied with sweets. Should the other children require a sweet at any time during the walk then they simply had to call for Susan.

Will steps it out

We start the walk by entering the church path and head towards the church door. Before we get to the door, on the left, is what has been described as the oldest living thing in East Sussex. Derek thought it was Ron and Ron insisted that it was Derek when, in fact, it is a large Yew tree.

Question 1 *How much does the tree measure around its girth?*
a]150feet(46 meters) b] 44feet(13.5 meters) c]10feet (3 meters) d]95feet (29meters)
Answer – b] 44 feet or 13.5 meters

It was surprising how many of the children got this first question correct. Will decided to measure it out with his own feet and got the correct answer, Sophie, Rachel and Meghan took one look at it and decided from the off and Jack took advice from his dad. It is believed that the tree was a 'hanging tree' and after much discussion we leave the churchyard and head towards the back of the church and out onto the road. Here we turned left, now walking along the road edge. For a small village the roads here are quite busy so care is needed.

After just a few hundred yards I noticed that a few of the children had bags of sweets. It is obvious that Susan is a soft touch with the children. We now come to a public footpath signpost where we will be turning left.

Question 2 *How far is it from this signpost to Battle?*
a]4 miles b]14 miles c]2 miles or d] 3½ miles
Answer – d] 3½ miles

---

[174] 'The Sussex Weather Book' by Ogley, Currie and Davison ISBN 9781872337302 Page 126

This was purely an observation question as the answer is carved into the signpost, as was the answer to the next question, because what I was attempting to do was to get the children to look at their surroundings and remember what they could see. There was no prize for getting the answers correct and I was very pleased with the overall effect the questions were having with the children. As I said the next question was also very visual:

Question 3 *We are about to go onto a named walk. What is the name?*
a]The Long Walk b]The Easy Walk c]The Up Hill Walk or d] Bexhill 1066 Walk
Answer *– d] Bexhill 1066 Walk*

We turn left and pass through a kissing gate. Anyone who has read our stories will be aware of what a kissing gate is but it didn't occur to me that our overseas guests Rachel, Sophie and Meghan may not have seen or even heard of a 'kissing gate'. So an explanation was needed. Unfortunately my explanation was misinterpreted by some when Dick refused to pass through the gate, if I intended to give him a kiss. Thankfully the girls accepted the explanation of Ron and all seemed pretty relieved to be through it and heading along the narrow grassy lane.

We all say hello to the goats

Walking past the Broad Beans

Although I work at a school it's been many years since I've been accompanied by so many children and I'm always stunned at how inquisitive children can be. All the way round these two short miles the children kept asking questions about everything they saw. Little Jack, Dick's son, needed to know everything about everything. His constant questions beginning with why or how seemed to get everyone talking. I spent a quite a few moments with Sophie, from Canada, who clearly and eloquently explained a number of things about her home town of Vancouver. She freely spoke about her school life and her friends, her likes and dislikes and I felt honoured that she could speak to me so freely after only meeting me for the first time a couple of hours ago.

Just to our left, as we walk along the lane is a paddock, with miniature ponies, and just next to these ponies is another paddock which contained three goats. Whilst the ponies didn't respond to the children's calls the goats certainly did and didn't hesitate to climb onto the fence so that the children could stroke them. As we leave the goats I advise the children that we will be walking into fields that contain some crops and that they should try to remember the names of these crops. A question is asked about them in the questionnaire. The first field we come to is full of broad beans. Most of the children didn't like broad beans. In Canada, Meghan advised me, that they are just called beans. Ron told me, when we checked out this walk a couple of weeks ago, that usually these bean plants are covered in black fly. When I said that in my garden, I had broad beans and I had black fly but thought that they would be eaten by ants. "Oh, no they won't," explains Ron, "the ants protect the black fly because they give off a sugary substance that the ants like." When I get home I'll have to spray my plants with insecticide. But I reminded everyone to keep a note of the name of this crop.

At the corner of this field of broad beans is a stile leading into open pasture. I turn to Ron because I'm not exactly sure of which direction we go in. "'ain't yer brought the map?" asks Ron. "Well, no," I try to explain, "I thought I'd know the way, after all it's only been a couple of weeks since we were last here. But it seems to look a bit different somehow." I have a rough idea that we need to follow a faint pathway, across the middle of the field and enter a wood at the other side. Ron takes me to one side. "Yer mean ter say we got all these people with us, with all these kiddies an' you aint got the map? We gets lost with a map, think 'ow far we can get lost without a bugger." I'm not sure if Ron is angry or not. "I did bring a map," I offer in way of an explanation,

Jack and his dad sit awhile

"but I left it in the boot of the car." Before Ron can say anymore, and I've noticed the children had stopped to listen to what we were saying, I said in an assertive voice, "ok, everyone, we now walk across this pasture and head towards the wood opposite," hoping that I not only sound convincing but I also know what I'm doing. I'm sure Ron isn't convinced.

As we approach the other side of the pasture I recognise the board inside the wood and heave a sigh of relief. Ron stands and shakes his head. My wife comes over and asks what the problem is. I explain about leaving the map in the car and she has a go at me as well. I can't win, so I frantically try to remember everything about the walk so that I don't have to ask Ron directions again. Hopefully, as we walk, things will look familiar. Right now we are heading towards a pond. But before we do....

Question 4 *What is the name of the wood we are about to walk through?*
Answer – *Forewood*

The chestnut trees from this wood, which was around at the time of the Battle of Hastings in 1066, used to be prepared for fence posts and the other, unwanted trees were converted to charcoal[175] in large charcoal burners. Forewood, is now in the capable hands of the RSPB which bring us to the next question:

Question 5 *What do the initials R S P B stand for?*
Answer – *Royal Society for the Protection of Birds*

---

[175] http://www.forewood.co.uk/theforewood.htm visited 18/07/2010

As we walk down the slope into the wood I warn the grown ups that at the bottom of this slope is a pond which, I believe, is called Asten Brook[176] and although very picturesque the thought of children and water still worries me. But my fears were not founded. All the children, even the older ones, managed to steer clear of any mishaps as we spent a few minutes at the water, looking at the wildlife and just resting for a little while.

One of many seats

We leave the little brook and head slightly uphill along a clear path. I can't really remember this path being so steep and the fact that we have Derek with us is a little worrying for me. Derek is the elder of the group and I need to make sure he isn't suffering. It has started to get pretty warm as the time approaches midday but I'm sure, just ahead is a wooden seat. Derek can rest there if he wants too. But we seem to walk for some way and we haven't reached the seat yet? Doubt starts to creep in but I daren't mention it to anyone just in case. So we keep walking and, thankfully, come to the wooden seat. But I needn't have worried because Derek said he was o.k. "If I sit down now," says Derek, "I'll never get back up again. I'm fine, really I am." So we don't stop for a rest but turn left here and head into the shade of the trees again.

Sophie, the little girl from Canada has caught me up and borrowed my thumbstick. All the way through this part of the walk she didn't stop talking about her home. The family are returning to Canada at the end of next week and I suspect that they have had a really good time with gran and granddad and may find it a little difficult to return. We now come to a signpost where we need to turn left, again. It is just past here that we need to cross over Powder Mill Stream for the first time....

Question 6 – *What do we walk on to cross Powder Mill Stream?*
a]a tunnel b]a bridge c]a road d]a gate
Answer – *b]a bridge*

We cross the stream for the first time!

I inform the children that they should keep a check on how many times we cross this stream as it is a question further on in the walk. "This is the first time we have crossed the stream. So remember, one." "Actually, your wrong it's twice," interrupts Marian. "I'm afraid it's only once." I correct her. "No it's not," she argues, "the stream must fill the pond we've just been to, so we must have crossed the stream twice now." "The stream is called Powder Mill Stream and, as far as I'm aware, doesn't feed the brook but flows to join the Combe Haven River. We cross it here and we cross it

---

[176] Ibid

A butterfly takes a break

Walking in single file

again further on in our walk. I can show you the route of our walk on an Ordinance Survey map that I have back at the car which will prove to you that we actually cross the stream twice. Now shall we continue?" "'ave we got a map?" asks Ron in a whisper. "We have, but I'm not sure if it's an Ordinance Survey map," I reply, "perhaps Marian won't ask when we get back to the car." "Bet she does," chuckles Ron.

Once everyone is over the stream we turn right and head along the field edge walking parallel with Powder Mill stream. "Try to remember the crops," I call out. "You'll see some more along this part of the walk." As we continue I notice that I am getting ahead of the others. But it is so nice and peaceful out here that you can get lost in the atmosphere and, although people are with me they're not, if you know what I mean. I have found recently, even when I'm walking with Ron, I'm on my own, with my own thoughts, ideas, sights and smells. I can walk for ages with people but not see or hear them. Is that strange? Is it a sign of dementia, of getting old or is it a natural thing? Who knows? But I must wait for everyone to catch up. Young Jack has decided to re-grass the area and our overseas contingent are marvelling at the abundance of butterflies and dragonflies that they have managed to see.

When we got home and I spoke to my wife about this walk she told me that this part was the least enjoyable. When I asked why she said that everyone got spread out. "We were all walking in single file," she continued, "and we tended to loose that togetherness feeling. Which was a shame, because Jack was keeping everyone amused at the back of the procession but we couldn't hear what the people at the front were saying." But unfortunately the pathway was very narrow and the only way we could get to the next part of the walk was to follow each others footsteps. But eventually everyone caught up and we headed for the next crossing of Powder Mill stream where we will re-enter the wood and come away from the crops so the next question was:

Question 7 – *Can you name the crops that we have passed?*
Answer – *Broad Beans, Barley and Wheat*

"Actually there was four," says Marian. "I'm sorry Marian, but there were only three actual crops." "I counted four," she continues, "the three you just said and corn." "I think you'll find that the corn you saw was only growing on the edge of the field and was probably a residue of last year's crop," I notice that no one is agreeing or disagreeing with me and hope I haven't made a mistake. But for heavens sake it's only a questionnaire for children it doesn't have to be written in tablets of stone and I was getting a little frustrated with her comments. Perhaps she was just doing it to 'wind me up'?

As we turn right and cross over Powder Mill stream for the second and final time we head back into Forewood. Just as we do there is a signpost, next to the entrance sign which gives the answer to the next visual question. To assist the children I have put a photograph of the post in the questionnaire.

Question 8 – *As we re-enter the wood there is a signpost which advises that certain things are not permitted past the sign. One is horses, what is the other?*
Answer – *Cyclists.*

The sign for Q.8

I notice that Marian is not looking at the post but is looking at something else, before the bridge. "You're looking at the wrong thing, Marian, that's why I put a photograph of the signpost in the questionnaire" I advise. "I'm looking at this post, it tells me the same thing, doesn't it?" is her reply. I refuse to argue anymore. The next question is, again, visual:

Question 9 – *What animal is permitted in the wood?*
Answer – *Dogs on a lead*

We now make our way back through the wood. The instructions for this walk actually go a bit wrong here. Our instructions read as follows, '....*turn right over the footbridge and follow the direction marker right, follow the next direction marker left and drop downhill...* '[177] If you follow these instructions you will not end up where you want to be. Trust me, we got lost when we came here the first time. What you have to do is turn right over the footbridge, follow the direction marker right, do not turn left but stay on this path. If you follow this footpath all the way downhill you end up back at the wooden seat that I wanted to give Derek a rest at, just after the pond. Do you remember the seat? Once back at the seat we turn right and follow the same path we did earlier but instead of crossing Powder Mill stream again, just before the bridge, we turn left, over the stile and follow the stream back to our starting point via a few kissing gates. This was another part of the walk that bothered me simply because of the water but, as everyone told me before the walk I had nothing to worry about. All the children were great. Jack, Will Sophie and Rachel just didn't stop nattering and because Meghan was so quiet it was really noticeable. I thought that her quietness may be because she wasn't

Derek manages the last stile

---

[177] 'Kiddiwalks in East Sussex' by Len Markham Page 47 Instruction 4

enjoying the walk but mum told me that she has always been the quiet one in the family and that her sisters made up for her. Just before we get to the car we have to pass the remains of Crowhurst Manor which is an ideal place for a photo opportunity so, below, is the whole group, minus yours truly, taking a pose in true professional manner.

We did stop at the Plough in Crowhurst for a well earned drop of refreshment and then headed back to the King's Head, in Hailsham where everyone was presented with a certificate and rosette and our hosts, Helen and Darren, along with Steve had laid on a lovely barbecue for one and all to enjoy. The end, I believe, to a great little walk with some great company. Thank you all.

And that, I'm afraid, concludes our stories.

The whole group

The children with certificates

WALKS THAT DIDN'T MAKE IT

Every now and again both Ron and I would like to carry out a walk but for one reason or another it doesn't come off. The 'Kiddies Walk' in this book very nearly didn't happen because we thought that the walk we chose was not suitable. Luckily we managed to find another one reasonably quickly. But sometimes things do not work out quite so well.

Right from the start of the writing for this book I wanted to be able to 'Walk the Bounds' of Hailsham, but try as I might I could not find a complete and easily understood map for the whole Parish. Some weeks ago a friend of ours, whilst checking the quality of our local brew, told me that he had, in his possession a little book that might interest Ron and me. "I'll bring it over to the pub the next time I'm in," says Alan, "nice little book, it is, all about Hailsham." But it was some time before I set my eyes on the book but what a treat it was. The title is 'Everything Except 'Poor Law'' and is written by 'Tom Collbran's daughter of Hailsham.[178] What Alan handed me was what looked like, a photocopy of the original (?) and it is full to the brim of stories of our home town that are told by Florence M Farrant. It is written in a way that takes you back in time. I will just give you a taster by the first few lines taken from the Forward of the 'book'.........

This is not a book; it has no plot nor is it a 'literary effort' in any way. It is 'Jus Nabbling', and I was terrified into jotting things down by Doris, and by Doris Walker, so they can take the blame for all its errors, and can go to Lewes jail for me if any libel case comes up at 'Hailsham Petty Sessions'.......

It concludes with the words: *'Nuff Sed'.*

Just the forward makes you want to read more, and more there is. But, I hear you ask, what has this to do with Ron and me going for a walk. Well, whilst reading of some of Florence's stories, I started to think about the events that were explicitly told by her in the 'book' that will never happen again, because the tradition has been lost. And that doesn't seem right to me. So I started to look into the possibility of reliving just one event from the 'book' – Beating the Bounds. Which, for those who are not aware of the event, involves walking around the boundary of the parish, beating sticks on certain landmarks? Now that seems like a thing that Ron and I could do. But how do I find out where the parish boundary is?

The Town Council couldn't help but if I wanted the Mayor of Hailsham to write a few words for insertion in the book he '...*would be only too happy to*

---

[178] Printed by Jenners of Hailsham but I'm unable to establish if it was ever published although the local library has a copy?

oblige.' But he couldn't supply a map of the Parish he serves?? I was then directed to Wealden District Council who, with the help of the young lady on the front desk could supply me with a map. Unfortunately it was a map of the town boundary and not a map of the Parish, but thank you WDC for your help. At least you tried. I then took a visit to our local library. Here the librarians were very helpful and allowed me to peruse the maps, held under lock and key. Unfortunately the maps they had, although of the parish and of the date I was looking for, were on so many pages that I would have needed a haversack to carry them with me. I thought about copying them into a smaller scale by hand but….. The next suggestion was to head towards Lewes and The Public Records Office. This was a brilliant idea but just to be permitted into their Search Room I first had to supply two items bearing my address as well as a driving licence or a passport so that I could prove not only who I was but where I came from. As that meant another drive back home and a drive back to Lewes with the chance that they might not have the map I'm looking for I decided not to go there. So, I'm afraid the 'Bounds Walk' was not done.

Another walk that didn't make it was, in fact, suggested by a couple of ladies who wished to walk through the bluebells in the spring. I managed to find a nice walk which included a visit to a windmill that may have had connections with my relatives from West Hoathly. Everyone was looking forward to the walk. A date was arranged, well in advance, but on the day that the walk was to be completed both ladies couldn't make it. So we made another date. Again, due to circumstances beyond the ladies control, the walk had to be cancelled. By now the bluebells had died. So the 'Bluebell Walk' was a no, no.

A drinking friend of ours suggested that we 'do' a 'Railway Walk'. This involved climbing aboard a train at one station, travelling in the train to another station and then walking back to the first station. It seemed a very good idea at the time. I managed to find a suitable train/walk with the aid of my many walking books to discover that what our friend was suggesting was a trip on a steam train, which involved an organised brewery trip along the 'Bluebell Line' and then walking back. After they had drunk copious amounts of beer….. I don't think so.

After our last 'Dog Walk', and the number of miles we managed to make my son's two Labradors walk, I had to think twice about doing it again. It was with some hesitation that my son, Anthony, agreed to let us take his two dogs out but I had to assure him that it wouldn't be too far. "After all," he reminds me, "the last walk they did with you and Ron they slept for three days afterwards!" Unfortunately Tess and Pip are that much older now and I just couldn't let them go through it again so I shelved the idea.

You will have noticed that we have not done anything 'funny' in this book. This must be due to me not drinking alcohol because everyone knows that once the amber nectar hits the spot I'm likely to agree to anything. And it's not for the want of trying because ballooning as well as abseiling has been mentioned over the King's Head. But apart from the 'Charity Walk' this year it's different. We have not done a 'Fancy Dress Walk' – I nearly flew over the cliffs when I dressed in a tutu and wings one Christmas, and anything to do with horses is a definite no as is pretend ice skating, although we did have some fun at the time of these events, but I always seemed to regret it afterwards..

Another book that found its way onto my bookshelf was 'Ten Adventurous Walks in West Sussex'[179]. This book contained some fantastic walks but the shortest was 10 miles (16 km) and the longest was 14½ miles. As you all know we can get lost in a short walk of 3 miles or less. Just think how many times we could be lost on a walk that was 14½ miles long. We would be out for days.

I also considered completing a 'Challenging Walk'. In a book titled 'Best Sussex Walks'[180] there is such a walk and would you believe its 30 miles in length. I'm not joking. But it was whilst I very briefly considered this walk that it suddenly hit me that most of the walks I have completed with Ron are all pretty challenging in one way or another. So I soon put that book back on the shelf.

A 'City Walk' was also discussed at various times. The nearest city to us is, of course, Brighton. Anyone who has visited Brighton will know that whilst it is a lovely? city it is very compact. Now people living in Brighton who read this will be angrily putting pen to paper and writing to me extolling the virtues of their fair city but a walk round Brighton, to me, is mainly a shopping trip. I know there are some historical places of interest in Brighton but we never got to do this one.

A picture walk was discussed. The idea was that we would take a group of people with us to a location in a minibus and they would paint a scene from that location. But, unfortunately one of the people we were going to take died suddenly and the idea didn't seem so good any more.

........and finally

So the time has come to call it a day. In some ways I will miss having to write about all we see and all the things that Ron and I speak about. I will, as long as health lets me, continue to walk with Ron and meet many, many new friends and visit some sacred places as well as some public houses, after all apart from getting some exercise that's what walking is all about. And I have enjoyed the last few years. With the help of Ron I have learnt a lot about Sussex, I have been very lucky and seen things in the countryside that, perhaps, a lot of people will never see unless they go out and look for it.

But most of all I have met a lot of people who have inspired me, encouraged me, made me laugh and at times made me sad. But everyone we have met has taken the time to speak to Ron and me, to talk about all things and anything, which, hopefully, should the younger generation pick up this book and read it will encourage them that there is more fun to be had in the great outdoors rather than being shut inside with a games machine, a computer or a television.

---

[179] Written by Raymond Hugh and published by Morning Mist Publications – ISBN 1874476012
[180] Written by David Bathurst and published by Summersdale – ISBN 978184024306

Bibliography

Many people have asked me where it is I get my information from. To be honest a lot of the information about places we visit whilst on our walks comes from the numerous books on Sussex that I have in my own personal 'library'. Of course, some of the facts[?] and figures are 'word of mouth' from people that Ron and I have met but if this was the case then I have attempted to verify the information, again, from books that I have at home. So, just to give you some idea on the extent that I have available to research the areas we visit I give you, below, a comprehensive list of the books that I have had to refer to. I have not put them in any special order apart from the order that they are in my bookcase:

A Dictionary of Sussex Folk Medicine by Dr. Andrew Allen published by Countryside Books 1995

Hidden Sussex Day by Day by Warden Swinfen & David Arscott published by BBC Radio Sussex 1987

Pub Walks in East Sussex by Mike Power published by Power Publications updated 2003

Kiddiwalks in East Sussex by Len Markham published by Countryside Books 2006

The Lore of the Land by Westwood and Simpson published by Penguin Books paperback 2006

The Strange Laws of Old England by Nigel Cawthorne published by Portrait, an imprint of Piatkus Books Ltd reprint 2006

I Never Knew That about England by Christopher Winn published by Ebury Press 2005

A Thousand Years of the English Parish by Anthea Jones published by The Windrush Press 2000

Family Names and Family History by David Hey published by Hambledon and London 2000

The Life of a Man – Ron Spicer 1929-1996 – by Doris Spicer published by Country Books 1997

Walks in Sussex by Norman Willis published by Spurbooks Ltd 1997

Complete Verse – Hilaire Belloc Introduced by A.N. Wilson published by Pimlico 1991

The Green Roof of Sussex by Charles Moore published by Middleton Press 1984

The Guide to Sussex – Part of the 'Little' series published by Methuen & Co. 9th edition 1938

Ashdown Forest by Garth Christian published by The Society of Friends of Ashdown Forest second edition 1968

Debrett's *People of Sussex* edited by Juliet Hime published by Debrett's Peerage Ltd 1991

The History of a Village Band 1896-1996 by Judith Kinnison Bourke published by the Warbleton and Buxted Band 1996

Battlefield Walks in Kent and Sussex by Rupert Matthews published by Francis Lincoln Ltd. 2008

Sussex and South Downs – Jarrold Short Walk Series published by Jarrold Publishing reprinted 2007

Pub Walks in West Sussex by Mike Power published by Power Publications 3rd edition April 2004

Captain Swing in Sussex and Kent by Mike Matthews published by The Hastings Press 2006

Frant – the Story of a Wealden Parish by Patricia Wright revised and updated 2009

An Illustrated Guide to East Sussex – a Crabtree Holiday Guide published by Crabtree Press 7th edition 1956

Walking at Weekends by SPB Mais published by Southern Railway (undated)

50 Walks in Sussex – published bt AA Publishing 2001

Ghost Hunter Walks in Sussex by Rupert Matthews published by SB Publications

South Sussex Walks by Lord Teviot and Michael B Quinion published by BBC Radio Brighton 1970

Pub Walks in the South Downs by Ben Perkins published by Countryside Books updated 2000

Footpaths for Fitness – East Sussex by Len Markham published by Countryside Books 2008

Village Walks in East Sussex by Ben Perkins published by Countryside Books 1998

Village Walks in West Sussex by Douglas Lasseter published by Countryside Books 1997

Best Sussex Walks by David Bathurst published by Summersdale 2003

Adventurous Pub Walks in Sussex by Ben Perkins published by Countryside Books 2005

Sussex as She Wus Spoke by Tony Wales published by SB Publications reprint 2001

Dead & Buried in Sussex by David Ascott published by SB Publications 1997

Villages of Sussex, Photographic Memories by Anthony Bryan published by Frith Book Co. 2001

A Sussex Garland by Tony Wales published by Countryside Books 2nd edition 1986

Women of Victorian Sussex by Helena Wojtczak published by The Hastings Press (signed copy) 2003

Sequestered Vales of Sussex by JB Paddon published by the West Sussex Guardian

Favourite Sussex Recipes compiled by Pat Smith published by J Salmon Ltd

Argus East Sussex Walks by Ben Perkins published by Southern Publishing and reprinted from the Evening Argus 1995

Pathfinders Guide Surrey and Sussex Walks published by Jarrold Publishing 2004

West Sussex Inns by Brigid Chapman published by Countryside Books 1988

Pub Walks in Kent by David Hancock published by M Power Publications 1994

Walks into History – Sussex by John Wilks published by Countryside Books 2003

Sussex Legends & Folklore by J Moore published by James Pike 1976

Pathfinders Guide More Sussex Walks published by Jarrold Publishing 2004

The Four Men by H Belloc published by Thomas Nelson & Sons (no date)

Our Sussex Parish by Thomas Geering published by Houghton Mifflin Co. 1925

The Sussex Bedside Anthology compiled by Margaret Goldsworthy published by The Arundel Press 1950

The County of Sussex by H Belloc published by Cassell & Co. 1936

Secret Sussex by Hardiman Scott published by the Batchworth Press 1949

Highways and Byways in Sussex by EV Lucas published by MacMillan & Co 1935

An Eccentric Tour of Sussex by Peter Bridgewater published by Snake River Press 2007

Curious Sussex by Mary Delorme

West Sussex in Character by Fred Lilley published by Southern Heritage Books 1996

Christmas Past in Sussex compiled by Fran & Geoff Doel published by Tempus Publishing 2005

West Sussex in Living Memory by West Sussex Federation of Women's Institutes published by Countryside Books 1993

East Sussex in Living Memory by East Sussex Federation of Women's Institutes published by Countryside Books 1995

Sussex by Esther Meynell published by Robert Hale Ltd second impression 1947

A Place in Time by Colin J Huggett published by the author 2002

Under the Eagle by Colin J Huggett published by the author 2004

East Grinstead and its Environs compiled by David Gould published by Tempus Publishing 2001

Sussex Celebrities by Fred Lilley published by SB Publications 2000

Sussex Tales of Mirth and Mayhem by Tony Wales published Countryside Books 2001

Robert Tressell's Hastings by Trevor Hopper published by Fanter Books 2005

A Saunterer in Sussex by AA Evans published by Methuen & Co. 1935

Sussex Music by Marcus Weeks published by Snake River Press 2008

Hailsham in Old Picture Postcards compiled by Hailsham Historical Society published by the European Library

100 Walks in Southeast England an AA publication (undated)

Silly Sussex by Judy Moore published by SB Publications 2004

Made in Sussex by Elizabeth Wright published by SB Publications 2000

Around Hailsham by Barry K Russell & Alan Gillet published by Sutton Publishing 1991

Around Heathfield in Old Photographs collected by Barry K Russell & Alan Gillet published by Sutton Publishing reprinted 1991

East Grinstead in Old Photographs by David Gould published by Sutton Publishing 1995

The Diary of Thomas Turner 1754-1765 edited by David Vaisey first published by Oxford University Press 1984 this edition published by CTR Publishing 1994

What the Vicar Saw by David Arscott published by Pomegranite Press (ex library)

10 Adventurous Walks in West Sussex by Raymond Hugh published by Morning Mist Publishing 1992

The West Sussex Village Book by Tony Wales published by Countryside Books new edition 1999

Around Hailsham in Old Photographs collected by Barry K Russell & Alan Gillet published by Sutton Publishing 1991

Sussex by SPB Mais published by The Richard Press Ltd. reprint 1950

Early to Rise – A Sussex Boyhood by Bob Copper published by Book Club Associates by arrangement with William Heinemann Ltd 1976

The South Downs Way by Jim Manthorpe published by Trailblazer Publications second edition 2007

West Hoathly School – The Story so Far by Basil Cridland published by West Hoathly School 2001

The Story of a Forest Village – West Hoathly by Ursula Ridley Published by The Friends of the Priest House 1971 this copy is one of a limited edition of 100

Portrait of Sussex by Cecile Woodford published by Robert Hale third edition 1984

People of Hidden Sussex by Warden Swinfen & David Arscott published by BBC Radio Sussex 1985

A History of Sussex by JR Armstrong published by Phillimore fourth edition 1995

Sussex Teashop Walks by Jean Patefield published by Countryside Books updated 2005

Classic Walks in Sussex by Ben Perkins published by SB Publications reprint 2007

Sussex Memorabilia by Sandy Hernu published by SB Publications 2002

Sussex Tales of Mystery and Murder by WH Johnson published by Countryside Books 2002

A Dictionary of Sussex Dialect by The Reverend WD Parish first published in 1875 but my book was published by Snake River Press 2008

The Sussex Weather Book by Bob Ogley, Ian Currie and Mark Davison published by Froglets Publications and Frosted Earth 1991

Pub Strolls in East Sussex by Ben Perkins published by Countryside Books reprint 2006

West Sussex Land Tax 1785 by A Readman, L Falconer, R Ritchie & P Wilkinson published by Sussex Record Society 2000

Mid Sussex Poor Law Records 1601-1835 by N Pilbeam & I Nelson published by Sussex Record Society Volume 83 1999

East Sussex Land Tax 1785 by Roger Davey published by Sussex Record Society 1991

Sussex Customs, Curiosities& Country Lore by Tony Wales published by Ensign Publications 1990

Hailsham and its Environs by Charles A Robertson (signed copy) published by Phillimore 1982

A Sussex Life – Memories of Gilbert Sargent edited by Dave Arthur published by Barrie & Jenkins 1989

Sussex People and History by Denys Skinner published by The Crowood Press 2002

A Grim Almanac of Sussex by WH Johnson published by Sutton Publishing 2007

An Historical Atlas of Sussex –edited by Kim Leslie and Brian Short published by Phillimore 1999

Hidden Sussex –by Warden Swinfen & David Arscott published by BBC Radio Sussex 1984

The Domesday Book - edited by Thomas Hinde published by Coombe Books 1999

Sussex Place Names by Judith Glover published by Countryside Books reprint 2002

The Local Historian's Encyclopedia by John Richardson published by Historical Publications Third edition 2003

….to be honest I really didn't realise how many books I have until I started to compile this list. I also use the Internet a great deal and, if this is the case, I have added the web address as a footnote at the bottom of the relevant page. Apart from and as well as all of the above we have also used the numerous pamphlets/booklets that can be purchased at all the churches we have visited (whenever they are available). And lastly I am also in possession of a number of computer discs giving most of the Sussex Census returns since 1840 to 1900 which I have used on a few occasions. Should anyone wish to borrow any of the above just let me or Ron know. Thanks.